The Best 1001 Short, Easy Recipes

That Everyone Should Have

Cookbook Resources, LLC
Highland Village, Texas

The Best 1001 Short, Easy Recipes
That Everyone Should Have

Printed April 2011

International Standard Book Number: 978-1-59769-092-8

Library of Congress Control Number: 2010938665

Cover and Illustrations by Nancy Bohanan

Edited, Designed, Published and Manufactured in the United States of America
Cookbook Resources, LLC
541 Doubletree Drive
Highland Village, Texas 75077
Toll free 866-229-2665

www.cookbookresources.com

cookbook resources LLC
Bringing Family and Friends to the Table

Short, Easy... and Delicious!

The dining table is as important now as it has ever been in spending time together as a family. It is a place where parents and children gather to discuss the happenings in their days and lives and to share their accomplishments with the people who matter most. And every minute spent around the table strengthens the family bond, enriches those relationships and brings family members closer together.

In this fast-paced world, we are faced with the challenge of balancing work and family and making sure our children can take advantage of the many opportunities available to them. That often means shuttling from school to music lessons to soccer games, and with all the rushing around, it's difficult to get home-cooked meals and the entire family to the table at the same time.

We're here to make that easier. The meals you'll create using *The Best 1001 Short, Easy Recipes* make family dinners a reality with minimal time and effort. These simple recipes made with readily available ingredients are so quick that your family can accomplish all they need to in a day and still come together at the end of it for some quality time and delicious food.

Table of Contents

Appetizers, Munchies & Beverages

Hot-to-Trot Dip

1 pound ground beef
2 (16 ounce) packages cubed processed cheese
1½ cups salsa
Several drops hot sauce

- Brown ground beef and drain well.
- In saucepan, heat cheese and salsa until cheese melts. Add hot sauce.
- Combine meat and cheese mixture.
- Serve hot with tortilla chips.

Zippy Cheese Dip

1 pound lean ground beef
½ pound hot pork sausage
1 (8 ounce) jar hot salsa
1 (32 ounce) carton cubed processed cheese

- Brown ground beef and sausage in large skillet. Stir until meats crumble and drain.
- Add salsa and cheese. Cook over low heat and stir constantly until cheese melts.
- Serve warm with chips.

Fiesta Dip

1 (15 ounce) can tamales
1 (16 ounce) can chili without beans
1 cup salsa
2 (5 ounce) jars sharp processed cheese spread
1 cup finely chopped onion

- Mash tamales with fork.
- In saucepan, combine all ingredients and heat to mix.
- Serve hot with crackers or chips.

Indian Corn Dip

1 pound lean ground beef
½ onion, chopped
1 (15 ounce) can whole kernel corn, drained
1 (12 ounce) jar taco sauce
¼ cup water

- In skillet, brown beef and onion and add corn, taco sauce and water.
- Simmer mixture for 15 to 20 minutes.
- Serve with tortilla chips.

Hot Sombrero Dip

2 (15 ounce) cans bean dip
1 pound lean ground beef, cooked
1 (4 ounce) can green chiles
1 cup hot salsa
1½ cups shredded cheddar cheese

- Layer bean dip, ground beef, chiles and salsa in 3-quart baking dish and top with cheese.
- Bake at 350° just until cheese melts, about 10 or 15 minutes.
- Serve with tortilla chips.

Spicy Beef-Cheese Dip

1 (10 ounce) can tomatoes and green chiles
½ teaspoon garlic powder
2 (16 ounce) packages cubed processed cheese
1 pound lean ground beef, browned, drained

- In large saucepan, place tomatoes and green chiles, garlic and cheese and heat on low until cheese melts. (Use Mexican processed cheese if you like it really spicy.)
- Add ground beef and mix well.
- Serve with tortilla chips.

Great Balls of Fire

1 pound lean hot sausage
3 green onions with tops, chopped
1 (4 ounce) can diced tomatoes and green chiles
2 (16 ounce) packages cubed processed cheese

- Brown sausage and onion in large skillet and drain off fat.
- Add tomatoes and green chiles and mix.
- Add cheese to sausage mixture and cook on low heat until cheese melts.
- Serve hot in chafing dish with large chips.

Pep-Pep-Pepperoni Dip

2 (8 ounce) packages cream cheese
1 (3.5 ounce) package pepperoni slices
1 (12 ounce) bottle chili sauce
1 bunch fresh green onions with tops, chopped

- Use mixer to beat cream cheese until smooth and creamy.
- Cut pepperoni slices into smaller chunks.
- Add pepperoni, chili sauce and green onions to cream cheese and mix well.
- Refrigerate and serve with chips.

Vegetable Dip

You will hear the family saying, "You mean this is spinach!"

1 (10 ounce) package frozen chopped spinach, thawed, well drained
1 bunch fresh green onions with tops, chopped
1 (1 ounce) packet dry vegetable soup mix
1 tablespoon lemon juice
2 (8 ounce) cartons sour cream

- Squeeze spinach in paper towels to drain thoroughly.
- In medium bowl, combine all ingredients and add a little salt. (Adding several drops of hot sauce is also good.)
- Cover and refrigerate.
- Serve with chips.

Crunchy Veggie Dip

1 (10 ounce) package frozen, chopped spinach, thawed, well drained
1 (16 ounce) carton sour cream
1 (1 ounce) package dry vegetable soup mix
1 bunch fresh green onions with tops, chopped
¾ cup chopped pecans

- Squeeze spinach in paper towels to drain thoroughly.
- Combine all ingredients and mix well.
- Refrigerate for several hours before serving.

Green Wonder Dip

1 (10 ounce) package frozen chopped spinach, thawed
1 (1 ounce) package dry vegetable soup mix
½ cup minced onion
1 cup mayonnaise
1 cup sour cream

- Squeeze spinach in paper towels to drain thoroughly.
- Combine all ingredients and mix well.
- Cover and refrigerate overnight.
- Serve with crackers, chips or raw vegetable sticks.

Avocado-Onion Dip

1 (1 ounce) package dry onion soup mix
1 (8 ounce) carton sour cream
½ cup mayonnaise
2 ripe avocados, mashed
1 tablespoon lemon juice

- Mix all ingredients and work quickly so avocados do not turn dark.
- Serve with wheat crackers.

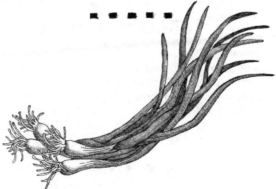

Avocado Olé

3 large ripe avocados, mashed
1 tablespoon fresh lemon juice
1 (1 ounce) package dry onion soup mix
1 (8 ounce) carton sour cream

- Combine avocados with lemon juice.
- Stir in soup mix and sour cream. (Add a little salt if desired.)
- Serve with chips or crackers.

Spinach-Cheese Dip

1 (10 ounce) package frozen chopped spinach, thawed
2 (8 ounce) packages cream cheese, softened
1 (1 ounce) package dry vegetable soup mix
1 (8 ounce) can water chestnuts, chopped

- Squeeze spinach in several paper towels to drain thoroughly.
- In mixing bowl, beat cream cheese until smooth. Fold in spinach, soup mix and water chestnuts and refrigerate.
- Serve with chips or crackers.

Spinach-Artichoke Dip

2 (10 ounce) packages frozen spinach, thawed, drained
1 (14 ounce) jar marinated artichoke hearts, drained, finely chopped
1 cup mayonnaise
2 cups shredded mozzarella cheese

- Squeeze spinach in paper towels to drain thoroughly.
- Combine all ingredients and mix well.
- Cover and refrigerate.
- Serve with chips.

Onion-Guacamole Dip

1 (8 ounce) carton sour cream
1 (1 ounce) package dry onion soup mix
2 (8 ounce) cartons prepared avocado dip
2 green onions with tops, chopped
½ teaspoon crushed dillweed

- Mix all ingredients and refrigerate.
- Serve with chips.

Sassy Onion Dip

Plain and simple but great!

1 (8 ounce) package cream cheese, softened
1 (8 ounce) carton sour cream
½ cup chili sauce
1 (1 ounce) package dry onion soup mix
1 tablespoon lemon juice

- In mixing bowl, beat cream cheese until fluffy. Add sour cream, chili sauce, soup mix and lemon juice and mix well.
- Cover and refrigerate. Serve with strips of raw zucchini, celery, carrots, etc.

Creamy Onion Dip

2 (8 ounce) packages cream cheese, softened
3 tablespoons lemon juice
1 (1 ounce) package dry onion soup mix
1 (8 ounce) carton sour cream

- Use mixer to beat cream cheese until smooth.
- Add lemon juice and soup mix. Gradually fold in sour cream and blend well.
- Refrigerate and serve with chips, crackers or fresh vegetables.

Crunchy Asparagus Dip

1 (14 ounce) can asparagus spears, drained, chopped
½ cup mayonnaise
¼ teaspoon hot sauce
½ cup chopped pecans

- Combine all ingredients in medium bowl and refrigerate.
- Serve with wheat crackers.

Hot Broccoli Dip

2 (16 ounce) packages cubed Mexican processed cheese
1 (10 ounce) can golden mushroom soup
1 (10 ounce) package frozen chopped broccoli, thawed, drained

- In saucepan, melt cheese with soup and stir in broccoli.
- Heat thoroughly.
- Serve hot with chips.

Zippy Broccoli-Cheese Dip

1 (10 ounce) package frozen chopped broccoli, thawed, drained
2 tablespoons (¼ stick) butter
2 ribs celery, chopped
1 small onion, finely chopped
1 (16 ounce) package cubed mild Mexican processed cheese

- Make sure broccoli is thoroughly thawed and drained.
- Place butter in large saucepan and sauté broccoli, celery and onion at medium heat for about 5 minutes. Stir several times.
- Add cheese. Heat just until cheese melts and stir constantly.
- Serve hot with chips.

TIP: If you want the "zip" to be zippier, use hot Mexican processed cheese instead of mild.

Cucumber Dip

2 medium cucumbers
2 (8 ounce) packages cream cheese, softened
Several drops hot sauce
1 (1 ounce) package dry ranch-style salad dressing mix
½ teaspoon garlic powder

- Peel cucumbers, cut in half lengthwise and scoop out seeds.
- Grate cucumbers into very fine pieces.
- In mixing bowl, combine cream cheese, hot sauce, dressing mix and garlic powder and beat until creamy.
- Combine cucumbers and cream cheese mixture and mix well. (Add ½ cup chopped pecans to make this dip even better.)
- Serve with chips.

TIP: This dip makes great "party" sandwiches when spread on thin slices of white bread. If you do use it for sandwiches, make sure you use paper towels to squeeze all the water out of the cucumbers.

Artichoke-Bacon Dip

1 (14 ounce) jar marinated artichoke hearts, drained, chopped
1 cup mayonnaise
2 teaspoons Worcestershire sauce
5 slices bacon, cooked crisp, crumbled

- In large bowl, combine all ingredients.
- Pour into buttered 8-inch baking dish.
- Bake at 350° for 12 minutes.
- Serve hot with crackers.

Creamy Ham Dip

2 (8 ounce) packages cream cheese, softened
2 (6 ounce) cans deviled ham
2 heaping tablespoons horseradish
¼ cup minced onion
¼ cup finely chopped celery

- In mixing bowl, beat cream cheese until creamy.
- Stir in ham, horseradish, onion and celery.
- Refrigerate and serve with crackers.

TIP: This will also make great little sandwiches with party rye bread.

Ham-It-Up Dip

1 (16 ounce) carton small-curd cottage cheese
2 (6 ounce) cans deviled ham
1 (1 ounce) package dry onion soup mix
½ cup sour cream
2 tablespoons lemon juice

- Blend cottage cheese in blender or with mixer.
- Add ham, soup mix, sour cream and lemon juice and mix well.
- Serve with crackers.

TIP: I like to add a little "zip" to this dip with several dashes of hot sauce.

Zesty Clam Dip

1 (15 ounce) can New England clam chowder
1 (8 ounce) and 1 (3 ounce) package cream cheese, softened
2 tablespoons minced onion
2 tablespoons prepared horseradish
2 tablespoons marinade for chicken

- Combine all ingredients and blend in food processor until smooth.
- Serve with raw vegetables or chips.

Velvet Clam Dip

1 (8 ounce) and 1 (3 ounce) package cream cheese
¼ cup (½ stick) butter
2 (6 ounce) cans minced clams, drained
½ teaspoon Worcestershire sauce

- Melt cream cheese and butter in double boiler.
- Add minced clams and Worcestershire sauce.
- Serve hot.

Favorite Standby Shrimp Dip

2 cups tiny, cooked shrimp, finely chopped
2 tablespoons horseradish
½ cup chili sauce
¾ cup mayonnaise
1 tablespoon lemon juice

- Combine all ingredients with a few sprinkles of salt and refrigerate. (If shrimp has been frozen, be sure to drain well.)
- Serve with cucumber or zucchini slices.

Horsey Shrimp Dip

1 (6 ounce) can tiny, cooked shrimp, chopped, drained
3 tablespoons cream-style horseradish
⅓ cup mayonnaise
½ teaspoon Cajun seasoning

- Combine shrimp, horseradish, mayonnaise and seasoning.
- Refrigerate and serve with crackers.

Chunky Shrimp Dip

2 (6 ounce) cans tiny, cooked shrimp, drained
2 cups mayonnaise
6 green onions with tops, finely chopped
¾ cup chunky salsa

- Crumble shrimp and stir in mayonnaise, onion and salsa.
- Refrigerate for 1 to 2 hours.
- Serve with crackers.

Hurrah for Shrimp

1 (8 ounce) package cream cheese, softened
½ cup mayonnaise
1 (6 ounce) can tiny, cooked shrimp, drained
1¼ teaspoons Creole (or Cajun) seasoning
1 tablespoon lemon juice

- Blend cream cheese and mayonnaise in mixing bowl until creamy.
- Add shrimp, seasoning and lemon juice and whip only until they mix well.
- Serve with chips.

TIP: *The Creole (or Cajun) seasoning is the key to this great dip!*

Gitty-Up Crab Dip

1 (8 ounce) package cream cheese, softened
3 tablespoons salsa
2 tablespoons prepared horseradish
1 (6 ounce) can crabmeat, drained, flaked

- Use mixer to beat cream cheese until smooth and creamy.
- Add salsa and horseradish and mix well.
- Stir in crabmeat and refrigerate.
- Serve with assorted crackers.

Hot Rich Crab Dip

1 (10 ounce) can cheddar cheese soup
1 (16 ounce) package cubed Mexican processed cheese
1 (6 ounce) can crabmeat, flaked, drained
1 (16 ounce) jar salsa

- In microwave-safe bowl, combine soup and processed cheese.
- Microwave at 1-minute intervals until cheese melts.
- Add crabmeat and salsa and mix well.
- Serve hot with chips.

Cheesy Crab Dip

1 (6 ounce) roll processed garlic cheese, diced
1 (10 ounce) can cream of mushroom soup
1 (6 ounce) can crabmeat, drained
2 tablespoons sherry

- In medium pan, combine all ingredients and heat until cheese melts.
- Keep warm in chafing dish and serve with assorted crackers.

Unbelievable Crab Dip

1 (16 ounce) package cubed processed cheese
2 (6 ounce) cans crabmeat, drained, flaked
1 bunch fresh green onions with tops, chopped
2 cups mayonnaise
½ teaspoon seasoned salt

- Melt cheese in top of double boiler. Add crabmeat, onions, mayonnaise and seasoned salt.
- Serve hot or at room temperature with assorted crackers.

TIP: Don't count on your guests leaving the table until this dip is gone!

Jump-In Crab Dip

1 (6 ounce) can white crabmeat, drained, flaked
1 (8 ounce) package cream cheese
½ cup (1 stick) butter

- In saucepan, combine crabmeat, cream cheese and butter.
- Heat and mix thoroughly.
- Transfer to hot chafing dish. Serve with chips.

TIP:　*This is so good you will wish you had doubled the recipe!*

Crab Dip

1 (16 ounce) box processed cheese
2 (6 ounce) cans crabmeat, drained, flaked
1½ cups mayonnaise
1 bunch fresh green onions with tops, chopped
5 to 10 drops hot sauce

- In double boiler, combine all ingredients.
- Heat on low until cheese melts and ingredients blend well.
- Serve with chips.

Crab-Cream Cheese Dip

1 (6 ounce) can white crabmeat, drained, flaked
1 (8 ounce) package cream cheese
½ cup (1 stick) butter

- In saucepan, combine crabmeat, cream cheese and butter.
- Heat and mix thoroughly.
- Transfer to chafing dish and serve with chips or crackers.

Crab Dip Kick

1 (8 ounce) package cream cheese, softened
3 tablespoons salsa
2 tablespoons horseradish
1 (6 ounce) can crabmeat, drained, flaked

- In mixing bowl, beat cream cheese until creamy.
- Add salsa and horseradish and mix well.
- Stir in crabmeat and refrigerate.
- Serve with assorted crackers.

Tasty Tuna Dip

1 (6 ounce) can tuna in spring water, drained, flaked
1 (1 ounce) package dry Italian salad dressing mix
1 (8 ounce) carton sour cream
¼ cup chopped black olives, drained

- Combine all ingredients and stir until they blend.
- Refrigerate for 8 hours.
- Serve with melba rounds.

Tuna-Avocado Dip

2 medium avocados
1 (6 ounce) can white tuna, drained
½ cup creamed cottage cheese
2 tablespoons lemon juice
Salt and pepper

- Peel and cut avocados in chunks.
- In mixing bowl, combine tuna, cottage cheese, lemon juice and salt and pepper and beat. (Mixture will not be smooth – a little texture should remain.)
- Fold in avocados.
- Serve with crackers.

Easy Tuna Dip

1 (6 ounce) can tuna, drained
1 (1 ounce) package dry Italian salad dressing mix
1 (8 ounce) carton sour cream
2 green onions with tops, chopped

- Combine all ingredients and mix well.
- Set aside several hours before serving.

Tasty Tuna Spread

1 (6 ounce) can solid white tuna, drained, flaked
1 (1 ounce) package dry Italian salad dressing mix
1 tablespoon lemon juice
1 (8 ounce) carton sour cream
3 green onions with tops, chopped

- Combine all ingredients and stir until they blend.
- Refrigerate and serve with melba rounds.

Mexican Cheese Dip

1 (16 ounce) package shredded cheddar cheese
1 (5 ounce) can evaporated milk
1 teaspoon cumin
1 tablespoon chili powder
1 (10 ounce) can tomatoes and green chiles

- Melt cheese with evaporated milk in double boiler.
- In blender, mix cumin, chili powder and tomatoes and green chiles. (Add dash of garlic powder if you like.)
- Add tomato mixture to melted cheese and mix well.
- Serve hot with chips.

Roasted Garlic Dip

4 or 5 unpeeled whole garlic cloves
2 (8 ounce) packages cream cheese, softened
¾ cup mayonnaise
1 (7 or 9 ounce) jar roasted sweet red peppers, drained, coarsely chopped
1 bunch fresh green onions with tops, chopped

- Preheat oven to 400°.
- Lightly brush outside of garlic cloves with a little oil and place in shallow baking pan.
- Heat about 10 minutes and cool.
- Press roasted garlic out of cloves.
- Beat cream cheese and mayonnaise until creamy. Add garlic, red peppers and onions and mix well. (Roasted peppers are great in this recipe, but if you want it a little spicy, add several drops of hot sauce.)
- Sprinkle with red pepper or paprika and serve with chips.

Pepper Pot-Bean Dip

1 (15 ounce) can refried beans
1 (16 ounce) package cubed Mexican processed cheese
½ cup (1 stick) butter
1 teaspoon garlic powder

- In large double boiler, combine all ingredients.
- Heat on low and stir often until cheese and butter melt.
- Serve hot in chafing dish with tortilla chips.

The Big Dipper

1 (15 ounce) can chili without beans
1 (10 ounce) can tomatoes and green chiles
1 (16 ounce) package cubed processed cheese
½ cup chopped green onions
½ teaspoon cayenne pepper

- In saucepan, combine all ingredients.
- Heat just until cheese melts and stir constantly.
- Serve warm with assorted dippers or toasted French bread sticks.

Velvet Dip

2 (16 ounce) packages cubed Mexican processed cheese
2 cups mayonnaise
1 (4 ounce) jar chopped pimentos, drained
1 (7 ounce) can diced green chiles

- Place cheese in saucepan and melt over low heat.
- Add mayonnaise, pimentos and chiles and mix well.
- Serve with chips.

Monterey Jack's Dip

1 (8 ounce) package cream cheese, softened, whipped
1 (16 ounce) can chili without beans
1 (4 ounce) can diced green chiles
1 (8 ounce) package grated Monterey Jack cheese
1 (4 ounce) can chopped black olives

- Preheat oven to 325°.
- In 7 x 11-inch glass baking dish, layer cream cheese, chili, chiles, cheese and black olives.
- Bake uncovered at 325° for 30 minutes.
- Serve with chips.

Curry Lover's Veggie Dip

1 cup mayonnaise
½ cup sour cream
1 teaspoon curry powder
¼ teaspoon hot sauce
1 teaspoon lemon juice

- Combine all ingredients and mix until they blend well.
- Sprinkle with a little paprika for color.
- Cover and refrigerate.
- Serve with raw vegetables.

La Cucaracha

1 (12 ounce) package chorizo, sliced or chopped
1 (16 ounce) box Mexican processed cheese
1 (15 ounce) can stewed tomatoes

- Saute chorizo, cook and drain.
- In double boiler, melt cheese and tomatoes and stir constantly over medium heat.
- Combine chorizo, cheese and tomatoes and mix well.
- Serve with tortilla chips.

Creamy Cucumber Spread

1 (8 ounce) package cream cheese, softened
½ cup mayonnaise
1 teaspoon seasoned salt
1 cup seeded, chopped cucumbers

- With mixer, beat cream cheese until creamy and add mayonnaise, seasoned salt and cucumber.
- Spread on crackers.

Green Olive Spread

1 (8 ounce) package cream cheese, softened
⅓ cup mayonnaise
¾ cup chopped pecans
1 cup chopped green olives, drained
¼ teaspoon black pepper

- In mixing bowl, blend cream cheese and mayonnaise until smooth.
- Add pecans, olives and black pepper, mix well and refrigerate.
- Serve on crackers or make sandwiches with party rye bread.

Olive-Cheese Appetizers

1 cup chopped pimento-stuffed olives
2 fresh green onions with tops, finely chopped
1½ cups shredded Monterey Jack cheese
½ cup mayonnaise

- Preheat oven to 375°.
- In large bowl, combine all ingredients and mix well.
- Spread on English muffins and bake at 375° until bubbly.
- Cut muffins into quarters and serve hot.

Tex-Mex Nachos

About 35 tortilla chips
1 (8 ounce) package shredded Monterey Jack cheese
2 tablespoons sliced jalapeno peppers
⅛ teaspoon chili powder
Bean Dip (recipe next page)

- Arrange chips in 9 x 15-inch baking dish and sprinkle with cheese.
- Top with jalapeno peppers and sprinkle with chili powder.
- Broil 4 inches from heat until cheese melts.

Bean Dip

1 (15 ounce) can Mexican-style chili beans
½ teaspoon ground cumin
½ teaspoon chili powder
¼ teaspoon dried oregano

- Drain beans and reserve 2 tablespoons liquid.
- Combine beans, reserved liquid, cumin, chili powder and oregano in food processor. Pulse several times until beans are partially chopped.
- Pour mixture into small saucepan and cook over low heat, stirring constantly until thoroughly heated.
- Serve with Tex-Mex Nachos.

Jack Quesadillas

¼ cup ricotta cheese, divided
6 (6 inch) corn tortillas
⅔ cup shredded Monterey Jack cheese, divided
1 (4 ounce) can diced green chiles, drained

- Spread 1 tablespoon ricotta over tortilla. Add 1 heaping tablespoon cheese and 1 tablespoon chiles. Place second tortilla on top.
- Repeat to make 2 more quesadillas.
- In heated skillet, add 1 quesadilla and cook for 3 minutes on each side.
- Remove from heat and cut into 4 wedges. Repeat with emaining quesadillas.
- Serve warm with salsa.

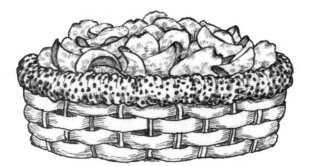

Cheese Strips

1 loaf thin-sliced bread
1 (8 ounce) package shredded cheddar cheese
6 slices bacon, fried, drained, coarsely broken
½ cup chopped onion
1 cup mayonnaise

- Remove crust from bread.
- Combine cheese, bacon, onion and mayonnaise and spread filling over bread slices.
- Cut each slice into 3 strips and place on baking sheet.
- Bake at 400° for 10 minutes.

TIP: For a special touch, add ⅓ cup slivered almonds, toasted.

Cheddar Toppers

1 cup chopped black olives
1 cup shredded cheddar cheese
½ cup mayonnaise
½ cup finely minced green olives

- Combine all ingredients and mix well.
- Spread mixture on English muffins and bake at 350° for 30 minutes.
- After baking, quarter muffins and serve as hors d'oeuvres.

Speedy Chili Con Queso

1 (16 ounce) package cubed processed cheese
½ cup milk
1 (12 ounce) jar salsa, divided

- In saucepan, melt cheese and milk in double boiler.
- Add about half of salsa.
- Serve with tortilla chips.

TIP: Taste and add more salsa as needed for desired heat!

Border Queso

1 (8 ounce) can jalapeno peppers with 1 tablespoon liquid
1 (16 ounce) package cubed processed cheese
1 (4 ounce) jar pimentos, drained, chopped
3 fresh green onions with tops, chopped

- Seed jalapeno peppers and chop. (Be sure to wear rubber gloves.)
- Combine peppers, cheese, pimentos and onion in saucepan.
- Heat on stove and stir constantly until cheese melts.
- Stir in reserved liquid.
- Serve with tortilla chips.

Ginger Cream Spread

1 (8 ounce) package cream cheese, softened
½ cup (1 stick) unsalted butter, softened
2 tablespoons milk
3 tablespoons finely chopped crystallized ginger

- Combine all ingredients in mixing bowl and beat until creamy.
- Spread on your favorite fruit or nut breads.

Orange-Cheese Spread

2 (8 ounce) packages cream cheese, softened
½ cup powdered sugar
1 tablespoon grated orange peel
2 tablespoons Grand Marnier
2 tablespoons frozen orange juice concentrate

- Blend all ingredients in mixing bowl until smooth and refrigerate.
- Spread on dessert breads to make sandwiches.

TIP: This spread is great on poppy seed buns and may also be used as dip for fruit.

Peanut Butter Spread

1 (8 ounce) package cream cheese, softened
12/3 cups peanut butter
½ cup powdered sugar
1 tablespoon milk

- With mixer, cream all ingredients.
- Serve spread with apple wedges or graham crackers.

Smoked Oyster Spread

1 (8 ounce) package cream cheese, softened
3 tablespoons mayonnaise
1 (3 ounce) can smoked oysters, chopped
½ teaspoon onion salt
2 tablespoons parmesan cheese

- Whip cream cheese and mayonnaise until creamy.
- Add oysters, onion salt and cheese.
- Mix well and dip or spread on crackers.

Quick Mix Dip

1 (8 ounce) package cream cheese, softened
1 cup mayonnaise
1 (1 ounce) package dry ranch-style salad dressing mix
½ onion, finely minced

- In mixing bowl, combine cream cheese and mayonnaise and beat until creamy.
- Stir in dressing mix and onion.
- Refrigerate and serve with fresh vegetables.

Confetti Dip

1 (15 ounce) can whole kernel corn, drained
1 (15 ounce) can black beans, drained
⅓ cup Italian salad dressing
1 (16 ounce) jar salsa

- Combine all ingredients and mix well.
- Refrigerate for several hours before serving.
- Serve with chips.

Artichoke-Blue Cheese Dip

½ cup (1 stick) butter
1 (14 ounce) can artichoke hearts, drained, chopped
1 (4 ounce) package blue cheese
2 teaspoons lemon juice

- In skillet, melt butter and mix in artichoke hearts.
- Add blue cheese and lemon juice.
- Serve hot in chafing dish.

Roquefort Dip

1 (8 ounce) package cream cheese, softened
2 cups mayonnaise
1 small onion, finely grated
1 (3 ounce) package roquefort cheese, crumbled
⅛ teaspoon garlic powder

- In mixing bowl, combine cream cheese and mayonnaise and beat until creamy.
- Add onion, roquefort (blue cheese) and garlic powder and mix well. Refrigerate.
- Serve with zucchini sticks, turnip sticks or cauliflower florets.

Blue Cheese Crisps

2 (4 ounce) packages crumbled blue cheese
½ cup (1 stick) butter, softened
1⅓ cups flour
⅓ cup poppy seeds
¼ teaspoon ground red pepper

- Beat blue cheese and butter at medium speed until fluffy.
- Add flour, poppy seeds and red pepper and beat until they blend.
- Divide dough in half and shape each portion into 9-inch log. Cover and refrigerate for 2 hours.
- Preheat oven to 350°.
- Cut each log into ¼-inch slices and place on ungreased baking sheet.
- Bake at 350° for 13 to 15 minutes or until golden brown and cool.

Hot Artichoke Spread

1 (14 ounce) can artichoke hearts, drained
1 cup mayonnaise
1 cup grated parmesan cheese
1 (1 ounce) package dry Italian salad dressing mix

- Remove tough outer leaves and chop artichoke hearts.
- Combine all ingredients and mix thoroughly.
- Pour into 9-inch square baking pan and bake at 350° for 20 minutes.
- Serve hot with assorted crackers.

Hot Artichoke-Chile Spread

1 (14 ounce) can artichoke hearts, drained
1 (4 ounce) can diced green chiles
1 cup mayonnaise
1 (8 ounce) package shredded mozzarella cheese
½ teaspoon garlic powder

- Remove any spikes or tough leaves from artichoke hearts and finely chop.
- Combine all ingredients and mix thoroughly.
- Pour into 9-inch square baking pan and sprinkle some paprika over top.
- Bake at 325° for 25 minutes.
- Serve hot with assorted crackers.

Chicken-Cheese Spread

2 (8 ounce) packages cream cheese, softened
¼ cup mayonnaise
2 tablespoons marinade for chicken
2 cups finely shredded, cooked chicken breasts
¼ cup chopped almonds, toasted

- In mixing bowl, combine cream cheese, mayonnaise and marinade for chicken and beat until creamy.
- Fold in shredded chicken and almonds.
- Spread on English muffin halves and toast. (Do not brown.)

Deluxe Pimento Cheese Spread

1 (16 ounce) package shredded sharp cheddar cheese
2 (4 ounce) jars diced pimentos, drained
1 cup salsa
¼ teaspoon freshly ground black pepper
3 tablespoons mayonnaise

- In large bowl, combine cheese, pimentos and salsa and mix well.
- Add pepper and mayonnaise and blend well.
- Refrigerate.
- Spread on wheat crackers or use to make sandwiches.

Walnut-Cheese Spread

¾ cup chopped walnuts
1 (16 ounce) package shredded cheddar cheese
3 green onions with tops, chopped
½ to ¾ cup mayonnaise
½ teaspoon liquid smoke

- Roast walnuts at 250° for 10 minutes.
- Combine all ingredients and let stand in refrigerator overnight.
- Spread on assorted crackers.

Smoky Gouda Spread

¾ cup chopped walnuts
1 (8 ounce) package smoked gouda cheese
1 (8 ounce) package cream cheese, softened
¼ cup sliced green onions

- Spread walnuts in shallow baking pan and bake at 325° for 10 minutes. Cool and set aside.
- Trim and discard outer red edge of gouda cheese and grate cheese.
- Use mixer to combine cream cheese and gouda cheese and mix well. Stir in walnuts and onions.
- Serve with apple wedges or crackers.

Tortilla Rollers

1 (8 ounce) package cream cheese, softened
1 (4 ounce) can chopped black olives, drained
1 (4 ounce) can diced green chiles, drained
1 (12 ounce) jar salsa
Flour tortillas

- Use mixer to beat cream cheese until smooth.
- Add black olives, green chiles and ¼ cup salsa to cream cheese and mix well.
- Spread cream cheese mixture on flour tortillas and roll up. Refrigerate for several hours.
- Slice tortilla rolls in ½-inch slices, insert toothpick in each slice and dip in salsa.

Poor Man's Paté

1 (16 ounce) roll braunschweiger, softened
1 (1 ounce) package dry onion soup mix
1 (8 ounce) carton sour cream
1 (8 ounce) package cream cheese, softened
Several dashes hot sauce

- Mash braunschweiger (goose liver) with fork.
- With mixer, beat soup mix, sour cream, cream cheese and hot sauce until fairly creamy.
- Add braunschweiger and mix well.
- Refrigerate and serve with chips.

Curried Wings

10 chicken wings
¼ cup (½ stick) butter, melted
¼ cup honey
¼ cup prepared mustard
1¼ teaspoons curry powder

- Cut off wing tips and discard. Cut wings in half at joint.
- Combine butter, honey, mustard and curry powder in large, resealable plastic bag.
- Add chicken to bag and seal.
- Refrigerate at least 2 hours and turn chicken occasionally.
- Remove chicken from marinade and discard marinade.
- Place chicken in greased 9 x 13-inch baking dish. Bake at 325° for 1 hour.

Chicken Lickers

2 white onions, sliced
10 to 12 chicken livers
4 strips bacon
⅓ cup sherry

- Place onion slices in shallow pan.
- Top each onion slice with chicken liver and ⅓-strip bacon.
- Pour sherry over all.
- Bake uncovered at 350° for about 45 minutes or until bacon is crisp and baste occasionally with pan drippings.

Raspberry-Glazed Wings

¾ cup seedless raspberry jam
¼ cup cider vinegar
¼ cup soy sauce
1 teaspoon garlic powder
1 teaspoon black pepper
16 (about 3 pounds) whole chicken wings

- In saucepan, combine jam, vinegar, soy sauce, garlic powder and black pepper. Bring to boil and boil 1 minute.
- Cut chicken wings into 3 sections and discard wing tips. Place wings in large bowl, add raspberry mixture and toss to coat.
- Cover and refrigerate for 4 hours.
- Line 10 x 15-inch baking pan with foil and grease foil.
- Use slotted spoon to place wings in pan and reserve marinade.
- Bake at 350° for 30 minutes and turn once.
- Cook reserved marinade for 10 minutes, brush over wings and bake for 25 minutes longer.

Tuna Melt Appetizer

1 (10 ounce) package frozen spinach, drained
2 (6 ounce) cans white tuna in water, drained, flaked
¾ cup mayonnaise
1½ cups shredded mozzarella cheese, divided

- Squeeze spinach in several paper towels to drain thoroughly.
- In large bowl, combine spinach, tuna, mayonnaise and 1 cup cheese and mix well.
- Spoon into buttered pie plate and bake at 350° for 15 minutes.
- Remove from oven and sprinkle remaining cheese over top.
- Return to oven and bake for another 5 minutes.
- Serve with crackers.

Garlic Shrimp

1 clove garlic, minced
⅔ cup chili sauce
½ pound thin bacon strips
1 pound medium shrimp, cooked

- Combine garlic and chili sauce and refrigerate for several hours.
- Broil bacon on 1 side only and cut in half.
- Dip shrimp in chili sauce and wrap with half bacon strip with uncooked side out.
- Fasten with toothpicks and refrigerate.
- Just before serving, broil shrimp until bacon is crisp.

Shrimp Squares Deluxe

1 (6 ounce) can shrimp, drained, chopped
1 cup mayonnaise
1 cup shredded cheddar cheese
10 to 12 slices white bread, trimmed, cut in squares

- Combine shrimp, mayonnaise and cheese and mix well.
- Spread shrimp mixture on bread squares and broil until bubbly.

Bacon-Oyster Bites

1 (5 ounce) can smoked oysters, drained, chopped
⅔ cup herb-seasoned stuffing mix
¼ cup water
8 slices bacon, halved, partially cooked

- Combine oysters, stuffing mix and water. Add 1 teaspoon water if mixture seems too dry.
- Form into balls, using 1 tablespoon mixture for each.
- Wrap half slice bacon around each and secure with toothpick.
- Place on rack in shallow baking pan.
- Cook at 350° for 25 to 30 minutes.

Hot Cocktail Squares

1 (4 ounce) can diced green chiles
1 (3 ounce) jar bacon bits
1 (16 ounce) package shredded cheddar cheese
7 eggs
Hot sauce

- In greased 7 x 11-inch baking dish, layer green chiles, bacon bits and cheese.
- Beat eggs well with fork and season with a little salt and several drops hot sauce.
- Pour over cheese and bake covered at 350° for 25 minutes.
- Uncover and bake another 10 minutes.
- Cut into squares and serve warm.

Chestnuts Under Wraps

1 (8 ounce) can whole water chestnuts, drained
¼ cup soy sauce
½ pound bacon, cut in thirds

- Marinate water chestnuts for 1 hour in soy sauce.
- Wrap one-third slice bacon around each water chestnut and fasten with toothpick.
- Bake at 375° for 20 minutes or until bacon is done.
- Drain and serve hot.

Bacon Nibblers

1 (16 ounce) package sliced bacon
1½ cups packed brown sugar
1½ teaspoons dry mustard
¼ teaspoon black pepper

- Cut each bacon slice in half. Combine brown sugar, dry mustard and black pepper in shallow bowl.
- Dip each half slice bacon in brown sugar mixture and press down so bacon coats well.
- Place each slice on baking sheet with sides and bake at 325° for 25 minutes or until bacon browns. Turn once.
- Immediately remove with tongs to layers of paper towels. (Bacon will harden and can be broken in pieces.)

Green Eyes

4 dill pickles
4 slices boiled ham
1 (3 ounce) package light cream cheese, softened
Black pepper

- Dry off pickles.
- Lightly coat one side of each ham slice with cream cheese and sprinkle on a little pepper.
- Roll pickle in ham slice coated with cream cheese.
- Refrigerate and slice into circles to serve.

Cocktail Ham Roll-Ups

1 (3 ounce) package cream cheese, softened
1 teaspoon finely grated onion
Mayonnaise
1 (3 ounce) package sliced ham
1 (15 ounce) can asparagus spears

- Combine cream cheese, grated onion and enough mayonnaise to make spreading consistency.
- Separate sliced ham and spread each with cream cheese mixture.
- Place 1 or 2 asparagus spears on each ham slice and roll.
- Cut each roll into 4 pieces.
- Spear each piece with toothpick for serving and refrigerate.

TIP: *This is great for a salad luncheon.*

Toasted Pepperoni

1 (5 ounce) box melba rounds
¾ cup chili sauce
5 ounces pepperoni rounds
1 cup shredded mozzarella cheese

- Spread melda rounds with chili sauce.
- Top melba rounds with pepperoni slices and sprinkle with cheese.
- Bake on baking sheet at 375° for 3 to 5 minutes.

Drunk Franks

1 (10 count) package wieners
½ cup chili sauce
½ cup packed brown sugar
½ cup bourbon

- Cut wieners into bite-size pieces.
- Combine chili sauce, sugar and bourbon in saucepan.
- Add wieners to sauce and simmer 30 minutes.
- Serve in chafing dish.

Party Smokies

1 cup ketchup
1 cup plum jelly
1 tablespoon lemon juice
¼ cup prepared mustard
2 (5 ounce) packages tiny smoked sausages

- In saucepan, combine ketchup, jelly, lemon juice and mustard, heat and mix well.
- Add sausages and simmer for 10 minutes.
- Serve hot with cocktail toothpicks.

Sausage Bites

1 (1 pound) package hot sausage
1 (16 ounce) package shredded Colby or cheddar cheese
3¾ cups biscuit mix
½ teaspoon garlic powder

- Combine all ingredients and knead thoroughly.
- Roll into 1-inch balls.
- Bake on baking sheet at 350° for 15 to 18 minutes or until light brown.

Sausage Pinwheels

2½ cups biscuit mix
⅔ cup milk
1 (16 ounce) package hot sausage, room temperature
1 green or red bell pepper, minced

- In medium bowl, combine biscuit mix and milk and mix well.
- Divide dough into 3 parts. Roll each piece of dough into thin rectangle.
- Crumble one-third sausage and one-third bell pepper on each piece of dough and pat down.
- Roll up like jellyroll, cover with foil and refrigerate overnight.
- Cut into thin slices and bake at 375° for 15 to 20 minutes.

Sausage-Pineapple Bits

1 pound link sausage, cooked, skinned
1 pound hot bulk sausage
1 (15 ounce) can crushed pineapple with juice
2 cups packed brown sugar
1 tablespoon marinade for chicken

- Slice link sausage into ⅓-inch pieces. Shape bulk sausage into 1-inch balls.
- In skillet, brown sausage balls.
- In large saucepan, combine pineapple, brown sugar and marinade for chicken.
- Heat, add both sausages and simmer for 30 minutes.
- Serve from chafing dish or small slow cooker with cocktail toothpicks.

TIP: This "sweet and hot" combination has a delicious flavor.

Pizza in a Bowl

1 pound lean ground beef
1 (26 ounce) jar marinara or spaghetti sauce
2 teaspoons dried oregano
1 (16 ounce) package shredded mozzarella cheese
¾ teaspoon garlic powder

- In a saucepan, cook beef over medium heat until no longer pink and drain.
- Stir in marinara sauce and oregano and simmer about 15 minutes.
- Gradually stir in cheese until it melts.
- Pour into fondue pot or small slow cooker to keep warm.
- Serve with Italian toast (Panetini – found in the deli).

No-Fuss Meatballs

1 (14 ounce) package frozen cooked meatballs, thawed
1 tablespoon soy sauce
½ cup chili sauce
⅔ cup grape or plum jelly
¼ cup dijon-style mustard

- In skillet, cook meatballs in soy sauce until heated through.
- Combine chili sauce, jelly and mustard and pour over meatballs.
- Cook and stir until jelly dissolves and mixture comes to a boil.
- Reduce heat, cover and simmer for about 5 minutes.

TIP: Be sure to have toothpicks ready for serving.

Mini Reubens

½ cup thousand island dressing
24 slices party rye bread
11/3 cups well drained, chopped sauerkraut
½ pound thinly sliced corned beef
¼ pound sliced Swiss cheese

- Spread dressing on slices of bread.
- Place 1 slice corned beef on bread and top with sauerkraut.
- Cut cheese same size as bread and place over sauerkraut.
- Place open-face sandwiches on baking sheet and bake at 375° for 10 minutes or until cheese melts.

Dried Beef and Chips

1 (8 ounce) package cream cheese, softened
1 (8 ounce) carton sour cream
1 (3 ounce) package dried beef, cubed
½ cup finely chopped pecans

- Use mixer to beat cream cheese and sour cream until smooth and creamy.
- Fold in dried beef chunks and pecans.
- Refrigerate and serve with chips.

Cucumber Squares

1 (8 ounce) package cream cheese, softened
½ teaspoon dillweed
3 medium cucumbers, peeled, grated
1 (1 ounce) package dry ranch-style salad dressing mix

- In mixing bowl, combine cream cheese and dillweed and beat until creamy.
- Fold in grated cucumbers and dressing mix.
- Spread on pumpernickel or rye bread slices.

Sweet Onions

5 Texas 1015 or Vidalia® onions, chopped
1 cup sugar
½ cup white vinegar
⅔ cup mayonnaise
1 teaspoon celery salt

- Soak onions in sugar, vinegar and 2 cups water for about 3 hours. Drain.
- Toss with mayonnaise and celery salt.
- Serve on crackers.

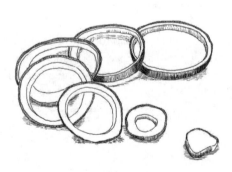

Onion Crisps

1 cup (2 sticks) butter, softened
2 cups shredded cheddar cheese
1 (1 ounce) package dry onion soup mix
2 cups flour

- Combine all ingredients and mix well. (Dough will be very thick.)
- Divide into 2 batches and form into 2 rolls. Refrigerate for 3 hours.
- Cut in ¼-inch slices.
- Bake at 350° for 12 to 15 minutes.

Great Guacamole

4 avocados, peeled
½ cup salsa
¼ cup sour cream
1 teaspoon salt

- Split avocados and remove seeds. Mash avocado with fork.
- Add salsa, sour cream and salt and stir.
- Serve with tortilla chips.

Caviar-Artichoke Delights

2 (8 ounce) packages cream cheese, softened
1 (14 ounce) can artichoke hearts, drained, chopped
½ cup finely grated onion
1 (3 ounce) jar caviar, drained
3 hard-boiled eggs, grated

- Beat cream cheese until smooth and add artichoke hearts and onion.
- Spread in 8 or 9-inch glass pie plate and refrigerate.
- Before serving, spread caviar on top of cream cheese mixture and place grated eggs on top.
- Serve with crackers.

Fruit 'n Crackers

1 (8 ounce) package cream cheese, softened
2 tablespoons orange juice
1½ teaspoons triple sec liqueur
1 (11 ounce) package wheat crackers
Several kiwi fruit

- Beat cream cheese, orange juice and triple sec.
- Lightly toast crackers at 350° for 10 minutes.
- Spread crackers with cream cheese mixture.
- Decorate tops of crackers with fruit.

Spicy Cheese Round

1 pound hot sausage
1 cup chunky hot salsa
1 (16 ounce) package cubed processed cheese
1 (16 ounce) package shredded sharp cheddar cheese
1 (16 ounce) package shredded mild cheddar cheese

- Brown sausage in large roasting pan and add salsa.
- Add processed cheese and turn burner on low. Stir constantly while cheese melts.
- Add cheddar cheeses while stirring. (It will be hard to stir, but you must keep stirring to keep cheese from burning.)
- Pour into bundt pan coated with non-stick vegetable spray and refrigerate overnight.
- Unmold onto platter. (It would be nice to place parsley around the ring.)
- To serve, cut slices of the cheese mold and serve with wheat crackers.

TIP: This is really a "big" party ring of seasoned cheese. The shape of the bundt pan makes it elegant as well as delicious.

Chipped Beef Ball

1 (8 ounce) package cream cheese, softened
2 teaspoons horseradish
1 teaspoon prepared mustard
¼ teaspoon garlic powder
1 (5 ounce) package dried beef, finely chopped

- In mixing bowl, blend cream cheese, horseradish, mustard and garlic powder and roll into ball.
- Roll ball in dried beef. (The best way to chop dried beef is with scissors.)
- Serve with crackers.

Ranch Cheese Ball

1 (1 ounce) package dry ranch-style salad dressing mix
2 (8 ounce) packages cream cheese, softened
¼ cup finely chopped pecans
1 (3 ounce) jar real bacon bits

- Use mixer to blend dressing mix and cream cheese.
- Roll into ball and then roll ball in pecans and bacon bits.
- Refrigerate several hours before serving.

Sausage Balls

1 pound hot pork sausage, uncooked
1 (16 ounce) package grated cheddar cheese
3 cups biscuit mix
⅓ cup milk

- Combine all ingredients and form into small balls. (If dough is a little too sticky, add 1 more teaspoon biscuit mix.)
- Bake at 375° for 13 to 15 minutes.

Olive-Cheese Balls

2¼ cups shredded sharp cheddar cheese
1 cup flour
½ cup (1 stick) butter, melted
1 (5 ounce) jar green olives

- In large bowl, combine cheese and flour. Add butter and mix well.
- Cover olives with mixture and form into balls.
- Bake at 350° for about 15 minutes or until light brown.

The Queen's Cheese Balls

½ cup (1 stick) butter, softened
1 (6 ounce) jar sharp processed cheese spread, softened
¼ teaspoon cayenne pepper
½ teaspoon salt
1 cup plus 2 tablespoons flour

- In bowl, mix butter, cheese spread, cayenne pepper and salt and work flour in gradually.
- Form into marble-size balls and flatten with fork.
- Bake at 400° for 6 to 8 minutes or until light brown.

Orange Dip for Apples

1 (8 ounce) package cream cheese, softened
1 (8 ounce) carton orange yogurt
½ cup orange marmalade
¼ cup finely chopped pecans

- Use mixer to beat cream cheese until smooth.
- Fold in yogurt, marmalade and pecans and refrigerate.
- Serve with apple slices.

Nutty Apple Dip

1 (8 ounce) package cream cheese, softened
1 cup packed brown sugar
1 teaspoon vanilla extract
1 cup finely chopped pecans

- In small mixing bowl combine cream cheese, sugar and vanilla and beat until smooth.
- Stir in pecans.
- Serve with sliced apples for dipping.

Caramel-Apple Dip

1 (8 ounce) package cream cheese, softened
1 cup packed brown sugar
1 teaspoon vanilla extract
½ cup chopped dry-roasted peanuts

- Combine cream cheese, brown sugar and vanilla with mixer and beat until creamy.
- Stir in peanuts. Refrigerate.
- Serve with crisp apple slices.

Fruit Dip for Nectarines

1 (8 ounce) package cream cheese, softened
2 (7 ounce) jars marshmallow cream
¼ teaspoon cinnamon
⅛ teaspoon ground ginger

- Use mixer to combine and beat all ingredients.
- Mix well and refrigerate.
- Serve with unpeeled slices of nectarines or any other fruit.

Kahlua Fruit Dip

1 (8 ounce) package cream cheese, softened
1 (8 ounce) carton whipped topping, thawed
⅔ cup packed brown sugar
⅓ cup Kahlua® liqueur
1 (8 ounce) carton sour cream

- With mixer, whip cream cheese until creamy and fold in whipped topping.
- Add sugar, Kahlua® and sour cream and mix well.
- Refrigerate 24 hours before serving with fresh fruit.

Peachy Fruit Dip

1 (15 ounce) can sliced peaches, drained
½ cup marshmallow cream
1 (3 ounce) package cream cheese, cubed
⅛ teaspoon ground nutmeg

- In blender or food processor, combine all ingredients.
- Serve with assorted fresh fruit.

Chocolate Fruit Dip

1 (8 ounce) package cream cheese, softened
¼ cup chocolate syrup
1 (7 ounce) jar marshmallow cream
Fruit

- In mixing bowl, beat cream cheese and chocolate syrup until smooth.
- Fold in marshmallow cream.
- Cover and refrigerate until ready to serve.
- Serve with apple wedges, banana chunks or strawberries.

Juicy Fruit

Delicious!

1 (8 ounce) package cream cheese, softened
2 (7 ounce) jars marshmallow cream
½ teaspoon cinnamon
⅛ teaspoon ground ginger

- With mixer, combine and beat all ingredients.
- Mix well and refrigerate.
- Serve with unpeeled slices of nectarines or apple slices.

Ginger-Fruit Dip

1 (3 ounce) package cream cheese, softened
1 (7 ounce) jar marshmallow cream
½ cup mayonnaise
1 teaspoon ground ginger
1 teaspoon grated orange rind

- Beat cream cheese at medium speed until smooth.
- Add marshmallow cream, mayonnaise, ginger and orange rind and stir until smooth.
- Serve with fresh fruit sticks.

Roasted Mixed Nuts

1 pound mixed nuts
¼ cup maple syrup
2 tablespoons brown sugar
1 (1 ounce) package dry ranch-style salad dressing mix

- In bowl, combine nuts and maple syrup and mix well.
- Sprinkle with brown sugar and salad dressing mix and stir gently to coat.
- Spread in greased 10 x 15-inch baking pan.
- Bake at 300° for 25 minutes or until light brown and cool.

Deviled Pecans

¼ cup (½ stick) butter, melted
1 tablespoon Worcestershire sauce
2 cups pecan halves
¼ teaspoon cayenne pepper

- In mixing bowl, combine butter and Worcestershire sauce and mix well.
- Add pecans, cayenne pepper and ¼ teaspoon salt.
- Stir and toss pecans until well coated.
- Roast on baking sheet at 350° for 15 minutes. Stir or shake pan occasionally.

Classy Red Pecans

¼ cup (½ stick) butter
1½ teaspoons chili powder
¾ teaspoon garlic salt
3 cups pecan halves

- In large skillet, melt butter.
- Stir in chili powder, garlic salt and pecans.
- Cook on medium heat. Stir pecans constantly for 4 or 5 minutes until brown and well coated with chili powder.

Toasted Pecans

12 cups pecan halves
½ cup (1 stick) butter
Salt

- Place pecans in large baking pan and toast at 250° for 30 minutes.
- Slice butter and spread in hot pan.
- Coat pecans completely with butter by stirring several times.
- After pecans and butter mix well, sprinkle with salt and stir often.
- Toast pecans 1 hour more until butter absorbs and pecans are crisp.

Sugared Pecans

½ cup packed brown sugar
¼ cup sugar
½ cup sour cream
⅛ teaspoon salt
3 cups pecan halves

- Combine sugars and sour cream and stir over medium heat until sugar dissolves.
- Boil sugar-sour cream mixture to soft-ball stage, add salt and remove from heat.
- Add pecans, stir to coat and pour on wax paper.
- Separate pecans carefully. (They will harden after several minutes.)

Honeycomb Pecans

2 cups sugar
2 tablespoons honey
2 teaspoons vanilla extract
1 teaspoon rum flavoring
3 cups whole pecans

- Combine sugar, honey and ½ cup water in saucepan and stir to mix.
- Bring mixture to boil (do not stir) and cook to soft-ball stage (240°).
- Remove from heat, add vanilla and rum flavoring and cool to lukewarm.
- Beat with mixer 2 to 3 minutes or until mixture turns creamy and stir in pecans until coated.
- Drop by heaping teaspoonfuls onto wax paper and cool.

Cinnamon Pecans

1 pound shelled pecan halves
1 egg white, slightly beaten with fork
2 tablespoons cinnamon
¾ cup sugar

- Combine pecan halves with egg white and mix well.
- Sprinkle with mixture of cinnamon and sugar and stir until all pecans are coated.
- Spread on baking sheet and bake at 325° for about 20 minutes.
- Cool and store in covered container.

Spiced Pecans

You can't eat just one!

2 cups sugar
2 teaspoons cinnamon
1 teaspoon ground nutmeg
½ teaspoon ground cloves
4 cups pecan halves

- Combine sugar, cinnamon, nutmeg, cloves, ½ cup water and ¼ teaspoon salt.
- Mix well, cover with wax paper and microwave on HIGH for 4 minutes.
- Stir and microwave another 4 minutes.
- Add pecans, quickly mix well and spread on wax paper to cool.
- Break apart and store in covered container.

Surprise Chocolates

2 pounds white chocolate
2 cups Spanish peanuts
2 cups small pretzel sticks, broken

- Melt chocolate in double boiler and stir in peanuts and pretzels.
- Drop by teaspoonfuls onto wax paper. (Work fast because mixture hardens quickly.)
- Place in freezer for 1 hour before storing at room temperature.

Scotch Crunchies

½ cup crunchy peanut butter
1 (6 ounce) package butterscotch bits
2½ cups frosted corn flakes
½ cup peanuts

- Combine peanut butter and butterscotch bits in large saucepan and melt over low heat.
- Stir until butterscotch bits melt and stir in cereal and peanuts.
- Drop by teaspoonfuls on wax paper.
- Refrigerate until firm and store in airtight container.

Tumbleweeds

1 (12 ounce) can salted peanuts
1 (7 ounce) can potato sticks, broken up
3 cups butterscotch chips
3 tablespoons peanut butter

- Combine peanuts and potato sticks in bowl and set aside.
- In microwave, heat butterscotch chips and peanut butter at 70% power for 1 to 2 minutes or until they melt and stir every 30 seconds.
- Add butterscorch mixture to peanut mixture and stir to coat evenly.
- Drop by rounded tablespoonfuls on wax paper-lined baking sheet.
- Refrigerate until set, about 10 minutes.

Butterscotch Peanuts

1 (12 ounce) package butterscotch morsels
2 cups chow mein noodles
1 cup dry-roasted peanuts

- In saucepan, heat butterscotch morsels over low heat until they completely melt.
- Add noodles and peanuts and stir until each piece is coated.
- Drop by teaspoonfuls on wax paper.
- Cool and store in airtight container.

White Chocolate Salties

8 (2 ounce) squares almond bark
1 (12 ounce) package salted Spanish peanuts
3 cups thin pretzel sticks, broken up

- Place almond bark in top of double boiler, heat and stir until almond bark melts.
- Remove from heat and cool 2 minutes.
- Add peanuts and pretzels and stir until coated.
- Drop by teaspoonfuls on wax paper and refrigerate 20 minutes or until firm.

Sweet and Sour Pickles

1 (1 quart) jar sliced dill pickles with juice
1½ cups sugar
½ cup white vinegar
¾ teaspoon mustard seeds

- Set aside juice and pickle jar and place pickles in bowl.
- Cover pickle slices with sugar and let soak overnight.
- Return pickles to jar.
- Heat pickle juice, vinegar and mustard seeds to a boil and pour over pickles.
- Let set overnight.

Simply Sweet Pickles

1 (1 gallon) jar whole dill pickles
5 pounds sugar
Hot sauce as needed
5 garlic cloves, chopped

- Drain pickles completely and slice.
- Layer pickles in 5 layers as follows: pickles, sugar, hot sauce and garlic.
- Pack firmly into original jar and close lid tightly.
- Set aside at room temperature for 6 days and turn jar upside down once a day.
- After sixth day, store in refrigerator.

Mexican Pick-Up Sticks

1 (7 ounce) can potato sticks
2 (12 ounce) cans Spanish peanuts
2 (3 ounce) cans french-fried onions
⅓ cup (⅔ stick) butter, melted
1 (1 ounce) package dry taco seasoning mix

- In 9 x 13-inch baking dish, combine potato sticks, peanuts and fried onions.
- Drizzle with melted butter and stir.
- Sprinkle with taco seasoning and mix well.
- Bake at 250° for 45 minutes and stir every 15 minutes.

Perfect Party Punch

1 (12 ounce) can frozen limeade concentrate
1 (46 ounce) can pineapple juice, chilled
1 (46 ounce) can apricot nectar, chilled
1 quart ginger ale, chilled

- Dilute limeade concentrate according to can directions.
- Add pineapple juice and apricot nectar and stir well.
- When ready to serve, add ginger ale

Great Fruit Punch

1 (46 ounce) can pineapple juice
2 (46 ounce) cans apple juice
3 quarts ginger ale
Fresh mint to garnish, optional

- Combine pineapple juice and apple juice and make ice ring with part of juice.
- Refrigerate remaining juice mixture and ginger ale.
- When ready to serve, combine juice mixture and ginger ale and place ice ring in punch bowl.

TIP: *If you don't have a round gelatin mold with hole in the middle, make the ice ring with any type of gelatin mold.*

Ruby Red Punch

1 (46 ounce) can pineapple-grapefruit juice
½ cup sugar
¼ cup cinnamon candies
1 quart ginger ale, chilled

- In large saucepan, combine pineapple-grapefruit juice, sugar and candies. Bring to a boil and stir until candies dissolve.
- Cool until time to serve and stir occasionally to completely dissolve candies.
- Add ginger ale just before serving.

Party Hardy Punch

1 (46 ounce) can pineapple juice
1 (46 ounce) can apple juice
3 quarts ginger ale, chilled
Pineapple chunks, optional

- Combine pineapple juice and apple juice in very large plastic container (or 2 plastic pitchers) and freeze.
- When ready to serve, place juice mixture in punch bowl and add chilled ginger ale.
- Stir to mix and garnish with pineapple chunks.

Piña Colada Punch

1 (46 ounce) can pineapple juice, chilled
1 (20 ounce) can crushed pineapple with juice
1 (15 ounce) can cream of coconut
1 (32 ounce) bottle lemon-lime carbonated drink, chilled

- Combine all ingredients.
- Serve over ice cubes.

Party Punch

1 (46 ounce) can pineapple juice
1 (46 ounce) can apple juice
3 quarts ginger ale, chilled

- Freeze pineapple and apple juices in their cans.
- One hour before serving, set out cans at room temperature.
- When ready to serve, place pineapple and apple juices in punch bowl and add chilled ginger ale. Stir to mix.

Cranberry Punch

2 (28 ounce) bottles ginger ale, chilled
1 (48 ounce) can pineapple juice, chilled
1 quart cranberry juice, chilled
1 quart pineapple sherbet, broken up

- Combine all ingredients in punch bowl and serve.

Pineapple-Citrus Punch

1 (46 ounce) can pineapple juice, chilled
1 quart apple juice, chilled
1 (2 liter) bottle lemon-lime carbonated beverage, chilled
1 (6 ounce) can frozen lemonade concentrate, thawed
1 orange, sliced

- Combine pineapple juice, apple juice, lemon-lime beverage and lemonade in punch bowl.
- Add orange slices for decoration.

Citrus Grove Punch

3 cups sugar
6 cups orange juice, chilled
6 cups grapefruit juice, chilled
1½ cups lime juice, chilled
1 liter ginger ale, chilled

- In saucepan, bring sugar and 2 cups water to boil and cook for 5 minutes. Cover and refrigerate until cool.
- Combine juices and sugar mixture and mix well.
- Just before serving, stir in ginger ale. Serve over ice.

Ginger Ale-Nectar Punch

1 (12 ounce) can apricot nectar
1 (6 ounce) can frozen orange juice concentrate, thawed
1 cup water
2 tablespoons lemon juice
1 (2 liter) bottle ginger ale, chilled

- Combine apricot nectar, orange juice concentrate, water and lemon juice and refrigerate.
- When ready to serve, stir in ginger ale.

Best Tropical Punch

1 (46 ounce) can pineapple juice
1 (46 ounce) can apricot nectar
3 (6 ounce) cans frozen limeade concentrate, thawed
3 quarts ginger ale, chilled

- Combine pineapple juice, apricot nectar and limeade concentrate and refrigerate.
- When ready to serve, add ginger ale.

Wine Punch

2 (12 ounce) cans frozen limeade concentrate
4 limeade cans white wine, chilled
2 quarts ginger ale, chilled
Lime slices

- Combine limeade, white wine and ginger ale in punch bowl.
- Serve with ice ring and lime slices.

Cranberry-Pineapple Punch

1 (48 ounce) bottle cranberry juice
1 (46 ounce) can pineapple juice
½ cup sugar
2 teaspoons almond extract
1 (2 liter) bottle ginger ale, chilled

- Combine cranberry juice, pineapple juice, sugar and almond extract and stir until sugar dissolves. Cover and refrigerate for 8 hours.
- When ready to serve, add ginger ale and stir.

Sparkling Cranberry Punch

Ice mold for punch bowl
Red food coloring
2 quarts cranberry juice cocktail, chilled
1 (6 ounce) can frozen lemonade concentrate, thawed
1 quart ginger ale, chilled

- Pour water in mold for ice ring and add red food coloring to make ice brighter and prettier.
- Mix cranberry juice and lemonade concentrate in pitcher. Refrigerate.
- When ready to serve, pour cranberry mixture into punch bowl and add ginger ale.
- Stir well and add ice mold to punch bowl.

Champagne-White Wine Punch

1 (750 ml) bottle dry white wine, chilled
1 cup apricot brandy
1 cup triple sec liqueur
2 (750 ml) bottles dry champagne, chilled
2 quarts club soda

- In large pitcher, combine white wine, apricot brandy and triple sec. Cover and refrigerate until ready to use.
- At serving time, add champagne and club soda, stir to blend and pour in punch bowl.
- Add ice ring to punch bowl and serve.

Sparkling Wine Punch

6 oranges with peel, thinly sliced
1 cup sugar
2 (750 ml) bottles dry white wine
3 (750 ml) bottles sparkling wine, chilled

- Place orange slices in large plastic or glass container and sprinkle with sugar.
- Add white wine, cover and refrigerate at least 8 hours.
- Stir in sparkling wine.

Champagne Punch

1 (750 ml) bottle champagne, chilled
1 (32 ounce) bottle ginger ale, chilled
1 (6 ounce) can frozen orange juice concentrate
Orange slices, optional

- Combine champagne, ginger ale and orange juice concentrate in punch bowl and mix well.
- Serve chilled and garnish with orange slices.

Creamy Strawberry Punch

1 (10 ounce) package frozen strawberries, thawed
½ gallon strawberry ice cream, softened
2 (2 liter) bottles ginger ale, chilled
Fresh strawberries, optional

- Process frozen strawberries in blender.
- Combine strawberries, chunks of ice cream and ginger ale in punch bowl.
- Stir and serve immediately.
- Garnish with fresh strawberries.

Best Coffee Punch

This is so good you will want a big glass of it instead of a punch cup full.

1 gallon very strong, brewed coffee
½ cup sugar
3 tablespoons vanilla extract
2 pints half-and-half cream
1 gallon vanilla ice cream, softened

- Add sugar to coffee and refrigerate. (Add more sugar if you like it sweeter.)
- Add vanilla and half-and-half.
- When ready to serve, combine coffee mixture and ice cream in punch bowl. Break up ice cream into chunks.

Mocha Punch

4 cups brewed coffee
¼ cup sugar
4 cups milk
4 cups chocolate ice cream, softened

- In container, combine coffee and sugar and stir until sugar dissolves.
- Refrigerate for 2 hours.
- Just before serving, pour into small punch bowl.
- Add milk and mix well.
- Top with scoops of ice cream and stir well.

Strawberry Fizz

2 (10 ounce) boxes frozen strawberries, thawed
2 (6 ounce) cans frozen pink lemonade concentrate, thawed
2 (2 liter) bottles ginger ale, chilled
Fresh strawberries, optional

- Process frozen strawberries in blender.
- Pour lemonade into punch bowl and stir in strawberries.
- Add chilled ginger ale and stir well.
- Garnish with fresh strawberries.

TIP: If you want an ice mold to go in the punch bowl, pour ginger ale in a ring mold or gelatin mold and freeze.

Orange Slush

2 cups orange juice
½ cup instant, non-fat dry milk
¼ teaspoon almond extract
8 ice cubes

- Combine all ingredients in blender and process on high until mixture is smooth and thick.
- Serve immediately.

Orange Lush

2 (6 ounce) cans frozen orange juice concentrate, thawed
1 pint cranberry juice
½ cup sugar
1 quart club soda, chilled

- Combine orange juice, cranberry juice and sugar and mix thoroughly.
- Just before serving, pour into punch bowl and stir in chilled club soda.

Limeade Cooler

1½ pints lime sherbet
1 (6 ounce) can frozen limeade concentrate
3 cups milk
Lime slices to garnish, optional

- Beat lime sherbet in mixing bowl and add limeade concentrate and milk.
- Blend all ingredients.
- Pour into 5 glasses and top each with additional scoop of lime sherbet.
- Serve immediately.

Peanut Power Shake

2 bananas, sliced
½ cup frozen orange juice concentrate, thawed
¼ cup peanut butter
¼ cup milk

- In blender, combine all ingredients. Cover and blend until smooth.
- Add 1 cup ice cubes and blend until smooth.

Holiday Egg Nog

1 gallon egg nog
1 pint whipping cream
1 quart brandy
½ gallon vanilla ice cream, softened
Nutmeg

- Combine all ingredients and mix well.
- Serve in individual cups, sprinkle with nutmeg and serve immediately.

Chocolate-Yogurt Malt

4 cups frozen vanilla yogurt
1 cup chocolate milk
¼ cup instant chocolate malted-milk drink mix
Mini-chocolate chips, optional

- Process yogurt, chocolate milk and drink mix in blender until smooth. Stop occasionally to scrape down sides.
- Serve immediately.
- Top with mini-chocolate chips.

Kahlua Frosty

1 cup Kahlua® liqueur
1 pint vanilla ice cream
1 cup half-and-half cream
⅛ teaspoon almond extract
1⅔ cups crushed ice

- Combine all ingredients in blender and process until smooth.
- Serve immediately.

Pink Fizz

3 (6 ounce) cans frozen pink lemonade concentrate
1 (750 ml) bottle pink sparkling wine
3 (2 liter) bottles lemon-lime carbonated beverage,
    divided, chilled

- Combine lemonade concentrate, wine and 2 bottles lemon-lime beverage in airtight container, cover and freeze 8 hours or until firm.
- Rest punch at room temperature for 10 minutes and place in punch bowl.
- Add remaining bottle lemon-lime beverage and stir until slushy.

Amaretto Cooler

1¼ cups amaretto
2 quarts cold orange juice
1 (15 ounce) bottle club soda, chilled
Orange slices, optional

- Combine all ingredients and stir well.
- Garnish with orange slices and serve over ice.

Lemonade Tea

2 family-size tea bags
½ cup sugar
1 (12 ounce) can frozen lemonade concentrate
1 quart ginger ale, chilled

- Steep tea in 3 quarts water and mix with sugar and lemonade.
- Add ginger ale just before serving.

Frosted Chocolate Milk

2 pints coffee ice cream
½ cup chocolate syrup
¼ cup instant coffee granules
2 quarts milk, divided

- In blender, process ice cream, chocolate syrup, coffee and half milk.
- Stir in remaining milk and refrigerate before serving.
- Serve in frosted glasses.

Tropical Smoothie

1½ heaping cups peeled, seeded ripe papaya
1 very ripe large banana
1½ heaping cups ripe cantaloupe, cut into chunks
1 (6 ounce) carton coconut cream pie yogurt
¼ cup milk

- Cut papaya into chunks.
- Place all ingredients in blender and purée until smooth.
- Pour into glasses and serve immediately.

Lemon-Banana Shake

1 (6 ounce) can frozen lemonade concentrate, thawed
1 cup diced bananas
1 quart vanilla ice cream
3 cups milk

- In mixing bowl, combine lemonade concentrate and bananas and beat until mixture is thick.
- For each milkshake, add 1 scoop vanilla ice cream and ¼ cup lemon-banana mixture in glass.
- Fill glass two-thirds full with milk and stir well.
- Top off with 1 more scoop of ice cream.

Banana Split Float

2 ripe bananas, mashed
3 cups milk
1 (10 ounce) package frozen sweetened strawberries, thawed
1½ pints chocolate ice cream, divided

- Place bananas in blender and add milk, strawberries and ½ pint chocolate ice cream.
- Process just until they blend.
- Pour into tall, chilled glasses and top each with scoop of chocolate ice cream.

Banana-Mango Smoothie

1 cup peeled, cubed ripe mango
1 ripe banana, sliced
⅔ cup milk
1 teaspoon honey
¼ teaspoon vanilla extract

- Arrange mango cubes in single layer on baking sheet and freeze about 1 hour or until firm.
- Combine frozen mango, banana, milk, honey and vanilla and pour into blender.
- Process until smooth.

Purple Shakes

1 (6 ounce) can frozen grape juice concentrate, thawed
1 cup milk
2½ cups vanilla ice cream
2 tablespoons sugar, optional

- In blender, combine all ingredients.
- Cover and blend at high speed for 30 seconds.
- Serve immediately.

Sweet Orange Fluff

1¾ cups milk
½ pint vanilla ice cream
⅓ cup frozen orange juice concentrate, thawed
1 teaspoon non-dairy creamer

- In blender, combine all ingredients. Blend until smooth.

Strawberry Smoothie

2 medium bananas, peeled, sliced
1 pint fresh strawberries, washed, quartered
1 (8 ounce) container strawberry yogurt
¼ cup orange juice

- Place all ingredients in blender and process until smooth.
- Serve as is or over crushed ice.

Pineapple-Strawberry Cooler

2 cups milk
1 (20 ounce) can crushed pineapple, chilled
½ pint vanilla ice cream
1 pint strawberry ice cream

- In mixing bowl, combine milk, pineapple and vanilla ice cream.
- Mix just until they blend.
- Pour into tall glasses and top with scoop of strawberry ice cream.

Kahlua

3 cups hot water
1 cup instant coffee granules
4 cups sugar
1 quart vodka
1 vanilla bean, split

- In large saucepan, combine hot water, coffee and sugar and mix well.
- Boil for 2 minutes and cool.
- Add vodka and vanilla bean.
- Pour into bottle or jar and let rest for 30 days before serving. Shake occasionally.

TIP: *If you happen to have some Mexican vanilla extract, make "instant" kahlua by using 3 tablespoons Mexican vanilla instead of 1 vanilla bean. You don't have to wait 30 days.*

Peppermint Hot Chocolate

3 cups hot milk, divided
8 small chocolate peppermint patties
Pinch salt
1 cup half-and-half cream

- Combine ½ cup hot milk with chocolate peppermint patties and stir well.
- Add pinch of salt and remaining hot milk.
- Simmer mixture but do not boil.
- Add half-and-half cream and serve.

Hot Cranberry Cider

1½ quarts cranberry juice
1 (12 ounce) can frozen orange juice concentrate, thawed
1½ orange juice cans water
½ teaspoon cinnamon

- Combine cranberry juice, orange juice and water in large saucepan. Bring to a boil to blend flavors.
- Add cinnamon and stir well.
- Serve hot.

Spanish Coffee

1 tablespoon sugar
4 cups hot, brewed coffee
¾ cup Kahlua® liqueur
Sweetened whipped cream

- Stir sugar into hot coffee and add Kahlua®.
- Pour into 4 serving cups.
- Top with whipped cream.

Praline Coffee

3 cups hot brewed coffee
¾ cup half-and-half cream
¾ cup packed light brown sugar
2 tablespoons butter
¾ cup praline liqueur

- Cook coffee, half-and-half, brown sugar and butter in large saucepan over medium heat and stir constantly. Do not boil.
- Stir in liqueur and serve with sweetened whipped cream.

Mexican Coffee

1 ounce Kahlua® liqueur
1 cup hot, black coffee
Ground cinnamon
Sweetened whipped cream

- Pour Kahlua® and coffee into tall mug.
- Sprinkle with cinnamon and stir.
- Top with whipped cream.
- If you need a shortcut, substitute frozen whipped topping, thawed.

Breakfast,
Brunch
& Breads

Sunrise Eggs

6 eggs
2 cups milk
1 pound sausage, cooked, browned
¾ cup grated processed cheese
6 slices white bread, trimmed, cubed

- Beat eggs and add milk, sausage and cheese.
- Pour mixture over bread and combine well.
- Pour into greased 9 x 13-inch baking pan and cover with foil.
- Bake at 350° for 20 minutes.
- Remove foil, turn oven up to 375° and bake for another 10 minutes.

Bacon-Sour Cream Omelet

5 strips bacon, fried, drained, crumbled
⅓ cup sour cream
3 green onions, chopped
1 tablespoon butter
2 eggs

- Combine bacon and sour cream.
- Sauté onions in remaining bacon drippings and add to bacon-sour cream mixture.
- Melt butter in omelet pan.
- Use fork to beat eggs with 1 tablespoon water, pour eggs into omelet pan and cook.
- When omelet is set, spoon sour cream mixture along center and fold omelet onto warm plate.

Breakfast Wake-Up

2 (7 ounce) cans diced green chiles
12 eggs
2 (16 ounce) packages shredded cheddar cheese
Salsa, optional

- Drain green chiles and save juice.
- In separate bowl, beat eggs with juice of green chiles and add a little salt and pepper.
- Spray 9 x 13-inch pan and spread half cheese in pan and layer chiles over top. Sprinkle with remaining cheese.
- Pour eggs over top and bake uncovered at 350° for 45 minutes.

A Better Scramble

1 (10 ounce) can cheddar cheese soup
8 eggs, lightly beaten
2 tablespoons (¼ stick) butter
Snipped chives

- Pour soup into bowl and stir until smooth.
- Add eggs and a little pepper and mix well.
- In skillet, melt butter.
- Pour in egg mixture and scramble over low heat until set.
- Sprinkle with chives.

Creamy Eggs on Toast

¼ cup (½ stick) butter
4 level tablespoons flour
2 cups milk
6 hard-boiled eggs, sliced

- Melt butter in skillet, stir in flour and add milk.
- Cook over medium heat and stir constantly until sauce thickens.
- Gently fold in egg slices.
- Serve over 6 slices toasted bread.

Mexican Breakfast Eggs

4 tablespoons (½ stick) butter
9 eggs
3 tablespoons milk
5 tablespoons salsa
1 cup crushed tortilla chips

- Melt butter in skillet.
- In bowl, beat eggs and add milk and salsa.
- Pour egg mixture into skillet and stir until eggs are lightly cooked.
- Stir in tortilla chips and serve hot.

Christmas Breakfast

12 to 14 eggs, slightly beaten
1 pound sausage, cooked, drained, crumbled
2 cups whole milk
1½ cups grated cheddar cheese
1 (5 ounce) box seasoned croutons

- Mix all ingredients and pour into 9 x 13-inch baking dish.
- Bake at 350° for 40 minutes.
- Let rest for about 10 minutes before serving.

Breakfast Bake

1 pound hot sausage, cooked, crumbled
1 cup grated cheddar cheese
1 cup biscuit mix
5 eggs, slightly beaten
2 cups milk

- Place sausage in sprayed 9 x 13-inch baking dish and sprinkle with cheese.
- In mixing bowl, combine biscuit mix, eggs and a little salt and beat well.
- Add milk to egg mixture and stir until fairly smooth. Pour over sausage mixture.
- Bake at 350° for 35 minutes. (You can mix this up the night before cooking and refrigerate. To cook the next morning, add 5 minutes to cooking time.)

TIP: This is a favorite for overnight guests and even special enough for Christmas morning.

Huevos Rancheros

4 corn tortillas
8 eggs
3 tablespoons oil
Enchilada sauce
1 cup grated Monterey Jack cheese

- Fry tortillas in hot oil and drain.
- Lightly scramble 2 eggs at a time and place eggs on each tortilla. Repeat process.
- Pour enchilada sauce over eggs.
- Top with cheese and serve with salsa.

Chile Rellenos

2 (7 ounce) cans diced green chiles, drained
1 (16 ounce) package shredded Monterey Jack cheese
4 eggs, beaten
½ cup milk

- In 7 x 11-inch baking dish, layer half green chiles, half cheese, then remaining chiles and cheese.
- Combine eggs, milk and a little salt and pepper in small bowl and mix well.
- Pour over layers of cheese and chiles.
- Bake uncovered at 350° for 30 minutes or until light brown and set.
- Cool for 5 minutes before cutting into squares.

Breakfast Tacos

4 eggs
4 flour tortillas
1 cup chopped, cooked ham
1 cup grated cheddar cheese

- Scramble eggs in skillet.
- Lay tortillas flat and spoon eggs over 4 tortillas.
- Sprinkle with ham and cheese and roll up to enclose filling.
- Place tacos in microwave-safe dish and microwave for 30 seconds or until cheese melts.
- Serve immediately.

Sunrise Tacos

4 eggs, scrambled
½ cup grated cheddar cheese, divided
½ cup salsa, divided
2 flour tortillas

- For each taco, spread half scrambled eggs, ¼ cup cheese and ¼ cup salsa on tortilla and roll up.

Bacon-Egg Burrito

2 slices bacon, cooked, chopped
2 eggs, scrambled
¼ cup shredded cheddar cheese
1 flour tortilla

- Sprinkle bacon, eggs and cheese in middle of tortilla. (Add taco sauce or salsa if you like.)
- Fold tortilla sides over and place seam side down on dinner plate.
- Microwave for 30 seconds or just until mixture heats thoroughly.

Mexican Eggs

4 corn tortillas
4 eggs
1 cup green chile salsa
½ cup grated longhorn cheese

- Dip tortillas in heated oil in skillet and remove quickly.
- Set tortillas in baking pan to keep warm.
- In skillet, fry eggs in a little butter until whites are set. Place fried egg on each tortilla.
- Heat salsa and spoon over each egg. Sprinkle grated cheese on top.
- Place baking pan under broiler just until cheese melts. Serve hot.

Homemade Egg Substitute

6 egg whites
¼ cup instant nonfat dry milk powder
2 teaspoons water
2 teaspoons oil
¼ teaspoon ground turmeric

- Combine all ingredients in blender and process 30 seconds.
- Refrigerate.

Green Chile Squares

2 cups diced green chiles
1 (8 ounce) package shredded sharp cheddar cheese
8 eggs, beaten
Salt and pepper
½ cup half-and-half cream

- Place green chiles in bottom of 9 x 13-inch baking pan and cover with cheese.
- Combine eggs, salt, pepper and cream and pour over chiles and cheese.
- Bake at 350° for 30 minutes.
- Let rest at room temperature for a few minutes before cutting into squares.

Glazed Bacon

1 pound bacon
⅓ cup packed brown sugar
1 teaspoon flour
½ cup finely chopped pecans

- Arrange bacon slices close together, but not overlapping, on wire rack over drip pan.
- In bowl, combine brown sugar, flour and pecans and sprinkle evenly over bacon.
- Bake at 350° for 30 minutes. Drain on paper towels.

Treasure-Filled Apples

6 tart apples
½ cup sugar
¼ cup cinnamon candies
¼ teaspoon ground cinnamon

- Cut tops off apples and set tops aside. Core apples to within ½ inch of bottom.
- Place in sprayed 8-inch baking dish.
- In bowl, combine sugar, candies and cinnamon and spoon 2 tablespoons mixture into each apple. Replace tops.
- Spoon any remaining sugar mixture over apples.
- Bake uncovered at 350° for 30 to 35 minutes or until apples are tender. Baste occasionally.

Spiced Pears

1 (15 ounce) can pear halves
⅓ cup packed brown sugar
¾ teaspoon ground nutmeg
¾ teaspoon ground cinnamon

- Drain pears, reserve syrup and set pears aside.
- Place syrup, brown sugar, nutmeg and cinnamon in saucepan and bring to a boil.
- Reduce heat and simmer uncovered for 5 to 8 minutes. Stir frequently.
- Add pears and simmer for another 5 minutes or until mixture heats through.

Curried Fruit Medley

1 (29 ounce) can sliced peaches
2 (15 ounce) cans pineapple chunks
1 (10 ounce) jar maraschino cherries
1 cup packed brown sugar
1 teaspoon curry powder
¼ cup (½ stick) butter, cut into pieces

- Drain all fruit and place in 9 x 13-inch baking dish.
- Combine brown sugar and curry and stir well. Sprinkle over fruit and dot with butter.
- Bake covered at 350° for 30 minutes or until thoroughly heated.

Apricot Bake

4 (15 ounce) cans apricot halves, drained, divided
1 (16 ounce) box light brown sugar, divided
2 cups round, buttery cracker crumbs, divided
½ cup (1 stick) butter, sliced

- Spray 9 x 13-inch baking dish and line with 2 cans drained apricots.
- Sprinkle half brown sugar and half cracker crumbs over apricots.
- Dot with half butter and repeat layers.
- Bake at 300° for 1 hour.

Mini Apricot Bake

2 (15 ounce) cans apricot halves, drained
¾ cup packed brown sugar
1 cup round, buttery cracker crumbs
½ cup (1 stick) butter, melted

- Butter 2-quart casserole and layer apricots, sugar and cracker crumbs until all ingredients are used.
- Melt butter and pour over casserole.
- Bake at 325° for 35 minutes or until cracker crumbs are slightly brown.
- Serve hot or room temperature.

Peach Bake

2 (15 ounce) cans peach halves, drained
1 cup packed brown sugar
1 cup round, buttery cracker crumbs
½ cup (1 stick) butter, melted

- Butter 2-quart casserole and layer peaches, sugar and cracker crumbs until all ingredients are used.
- Pour melted butter over casserole.
- Bake at 325° for 35 minutes or until cracker crumbs are slightly brown.
- Serve hot or at room temperature.

Pineapple-Cheese Casserole

1 cup sugar
5 tablespoons flour
2 (20 ounce) cans unsweetened pineapple chunks, drained
1½ cups grated cheddar cheese
1 stack round, buttery crackers, crushed
½ cup (1 stick) butter, melted

- Combine sugar and flour.
- Grease 9 x 13-inch baking dish and layer pineapple, sugar-flour mixture, grated cheese and cracker crumbs (in that order).
- Drizzle butter over casserole.
- Bake at 350° for 25 minutes or until bubbly.

TIP: *This is really a different kind of recipe and very good. It can be served at brunch and is also great with sandwiches at lunch.*

Crabmeat Quiche

3 eggs, beaten
1 (8 ounce) carton sour cream
1 (6 ounce) can crabmeat, rinsed, drained, flaked
½ cup grated Swiss cheese
1 (9 inch) unbaked piecrust

- In bowl, combine eggs and sour cream.
- Blend in crabmeat and cheese and add a little garlic salt and pepper.
- Pour into piecrust.
- Bake at 350° for 35 minutes.

Corned Beef Hash Bake

2 (15 ounce) cans corned beef hash, slightly warmed
Butter
6 to 8 eggs
⅓ cup half-and-half cream

- Spread corned beef hash in greased 9 x 13-inch pan.
- Pat down with back of spoon and make 6 to 8 deep hollows in hash large enough for egg to fit.
- Fill hollows with tiny dab of butter.
- Crack 1 egg into each hollow and cover with about 1 tablespoon cream.
- Bake uncovered at 350° for 15 to 20 minutes or until eggs set as desired.
- Divide into squares to serve.

Grits Souffle

1½ cups grits
1½ teaspoons salt
½ cup (1 stick) butter
1½ cups shredded cheddar cheese
5 eggs, beaten

- Boil grits in 6 cups salted water and drain.
- Stir in butter and cheese until cheese melts.
- Cool until lukewarm and stir in eggs.
- Pour into greased 2-quart baking dish and bake at 350° for 45 minutes.

Baked Grits

2 cups quick-cooking grits
4 cups water
2 cups milk
¾ cup (1½ sticks) butter
4 eggs, beaten

- Stir grits in water over medium heat for about 5 minutes.
- Add milk and butter, cover and cook another 10 minutes.
- Remove from heat and add eggs.
- Pour in buttered casserole dish and bake at 350° for 30 minutes.

Ranch Sausage-Grits

1 cup quick-cooking grits
1 pound pork sausage
1 onion, chopped
1 cup salsa
1 (8 ounce) package shredded cheddar cheese, divided

- Cook grits according to package directions and set aside.
- Cook and brown sausage and onion and drain well.
- Combine grits, sausage mixture, salsa and half of cheese and spoon into greased 2-quart baking dish.
- Bake at 350° for 15 minutes.
- Remove from oven, add remaining cheese and bake for another 10 minutes.
- Serve hot.

Chiffon Cheese Souffle

12 slices white bread, crusts trimmed
2 (5 ounce) jars sharp processed cheese spread, softened
6 eggs, beaten
3 cups milk
¾ cup (1½ sticks) butter, melted

- Spray 9 x 13-inch baking dish.
- Cut each bread slice into 4 triangles and place dab of cheese on each triangle.
- Place triangles evenly in layers in baking dish. (You could certainly make this in a souffle dish if you have one.)
- Combine eggs, milk, butter and a little salt and pepper and pour over layers.
- Cover and refrigerate 8 hours.
- Remove from refrigerator 10 to 15 minutes before baking and bake uncovered at 350° for 1 hour.

TIP: Wow! Is this ever good! This breakfast soufflé is light and fluffy but still very rich. I think it is the sharp cheese that gives it that special flavor.

Cinnamon Soufflé

1 loaf cinnamon-raisin bread
1 (20 ounce) can crushed pineapple with juice
1 cup (2 sticks) butter, melted
½ cup sugar
5 eggs, slightly beaten

- Slice very thin portion of bread crusts off.
- Tear bread into small pieces and place in buttered 9 x 13-inch baking dish.
- Pour pineapple and juice over bread and set aside.
- Cream butter and sugar.
- Add eggs to creamed mixture and mix well.
- Pour creamed mixture over bread and pineapple. Bake uncovered at 350° for 40 minutes.

TIP: If you have some pecans handy, ½ cup chopped pecans really adds extra texture and flavor.

Bacon-Cheese Stromboli

1 (10 ounce) tube refrigerated pizza dough
¾ cup shredded cheddar cheese
¾ cup shredded mozzarella cheese
6 bacon strips, cooked, crumbled

- On ungreased baking sheet, roll dough into 12-inch circle.
- On half dough, sprinkle cheeses and bacon to within ½ inch of edge.
- Fold dough over filling and pinch edges to seal.
- Bake at 400° for 10 minutes or until golden brown.
- Cut in pie slices and serve with marinara sauce.

Cheese Enchiladas

1 dozen corn tortillas
1 (8 ounce) package shredded cheddar cheese, divided
½ cup chopped onion, divided
2 (10 ounce) cans enchilada sauce

- Wrap tortillas in slightly damp paper towel. Place between 2 salad plates and microwave on HIGH for 45 seconds.
- Sprinkle ⅓ cup cheese and some onion on each tortilla and roll up.
- Place seam side down in 9 x 13-inch baking dish. Repeat with remaining tortillas.
- Pour enchilada sauce over tortillas and sprinkle with remaining cheese and onions.
- Cover and microwave on MEDIUM-HIGH for 5 to 6 minutes.

Praline Toast

½ cup (1 stick) butter, softened
1 cup packed brown sugar
½ cup finely chopped pecans
Bread slices

- Combine butter, sugar and pecans and mix well.
- Spread on bread slices.
- Toast in broiler until brown and bubbly.

French Toast

4 eggs
1 cup whipping cream
2 thick slices bread, cut into 3 strips
Powdered sugar
Maple syrup

- Place a little oil in skillet.
- Beat eggs, cream and pinch of salt to make batter.
- Dip bread and allow batter to soak in.
- Fry bread in skillet until brown, turn and fry other side. Transfer to baking sheet.
- Bake at 325° for about 4 minutes or until puffed.
- Sprinkle with powdered sugar and serve with maple syrup.

Orange-French Toast

1 egg, beaten
½ cup orange juice
5 slices raisin bread
1 cup crushed graham crackers
2 tablespoons butter

- Combine egg and orange juice.
- Dip each slice of bread in egg mixture and then in graham cracker crumbs.
- Fry in butter until brown.

Waffle Flash

2 eggs
1 cup milk
½ teaspoon vanilla extract
8 slices stale bread

- Heat waffle iron according to directions.
- Beat eggs, slowly add milk and vanilla and beat well.
- Remove crust from bread and butter both sides of bread.
- When waffle iron is ready, dip bread in egg mixture and place in waffle iron.
- Close lid and grill until light brown. Serve with syrup.

Light, Crispy Waffles

2 cups biscuit mix
1 egg
½ cup oil
1⅓ cups club soda

- Preheat waffle iron.
- Combine all ingredients in mixing bowl and stir by hand.
- Pour just enough batter to cover waffle iron and cook.

TIP: *To have waffles for a "company weekend", make them before the guests arrive.*
       Freeze the waffles separately on a cookie sheet and place in large plastic bags. To
       heat, bake at 350° for about 10 minutes.

Pecan Waffles

2 cups flour
½ cup oil
½ cup milk
⅔ cup finely chopped pecans

- Preheat waffle iron.
- In bowl, combine flour, oil and milk and mix well.
- Stir in chopped pecans.
- Pour approximately ¾ cup batter onto hot waffle iron and cook until brown and crispy.

Blueberry Coffee Cake

1 (16 ounce) package blueberry muffin mix with blueberries
⅓ cup sour cream
1 egg
⅔ cup powdered sugar
½ cup plus 1 tablespoon water

- Stir muffin mix, sour cream, egg and ½ cup water.
- Rinse blueberries from mix, drain and gently fold into batter.
- Pour into sprayed 7 x 11-inch baking dish.
- Bake at 400° for about 25 minutes and cool.
- Mix powdered sugar and 1 tablespoon water and drizzle over coffee cake.

Pineapple Coffee Cake

1 (18 ounce) box butter cake mix
½ cup oil
4 eggs, slightly beaten
1 (20 ounce) can pineapple pie filling

- In mixing bowl, combine cake mix, oil and eggs and beat well.
- Pour batter into greased, floured 9 x 13-inch baking pan.
- Bake at 350° for 45 to 50 minutes. Test with toothpick to make sure cake is done.
- With knife, punch holes in cake about 2 inches apart.
- Spread pineapple pie filling over cake while cake is still hot.

Cranberry Coffee Cake

2 eggs
1 cup mayonnaise
1 (18 ounce) box spice cake mix
1 (16 ounce) can whole cranberry sauce
Powdered sugar

- Preheat oven to 325°.
- Beat together eggs, mayonnaise and cake mix with mixer and fold in cranberry sauce.
- Pour into greased, floured 9 x 13-inch baking pan.
- Bake for 45 minutes. Test with toothpick to be sure cake is done.
- When cake is cool, dust with powdered sugar. (If you would rather have frosting than powdered sugar, use prepared frosting.)

Toasted French Bread

1 (16 ounce) loaf unsliced French bread
½ cup (1 stick) butter, softened
¾ cup grated parmesan cheese
1½ teaspoons hot sauce

- Slice bread in half horizontally, then quarter.
- Combine butter, parmesan cheese and hot sauce and spread over slices using all of mixture.
- Place on baking sheet and cook at 325° for 25 minutes or until bread heats well and is brown on top.

Parmesan Bread Deluxe

1 (16 ounce) loaf unsliced Italian bread
½ cup refrigerated creamy caesar dressing
⅓ cup grated parmesan cheese
3 tablespoons finely chopped green onions

- Cut 24 (½-inch thick) slices from bread. (Save remaining bread for other use.)
- In small bowl, combine dressing, cheese and onion.
- Spread 1 teaspoon dressing mixture on each bread slice.
- Place bread on baking sheet and broil 4 inches from heat until golden brown.
- Serve warm.

Cheesy Herb Bread

1 (16 ounce) loaf unsliced French bread
½ teaspoon garlic powder
1 teaspoon marjoram leaves
1 tablespoon dried parsley leaves
½ cup (1 stick) butter, softened
1 cup grated parmesan cheese

- Slice bread into 1-inch slices.
- Combine garlic, marjoram, parsley and butter.
- Spread mixture on bread slices and sprinkle with cheese.
- Wrap in foil and bake at 375° for 20 minutes. Unwrap and bake for 5 more minutes.

Garlic Toast

1 (16 ounce) loaf unsliced French bread
1 tablespoon garlic powder
2 tablespoons dried parsley flakes
½ cup (1 stick) butter, melted
1 cup grated parmesan cheese

- Slice bread into 1-inch slices diagonally.
- In small bowl, combine garlic powder, parsley and butter and mix well. Use brush to spread mixture on bread slices and sprinkle with parmesan cheese.
- Place on baking sheet and bake at 225° for about 1 hour.

Ranch French Bread

1 (16 ounce) loaf unsliced French bread
½ cup (1 stick) butter, softened
1 tablespoon dry ranch-style salad dressing mix

- Cut loaf in half horizontally.
- Blend butter and dressing mix and spread mixture on bread.
- Wrap bread in foil and bake at 350° for 15 minutes.

Cheese Drops

2 cups biscuit mix
⅔ cup milk
⅔ cup grated sharp cheddar cheese
¼ cup (½ stick) butter, melted

- Spray baking sheet with non-stick spray.
- Combine biscuit mix, milk and cheese. Drop 1 heaping tablespoon dough onto baking sheet for each biscuit.
- Bake at 400° for 10 minutes or until light brown.
- While warm, brush tops of biscuits with melted butter. Serve hot.

Bacon-Cheese French Bread

1 (16 ounce) loaf unsliced French bread
5 slices bacon, cooked, crumbled
1 (8 ounce) package shredded mozzarella cheese
½ cup (1 stick) butter, melted

- Slice bread into 1-inch slices and place sliced loaf on large piece of foil.
- Combine bacon and cheese and sprinkle between slices of bread.
- Drizzle butter over loaf and let some drip in between slices.
- Wrap loaf tightly in foil. Bake at 350° for 20 minutes or until it heats well.
- Serve hot.

Green Chile-Cheese Bread

1 (16 ounce) loaf unsliced Italian bread
½ cup (1 stick) butter, melted
1 (4 ounce) can diced green chiles, drained
¾ cup grated Monterey Jack cheese

- Slice bread into 1-inch slices almost all the way through.
- Combine melted butter, chiles and cheese and mix well.
- Spread cheese mixture between bread slices.
- Cover loaf with foil and bake at 350° for 25 minutes.

Poppy Seed Bread

3¾ cups biscuit mix
1½ cups shredded cheddar cheese
1 tablespoon poppy seeds
1 egg, beaten
1½ cups milk

- Combine all ingredients and beat vigorously for 1 minute.
- Pour into greased loaf pan.
- Bake at 350° for 50 to 60 minutes. Test for doneness with toothpick.
- Remove from pan and cool before slicing.

Poppy Seed-Onion Loaf

2 tablespoons instant minced onions
1 tablespoon poppy seeds
½ cup (1 stick) butter, melted
2 (12 ounce) cans refrigerated butter flake biscuits

- Combine onions and poppy seeds with butter.
- Separate each biscuit into 2 or 3 layers.
- Dip each biscuit piece in butter mixture and turn to coat.
- Place biscuit pieces on edge of loaf pan and pieces into 2 rows.
- Pour remaining butter mixture over top of loaf.
- Bake at 325° for 35 minutes. Serve warm.

Mozzarella Loaf

1 (16 ounce) loaf unsliced French bread
12 slices mozzarella cheese
¼ cup grated parmesan cheese
6 tablespoons (¾ stick) butter, softened
½ teaspoon garlic salt

- Cut loaf into 1-inch thick slices.
- Place mozzarella slices between bread slices.
- Combine parmesan cheese, butter and garlic salt and spread mixture on each slice of bread.
- Reshape loaf, press firmly together and brush remaining butter mixture on outside of loaf.
- Bake at 375° for 8 to 10 minutes.

Cheddar Cheese Loaf

3¾ cups biscuit mix
¾ cup shredded sharp cheddar cheese
1½ cups milk
2 small eggs
⅛ teaspoon ground red pepper

- Combine biscuit mix and cheese. Add milk, eggs and pepper and stir 2 minutes or until ingredients blend.
- Spoon into sprayed 9 x 5-inch loaf pan.
- Bake at 350° for 45 minutes. Cool before slicing.

Creamy Butter Bread

1 cup (2 sticks) butter, softened
2 cups flour
1 (8 ounce) carton sour cream

- Combine all ingredients and mix well.
- Drop by teaspoonfuls into miniature muffin cups.
- Bake at 350° for 20 minutes or until light brown.

Crunchy Breadsticks

1 (8 count) package hot dog buns
1 cup (2 sticks) butter, melted
Garlic powder
Paprika

- Take each half bun and slice in half lengthwise.
- Use pastry brush to butter each breadstick. Sprinkle lightly with garlic powder and paprika.
- Place on baking sheet and bake at 225° for 45 minutes.

Cheddar-Butter Toast

½ cup (1 stick) butter, softened
1¼ cups shredded cheddar cheese
1 teaspoon Worcestershire sauce
¼ teaspoon garlic powder
Thick-sliced bread

- Combine all ingredients and spread on thick-sliced bread.
- Turn on broiler to preheat. When oven is hot, turn off broiler and put toast in oven for about 15 minutes.

Crispy Herb Bread

1½ teaspoons basil
1 teaspoon rosemary
½ teaspoon thyme
¾ cup (1½ sticks) butter, melted
1 (8 count) package hot dog buns

- Combine basil, rosemary, thyme and butter and let stand several hours at room temperature.
- Spread butter mixture on buns and cut buns into strips.
- Bake at 300° for 15 to 20 minutes or until crisp.

Easy Cheesy Breadsticks

1½ cups shredded Monterey Jack cheese
¼ cup poppy seeds
2 tablespoons dry onion soup mix
2 (11 ounce) cans breadstick dough

- Spread cheese evenly in 9 x 13-inch baking dish. Sprinkle poppy seeds and soup mix evenly over cheese.
- Separate breadstick dough into strips. Stretch strips slightly until each is about 12 inches long.
- Place strips one at a time into cheese mixture. Turn to coat all sides.
- Cut into smaller 3 or 4-inch strips. Place on baking sheet and bake at 375° for 12 minutes.

Quick Pumpkin Bread

1 (16 ounce) package pound cake mix
1 cup canned pumpkin
2 eggs
⅓ cup milk
1 teaspoon allspice

- With mixer, beat all ingredients and blend well.
- Pour into greased, floured 9 x 5-inch loaf pan.
- Bake at 350° for 1 hour. Use toothpick to test for doneness.
- Cool and turn out onto cooling rack.

Sausage-Cheese Biscuits

1 (8 ounce) package grated cheddar cheese
1 pound hot bulk pork sausage
2 cups biscuit mix
¾ cup milk

- Combine cheese, sausage and biscuit mix. Stir in milk.
- Drop by teaspoonfuls on ungreased baking sheet.
- Bake at 400° until light brown and serve hot.

Quickie Hot Biscuits

1⅓ cups flour
1 (8 ounce) carton whipping cream
2 tablespoons sugar

- Combine all ingredients and stir until they blend well.
- Drop biscuits by teaspoonfuls onto sprayed baking sheet and bake at 400° for 10 minutes or until light brown.
- Serve with plain or flavored butters.

Garlic Biscuits

5 cups biscuit mix
1 cup shredded cheddar cheese
1 (14 ounce) can chicken broth with roasted garlic

- Combine all ingredients to form soft dough.
- Drop by heaping teaspoonfuls onto sprayed baking sheet.
- Bake at 425° for 10 minutes or until light brown.

French Onion Biscuits

2 cups biscuit mix
¼ cup milk
1 (8 ounce) container French onion dip
2 tablespoons finely minced green onion

- Mix all ingredients until soft dough forms.
- Drop dough by teaspoonfuls onto sprayed baking sheet.
- Bake at 400° for 10 minutes or until light brown.

Cream Cheese Biscuits

1 (3 ounce) package cream cheese, softened
½ cup (1 stick) butter, softened
1 cup flour
¼ teaspoon salt, optional

- Use mixer to beat cream cheese and butter.
- Add flour and mix well.
- Roll out dough to ½-inch thickness and cut out biscuits with small biscuit cutter.
- Place on greased baking sheet and bake at 350° for 20 minutes or until light brown.

Quick Sour Cream Biscuits

⅓ cup club soda
⅓ cup sour cream
½ tablespoon sugar
2 cups biscuit mix

- In mixing bowl, combine all ingredients with fork just until dry ingredients are moist.
- Turn bowl out onto lightly floured board and knead gently several times.
- Roll dough to 1-inch thickness and cut out biscuits with biscuit cutter.
- Place dough in sprayed 9 x 13-inch baking pan.
- Bake at 400° for 12 to14 minutes or until golden brown.

Sour Cream Biscuits

2 cups plus 1 tablespoon flour
3 teaspoons baking powder
½ teaspoon baking soda
½ cup shortening
1 (8 ounce) carton sour cream

- Combine flour, baking powder and baking soda, add a little salt and cut in shortening.
- Gradually add sour cream and mix lightly.
- Turn onto lightly floured board and knead a few times. Roll to ½-inch thickness.
- Cut with biscuit cutter and place biscuits on greased baking sheet.
- Bake at 400° for 15 minutes or until light brown.

Lickety-Split Biscuits

2 cups self-rising flour
4 tablespoons mayonnaise
1 cup milk

- Mix all ingredients and drop by teaspoonfuls on baking sheet.
- Bake at 425° until biscuits are golden brown.

Old South Sweet Potato Biscuits

1 (16 ounce) can sweet potatoes, drained
1 tablespoon sugar
¼ cup milk
1½ cups biscuit mix

- In mixing bowl, mash sweet potatoes, add sugar and milk and beat until creamy.
- Stir in biscuit mix with fork until most lumps are gone.
- Pour mixture onto floured wax paper and knead 5 to 6 times.
- Press down to about ½-inch thick and cut out biscuits with biscuit cutter or small glass.
- Bake at 450° for 10 to 12 minutes on ungreased baking sheet.

Cream Biscuits

2 cups flour
1 tablespoon baking powder
½ teaspoon salt
1 (8 ounce) carton whipping cream

- Combine flour, baking powder and salt.
- In mixing bowl, beat whipping cream only until it holds a shape.
- Combine flour mixture and cream and mix with fork.
- Put dough on lightly floured board and knead for about 1 minute. Pat dough to ¾-inch thickness. Cut out biscuits with small biscuit cutter.
- Place on baking sheet and bake at 375° for about 12 minutes or until light brown.

Maple Syrup Biscuits

2¼ cups biscuit mix
⅔ cup milk
1½ cups maple syrup

- Combine biscuit mix and milk and stir just until moist.
- On floured surface, roll dough to ½-inch thickness. Cut out biscuits with 2-inch biscuit cutter.
- Pour syrup into 7 x 11-inch baking dish. Place biscuits on top of syrup.
- Bake at 425° for 13 to 15 minutes or until biscuits are golden brown.

Date Biscuits

1 cup chopped dates
2 cups biscuit mix
½ cup grated American cheese
¾ cup milk

- Combine dates, biscuit mix and cheese.
- Add milk and stir well into moderately soft dough.
- Drop by teaspoonfuls onto sprayed baking sheet.
- Bake at 400° for 12 to 15 minutes and serve hot.

Come and Get 'em Biscuits

2 cups flour
¼ cup mayonnaise
1 cup milk

- Combine all ingredients and drop by teaspoonfuls on baking sheet.
- Bake at 425° until biscuits are golden brown.
- Serve with plain or flavored butters.

Corn Sticks

2 cups biscuit mix
1 (8 ounce) can cream-style corn
2 tablespoons minced green onion
Melted butter

- Combine biscuit mix, cream-style corn and green onions.
- Place dough on floured surface and cut into 3 x 1-inch strips. Roll strips in melted butter.
- Bake at 400° for 15 minutes.

Hush Puppies

1¼ cups yellow cornmeal
1 teaspoon salt
1 cup boiling water
½ onion, finely minced
1 egg, beaten

- Combine cornmeal and salt.
- Bring water to boil in saucepan, add cornmeal mixture and stir constantly.
- Cook until smooth and thick. Cool.
- Add onion and egg and mix thoroughly.
- Form into small balls, roll in flour and deep fry.

Spicy Cornbread Twists

3 tablespoons butter
⅓ cup cornmeal
¼ teaspoon cayenne pepper
1 (11 ounce) can refrigerated soft breadsticks

- Place butter in pie plate and melt in oven. Remove from oven.
- On wax paper, mix cornmeal and cayenne pepper.
- Roll breadsticks in butter and in cornmeal mixture.
- Twist breadsticks according to package directions and place on cookie sheet.
- Bake at 350° for 15 to 18 minutes.

Souper Sausage Cornbread

1 (10 ounce) can cream of celery soup
2 eggs
¼ cup milk
1 (8 ounce) package corn muffin mix
⅓ pound pork sausage, cooked, drained, crumbled

- In medium bowl, combine soup, eggs and milk.
- Stir in muffin mix just until it blends and fold in sausage.
- Spoon mixture into sprayed 9 x 13-inch baking pan.
- Bake at 400° for about 20 minutes or until golden brown.
- Cut into squares.

Cheddar Cornbread

2 (8.5 ounce) packages cornbread muffin mix
2 eggs, beaten
½ cup milk
½ cup plain yogurt
1 (14 ounce) can cream-style corn
½ cup shredded cheddar cheese

- In bowl, combine cornbread mix, eggs, milk and yogurt until blended.
- Stir in corn and cheese and pour into greased 9 x 13-inch baking dish.
- Bake at 400° for 18 to 20 minutes or until light brown.

Sour Cream Cornbread

1 cup self-rising cornmeal
1 (8 ounce) can cream-style corn
1 (8 ounce) carton sour cream
3 large eggs, lightly beaten
¼ cup oil

- Heat lightly greased 8-inch cast-iron skillet in oven at 400°.
- Combine all ingredients and stir just until moist.
- Remove prepared skillet from oven and spoon batter into hot skillet.
- Bake at 400° for 20 minutes or until golden.

Fried Cornbread

2 cups cornmeal
1¼ teaspoons salt
½ teaspoon sugar
1 teaspoon baking powder
Oil

- Combine cornmeal, salt, sugar and baking powder and add just enough boiling water to form fairly stiff dough.
- To fry, heat a little oil in skillet.
- Take heaping tablespoon dough and place in skillet. Pat down with back of spoon so it can be turned over and fried on the top side. (If the last few spoonfuls of cornbread get a little dry, add just a drip or 2 more water.)
- Brown on both sides and serve immediately.

TIP: *This is really an old-time recipe, and of course, we try not to fry things anymore. My husband just has to have this a couple times a year with the old standby red beans.*

Cheese Muffins

3¾ cups buttermilk biscuit mix
1¼ cups grated cheddar cheese
1 egg, beaten
1¼ cups milk
Dash chili powder

- In large bowl, combine all ingredients and beat vigorously by hand.
- Pour into greased muffin tins.
- Bake at 325° for 35 minutes.

Kids' Corn Dog Muffins

2 (6.5 ounce) packages cornbread muffin mix
2 tablespoons brown sugar
2 eggs
1 cup milk
1 (8 ounce) can whole kernel corn, drained
5 hot dogs, chopped

- In bowl, combine cornbread mix and brown sugar.
- Combine eggs and milk and blend with cornbread mixture.
- Stir in corn and hot dogs. (Batter will be thin.)
- Fill greased muffin cups three-fourths full. Bake at 400° for 16 to 18 minutes or until golden brown.

Salad Muffins

⅓ cup sugar
⅓ cup oil
¾ cup milk
2 eggs
2 cups biscuit mix

- In mixing bowl, combine sugar, oil and milk.
- Beat in eggs and biscuit mix and combine well. (Mixture will be a little lumpy.)
- Pour into greased muffin tins two-thirds full.
- Bake at 400° for about 10 minutes or until light brown.

Blueberry-Orange Muffins

1 (16 ounce) package blueberry muffin mix with blueberries
2 egg whites
½ cup orange juice
Orange marmalade

- Wash blueberries with cold water and drain.
- Stir muffin mix, egg whites and orange juice in bowl and break up any lumps.
- Fold blueberries gently into batter and pour into muffin tins (with paper liners) about half full.
- Bake at 370° for 18 to 20 minutes or until toothpick inserted in center comes out clean.
- Spoon orange marmalade over top of hot muffins.

Raspberry-Filled Blueberry Muffins

1(16 ounce) box blueberry muffin mix with blueberries
1 egg
⅓ cup red raspberry jam
¼ cup sliced almonds

- Rinse blueberries and drain.
- In bowl, combine muffin mix, egg and ½ cup water. Stir until moist and break up any lumps in mix.
- Place paper liners in 8 muffin cups. Fill cups half full with batter.
- Combine raspberry jam with blueberries and spoon mixture over batter.
- Cover with remaining batter and sprinkle almonds over batter.
- Bake at 375° for 18 minutes or until light brown.

Ginger-Raisin Muffins

1 (16 ounce) box gingerbread mix
1¼ cups lukewarm water
1 egg
2 (1.5 ounce) boxes seedless raisins

- Combine gingerbread mix, water and egg and mix well. Stir in raisins.
- Pour into sprayed muffin tins and fill half full.
- Bake at 350° for 20 minutes or when tested done with toothpick.

Popovers

2 cups flour
1 teaspoon salt
6 eggs, beaten
2 cups milk
Butter

- Combine flour and salt in bowl.
- Mix eggs and milk in separate bowl.
- Add flour mixture and mix well. (The batter will be like whipping cream.)
- Coat popover pans with butter and heat in oven. Fill each cup half full with batter.
- Bake at 425° for 20 minutes. Reduce heat to 375° and bake for 25 more minutes.
- Serve immediately.

Tea Cakes

1 cup flour
1 cup whipping cream
2 tablespoons sugar
⅛ teaspoon ground cinnamon

- Combine all ingredients and pour into greased mini-muffin cups.
- Bake at 375° for 10 to 15 minutes.

Butter Rolls

2 cups biscuit mix
1 (8 ounce) carton sour cream
½ cup (1 stick) butter, melted

- Combine all ingredients and mix well. Spoon into greased muffin tins and fill only half full.
- Bake at 400° for 12 to 14 minutes or until rolls are light brown.

Drunk Biscuits

3¼ cups biscuit mix
¼ teaspoon salt
1 teaspoon sugar
1⅔ cups beer

- Combine all ingredients and spoon into 12 sprayed muffin cups.
- Bake at 400° for 15 to 20 minutes or until biscuits are golden brown.

Mayo Muffins

1¼ cups flour
3 tablespoons mayonnaise
1 cup whole milk

- Combine all ingredients and spoon into sprayed muffin tins.
- Bake at 375° for 20 minutes or until muffins are light brown.

Soups,
Salads &
Sandwiches

Warm-Your-Soul Soup

Great flavor – great soup!

3 (15 ounce) cans chicken broth
1 (10 ounce) can Italian-style stewed tomatoes with liquid
½ cup chopped onion
¾ cup chopped celery
½ (12 ounce) box fettuccine

- In large soup kettle, combine chicken broth, tomatoes, onion and celery, bring to boil and simmer until onion and celery are almost done.
- Add pasta and cook according to package directions.
- Season with a little salt and pepper.

Swiss-Vegetable Soup

1 (1 ounce) package dry vegetable soup mix
3 cups water
1 cup half-and-half cream
1½ cups shredded Swiss cheese

- Combine soup mix and water in saucepan and bring to boil.
- Lower heat and simmer for 10 minutes.
- Add half-and-half and cheese and serve hot.

Tomato-French Onion Soup

1 (10 ounce) can tomato bisque soup
2 (10 ounce) cans French onion soup
Grated parmesan cheese
Croutons

- In saucepan, combine soups with 2 soup cans water and heat thoroughly.
- To serve, pour soup into individual bowls and top with croutons and cheese.

Beef-Noodle Soup

1 pound lean ground beef
1 (46 ounce) can cocktail vegetable juice
1 (1 ounce) package dry onion soup mix
1 (3 ounce) package beef-flavored ramen noodles
1 (16 ounce) package frozen mixed vegetables

- In large saucepan, cook beef over medium heat until no longer pink and drain.
- Stir in vegetable juice, soup mix, contents of noodle seasoning packet and mixed vegetables and bring to boil.
- Reduce heat and simmer, uncovered, for 6 minutes or until vegetables are tender.
- Return to a boil and stir in noodles.
- Cook for 3 minutes or until noodles are tender and serve hot.

Broccoli-Wild Rice Soup

This is a hearty and delicious soup that is full of flavor.

1 (6 ounce) package chicken-flavored wild rice mix
1 (10 ounce) package frozen chopped broccoli, thawed
2 teaspoons dried minced onion
1 (10 ounce) can cream of chicken soup
1 (8 ounce) package cream cheese, cubed

- In large saucepan, combine rice, rice seasoning packet and 6 cups water.
- Bring to a boil, reduce heat, cover and simmer for 10 minutes, stirring once.
- Stir in broccoli and onion and simmer 5 minutes.
- Stir in soup and cream cheese.
- Cook and stir until cheese melts.

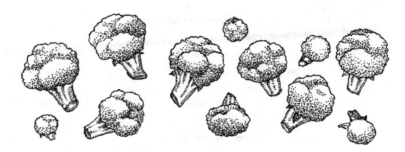

Creamy Cauliflower Soup

1 onion, chopped
½ teaspoon garlic powder
2 (14 ounce) cans chicken broth
1 large cauliflower, cut into small florets
1½ cups whipping cream

- Sauté onion and garlic powder in 1 tablespoon butter, stir in broth and bring to boil.
- Add cauliflower and cook, stirring occasionally, 15 minutes or until tender.
- Process soup in batches in blender until smooth and return to pan.
- Stir in cream and add a little salt and white pepper.
- Cook over low heat and stir often until thoroughly heated.

Cream of Zucchini Soup

1 pound fresh zucchini, grated
1 onion, chopped
1 (14 ounce) can chicken broth
½ teaspoon sweet basil
2 cups half-and-half cream, divided

- In saucepan, combine zucchini, onion, broth, basil and a little salt and pepper.
- Bring to a boil, simmer until soft, pour into food processor and purée.
- Gradually add ½ cup cream and blend. (You could add ¼ teaspoon curry powder if you like curry flavor.)
- Return zucchini mixture to saucepan and add remaining cream.
- Heat but do not boil.

Creamy Butternut Soup

4 cups cooked, mashed butternut squash
2 (14 ounce) cans chicken broth
½ teaspoon sugar
1 (8 ounce) carton whipping cream, divided
¼ teaspoon ground nutmeg

- In saucepan, combine mashed squash, broth, sugar and a little salt.
- Bring to a boil, gradually stir in half of whipping cream and cook until thoroughly heated.
- Beat remaining whipping cream and, when ready to serve, place dollop of whipped cream on soup and sprinkle with nutmeg.

Easy Potato Soup

1 (16 ounce) package frozen hash-brown potatoes
1 cup chopped onion
1 (14 ounce) can chicken broth
1 (10 ounce) can cream of celery
1 (10 ounce) can cream of chicken soup
2 cups milk

- In large saucepan, combine potatoes, onion and 2 cups water and bring to a boil.
- Cover, reduce heat and simmer 30 minutes.
- Stir in broth, soups and milk and heat thoroughly. (If you like, garnish with shredded cheddar cheese or diced, cooked ham.)

Navy Bean Soup

3 (16 ounce) cans navy beans with liquid
1 (14 ounce) can chicken broth
1 cup chopped ham
1 large onion, chopped
½ teaspoon garlic powder

- In large saucepan, combine all ingredients, add 1 cup water and bring to a boil.
- Simmer until onion is tender-crisp and serve hot with cornbread.

Peanut Soup

2 (10 ounce) cans cream of chicken soup
2 soup cans milk
1¼ cups crunchy-style peanut butter

- In saucepan on medium heat, blend soup and milk.
- Stir in peanut butter and heat until well blended.

Cold Cucumber Soup

3 medium cucumbers, peeled, seeded, cut into chunks
1 (14 ounce) can chicken broth, divided
1 (8 ounce) carton sour cream
3 tablespoons fresh chives, minced
2 teaspoon fresh dill, minced

- In blender, combine cucumbers, 1 cup chicken broth and a dash of salt, cover and process until smooth.
- Transfer cucumber mixture to medium bowl and stir in remaining chicken broth.
- Whisk in sour cream, chives and dill, cover and refrigerate well before serving.
- Garnish with dill sprig.

Chili-Soup Warmer

1 (10 ounce) can tomato bisque soup
1 (10 ounce) can chili
1 (10 ounce) can fiesta chili-beef soup
1 (15 ounce) can chicken broth

- In saucepan, combine all ingredients and add enough water to produce desired thickness of soup.
- Heat and serve hot with crackers.

Easy Chili

2 pounds lean ground chuck
1 onion, chopped
4 (16 ounce) cans hot chili beans with liquid
1 (1 ounce) package chili seasoning mix
1 (46 ounce) can tomato juice

- In Dutch oven, cook beef and onion, stir until meat crumbles and drain.
- Stir in beans, seasoning mix and tomato juice.
- Bring mixture to a boil, reduce heat and simmer, stirring occasionally, for 2 hours.

Stroganoff Stew

1 (1 ounce) package dry onion soup mix
2 (10 ounce) cans golden mushroom soup
2 pounds stew meat
1 (8 ounce) carton sour cream

- Combine soup mix, mushroom soup and 1 soup can water and pour over stew meat.
- Cover tightly and bake at 275° for 6 to 8 hours.
- When ready to serve, stir in sour cream, return mixture to oven until it heats thoroughly and serve over noodles.

Meat and Potato Stew

2 pounds beef stew meat
2 (15 ounce) cans new potatoes, drained
1 (15 ounce) can sliced carrots, drained
1 (10 ounce) can French-onion soup

- In large pot, cook meat with 2 cups water for 1 hour.
- Add potatoes, carrots and onion soup and mix well.
- Heat to a boil, reduce heat and simmer for 30 minutes.

Supper Gumbo

1 (10 ounce) can condensed pepper pot soup
1 (10 ounce) can condensed chicken-gumbo soup
1 (6 ounce) can white crabmeat, flaked
1 (6 ounce) can tiny, cooked shrimp

- Combine all ingredients with 1½ soup cans water.
- Cover and simmer for 15 minutes.

Chilled Squash Soup

2 pounds yellow squash, thinly sliced
1 onion, chopped
1 (14 ounce) can chicken broth
1 (8 ounce) package cream cheese, softened
¼ teaspoon freshly ground pepper

- Combine squash, onion and broth in saucepan and bring to a boil.
- Cover, reduce heat, simmer 10 minutes or until tender and set aside to cool.
- Spoon half of squash mixture and half of cream cheese into blender, process until smooth and stop once to scrape down sides. Repeat procedure.
- Stir in pepper and refrigerate.

Clam Chowder

1 (10 ounce) can New England clam chowder
1 (10 ounce) can cream of celery soup
1 (10 ounce) can cream of potato soup
1 (6 ounce) can chopped clams
1 (10 ounce) soup can milk

- Combine all ingredients in saucepan.
- Heat and stir.

Avocado-Cream Soup

4 ripe avocados, peeled, diced
1½ cups whipping cream
2 (14 ounce) cans chicken broth
1 teaspoon salt
¼ cup dry sherry

- In blender, cream half avocados and half cream. Repeat with remaining avocados and cream.
- Bring chicken broth to a boil, reduce heat and stir in avocado puree.
- Add salt and sherry and refrigerate thoroughly.
- To serve, place in individual bowls and sprinkle a little paprika on top.

Speedy Taco Soup

1 (12 ounce) can chicken with liquid
1 (14 ounce) can chicken broth
1 (16 ounce) jar mild thick and chunky salsa
1 (15 ounce) can ranch-style beans

- In large saucepan, combine all ingredients.
- Bring to a boil, reduce heat and simmer for 15 minutes.

Crab Bisque

1 (10 ounce) can cream of celery soup
1 (10 ounce) can pepper pot soup
1 pint half-and-half cream
1 (6 ounce) can crabmeat, drained, flaked
A scant ⅓ cup sherry

- In saucepan, mix soups and half-and-half, stir in crabmeat and heat through.
- Just before serving, add sherry and stir.

Strawberry Soup

1½ cups fresh strawberries
1 cup orange juice
¼ cup honey
½ cup sour cream
½ cup white wine

- Combine all ingredients in blender and purée.
- Refrigerate thoroughly and stir before serving.

Cold Strawberry Soup

2¼ cups strawberries
⅓ cup sugar
½ cup sour cream
½ cup whipping cream
½ cup light red wine

- Place strawberries and sugar in blender and purée.
- Pour strawberry mixture into pitcher, stir in sour cream and whipping cream and blend well.
- Add 1¼ cups water and red wine, stir and refrigerate.

Deviled Eggs

6 hard-boiled eggs
2 tablespoons sweet pickle relish
3 tablespoons mayonnaise
½ teaspoon prepared mustard

- Peel eggs and cut in half lengthwise.
- Remove yolks and mash with fork.
- Add relish, mayonnaise and mustard to yolks and place yolk mixture back into egg white halves.
- Sprinkle with paprika, if you like.

Shrimp-Stuffed Eggs

8 hard-boiled eggs
¼ cup mayonnaise
1 (6 ounce) can tiny, cooked shrimp, drained
2 tablespoons sweet pickle relish, drained

- Cut eggs in half lengthwise and set aside egg whites.
- In small bowl, mash egg yolks with mayonnaise.
- Add shrimp and pickle relish and mix well.
- Refill egg whites. Refrigerate.

Fancy Eggs

12 large hard-boiled eggs
1 (4 ounce) package crumbled blue cheese
¼ cup half-and-half cream
2 tablespoons lime juice
2 tablespoons black caviar

- Peel eggs and cut in half lengthwise.
- Carefully remove yolks and mash with fork.
- Add cheese, half-and-half and lime juice and stir until smooth.
- Spoon mixture back into egg whites, top with caviar and refrigerate.

Nutty Green Salad

6 cups torn mixed salad greens
1 medium zucchini, sliced
1 (8 ounce) can sliced water chestnuts, drained
½ cup peanuts
⅓ cup Italian salad dressing

- Toss greens, zucchini, water chestnuts and peanuts.
- When ready to serve, add salad dressing and toss.

Salad Surprise

1 (10 ounce) bag fresh spinach, washed, stemmed
1 pint fresh strawberries, stemmed, halved
1 large banana, sliced
⅔ cup chopped walnuts

- Combine all salad ingredients in large bowl.
- When ready to serve, toss with prepared salad dressing.

City-Slicker Salad

2 (10 ounce) packages fresh spinach
1 quart fresh strawberries, halved
½ cup slivered almonds, toasted
Poppy seed dressing

- Tear spinach into smaller pieces and add strawberries and almonds.
- Refrigerate and, when ready to serve, toss with poppy seed dressing.

Sesame-Romaine Salad

1 large head romaine lettuce
2 tablespoons sesame seeds, toasted
6 strips bacon, fried, crumbled
½ cup grated Swiss cheese

- Wash and dry lettuce and tear into bite-size pieces.
- When ready to serve, sprinkle sesame seeds, bacon and cheese over lettuce and toss with creamy Italian salad dressing.

Green and Red Salad

4 cups torn mixed salad greens
3 fresh green onions with tops, chopped
2 medium red apples with peel, diced
1 cup fresh raspberries
½ cup prepared poppy seed dressing

- In bowl, toss salad greens, onions and fruit.
- Drizzle with dressing and toss.

Merry Berry Salad

1 (10 ounce) package mixed salad greens
2 apples with peel: 1 red and 1 green, diced
1 cup shredded parmesan cheese
½ cup dried cranberries
½ cup slivered almonds, toasted
Poppy seed dressing

- In large salad bowl, toss greens, apples, cheese, cranberries and almonds.
- Drizzle prepared poppy seed dressing over salad and toss.

Swiss Salad

1 large head romaine lettuce
1 bunch fresh green onions with tops, chopped
1 (8 ounce) package of shredded Swiss cheese
½ cup toasted sunflower seeds

- Tear lettuce into bite-size pieces.
- Add onions, cheese and sunflower seeds and toss.
- Serve with vinaigrette salad dressing.

Vinaigrette for Swiss Salad:

⅔ cup salad oil
⅓ cup red wine vinegar
1 tablespoon seasoned salt

- Combine all ingredients and refrigerate.

Mandarin Salad

1 head red-tipped lettuce
2 (11 ounce) cans mandarin oranges, drained
2 avocados, peeled, diced
1 small red onion, sliced
Poppy seed salad dressing

- Combine all ingredients.
- When ready to serve, toss with poppy seed salad dressing.

Spinach-Orange Salad

1 (10 ounce) package spinach, stems removed
2 (11 ounce) cans mandarin oranges, drained
⅓ small jicama, peeled, cut into julienne strips
⅓ cup slivered almonds, toasted

- In large bowl, combine spinach, oranges, jicama and almonds.
- Toss with prepared vinaigrette salad dressing.

Strawberry-Spinach Salad

1 (10 ounce) package fresh spinach, washed, stemmed
1 small jicama, peeled, cut into julienne strips
1 pint fresh strawberries, stemmed, halved
2½ cups fresh bean sprouts

- Combine all ingredients in large bowl.
- Toss with prepared poppy seed salad dressing just before serving.

Spinach-Bacon Salad

1 (8 ounce) package fresh spinach
3 hard-boiled eggs, chopped
8 mushroom caps, sliced
1 (8 ounce) can sliced water chestnuts, drained

• Combine all ingredients and serve with Hot Bacon Dressing.

Hot Bacon Dressing for Spinach-Bacon Salad:

½ pound bacon, chopped
1 cup sugar
1⅓ cups white vinegar
5 teaspoons cornstarch

• Fry bacon until crisp, drain and leave bacon drippings in skillet.
• Add sugar and vinegar to skillet and stir well.
• Add 1 cup water and bring to a boil.
• Mix cornstarch with ⅔ cup water, stir until it dissolves and pour cornstarch mixture into skillet with dressing.
• Return to boil and simmer for 5 minutes.
• Remove from heat, return bacon to skillet and toss dressing into salad.

Broccoli-Pepperoni Salad

1 (1 pound) bunch broccoli
½ pound fresh mushrooms, sliced
6 ounces Swiss cheese, diced
1 (3 ounce) package sliced pepperoni, chopped

• Cut off broccoli florets and combine broccoli, mushrooms, cheese and pepperoni.
• Toss with Italian salad dressing.
• Refrigerate for at least 8 hours before serving.

Spinach-Apple Salad

1 (10 ounce) package fresh spinach
⅓ cup frozen orange juice concentrate, thawed
¾ cup mayonnaise
1 red apple with peel, diced
5 slices bacon, fried, crumbled

- Tear spinach into small pieces.
- Mix orange juice concentrate and mayonnaise.
- When ready to serve, peel and chop apple and mix with spinach. Pour orange juice-mayonnaise mixture over salad and top with bacon.

Green Pea Salad

1 (16 ounce) bag frozen green peas
1 bunch fresh green onions with tops, chopped
½ cup chopped celery
½ cup sweet pickle relish
Mayonnaise

- Mix peas, onions, celery and relish.
- Stir in enough mayonnaise to hold salad together and refrigerate.

Summertime Mushroom Salad

1 (8 ounce) package cream cheese, softened
½ cup mayonnaise
½ teaspoon salt
1 bunch fresh green onion with tops, chopped
4 cups fresh mushrooms, sliced

- In mixing bowl, blend cream cheese, mayonnaise and salt.
- Gently mix in onions and mushrooms.
- Refrigerate and serve on lettuce leaf.

Carrot Salad

3 cups finely grated carrots
1 (8 ounce) can crushed pineapple, drained
4 tablespoons flaked coconut
1 tablespoon sugar
⅓ cup mayonnaise

- Combine carrots, pineapple, coconut and sugar and mix well.
- Toss with mayonnaise and refrigerate.

Garlic Green Beans

3 (16 ounce) cans whole green beans, drained
⅔ cup oil
½ cup vinegar
½ cup sugar
5 cloves garlic, finely chopped

- Place green beans in container with lid.
- Mix oil, vinegar, sugar and garlic, pour over beans and sprinkle with a little salt and red pepper.
- Let set overnight in refrigerator.

Sunshine Salad

2 (15 ounce) cans mexicorn, drained
2 (15 ounce) cans peas, drained
1 (15 ounce) can kidney beans, rinsed, drained
1 (8 ounce) bottle Italian salad dressing

- In large bowl, combine corn, peas and beans.
- Pour dressing over vegetables and refrigerate for several hours before serving.

Easy Guacamole Salad

4 avocados, softened
1 (8 ounce) package cream cheese, softened
1 (10 ounce) can diced tomatoes and green chiles
1½ teaspoons garlic salt
About 1 tablespoon lemon juice

- Peel avocados and mash with fork.
- In mixing bowl, beat cream cheese until smooth, add avocados, tomatoes and green chiles, garlic salt and lemon juice and mix well.
- Serve on lettuce leaf with a few tortilla chips beside salad.

Broccoli-Waldorf Salad

6 cups fresh broccoli florets
1 large red apple with peel, chopped
½ cup golden raisins
½ cup chopped pecans
½ cup prepared coleslaw dressing

- In large bowl, combine broccoli, apple, raisins and pecans.
- Drizzle with dressing, toss to coat and refrigerate.
- Serve in pretty crystal bowl.

Avocado-Green Bean Salad

2 (15 ounce) cans French-cut green beans, drained
8 green onions with tops, chopped
¾ cup Italian salad dressing
2 avocados
1 (8 ounce) can artichoke hearts

- Place green beans and onions in serving dish, pour dressing over mixture and refrigerate several hours or overnight.
- When ready to serve, chop peeled avocados and artichoke hearts and stir in with beans and onions.

Grapefruit-Avocado Salad

2 (15 ounce) cans grapefruit sections, drained
2 ripe avocados, peeled, sliced
½ cup slivered almonds, chopped
Prepared poppy seed salad dressing

- Combine grapefruit, avocados and almonds.
- Toss with dressing.
- Serve on bed of lettuce.

Cucumber Salad

1 (3 ounce) package lime gelatin
2 medium cucumbers
1 tablespoon minced onion
½ cup mayonnaise
½ cup sour cream

- Dissolve gelatin in ¾ cup boiling water, mix well and bring to room temperature.
- Slice cucumber in half, remove seeds and grate.
- Add grated cucumber, onion, mayonnaise and sour cream to cool gelatin.
- Pour into square dish and refrigerate until set.

Dill Cucumbers

⅓ cup vinegar
2 tablespoons sugar
1 teaspoon dried dillweed
3 cucumbers, peeled, sliced

- Combine vinegar, sugar, dillweed, 1 teaspoon salt and ¼ teaspoon black pepper.
- Pour mixture over cucumbers.
- Refrigerate for 1 hour before serving.

TIP: *Add onion to cucumbers if you like.*

Stuffed Cucumber Slices

3 cucumbers, peeled
2 (3 ounce) packages cream cheese, softened
¼ cup stuffed green olives, chopped
½ teaspoon seasoned salt

- Halve cucumbers lengthwise and scoop out seeds.
- Beat cream cheese with mixer until creamy and add olives and seasoned salt.
- Fill hollows of cucumbers with cream cheese mixture.
- Press halves back together, wrap tightly in plastic wrap   and refrigerate.
- Remove plastic wrap and cut crosswise in ⅓-inch slices to serve.

Marinated Cucumbers

3 cucumbers, thinly sliced
2 (4 ounce) jars chopped pimentos, drained
⅔ cup oil
¼ cup white wine vinegar
1 (8 ounce) carton sour cream

- Combine cucumber and pimentos.
- Mix oil, vinegar and ½ teaspoon salt, pour over cucumbers and refrigerate for 1 hour.
- To serve, drain well and pour sour cream over cucumbers and toss.

Red Hot Onions

Great with barbecue!

3 large purple onions
2 tablespoons hot sauce
3 tablespoons olive oil
3 tablespoons red wine vinegar

- Cut onions into thin slices.
- Pour 1 cup boiling water over onions, let set for 1 minute and drain.
- Combine hot sauce, oil and vinegar and pour over onion rings in bowl with lid.
- Cover and refrigerate for at least 3 hours.
- Drain to serve.

Marinated Onion Rings

2 pounds white onion, thinly sliced
1 cup sugar
2 cups white vinegar
½ teaspoon salt

- Cover onions with boiling water, let stand for 5 minutes and drain.
- Combine sugar, vinegar and salt and pour over onions.
- Refrigerate.

Winter Salad

1 (15 ounce) can cut green beans, drained
1 (15 ounce) can English peas, drained
1 (15 ounce) can whole kernel corn, drained
1 (15 ounce) can jalapeno black-eyed peas, drained
1 (8 ounce) bottle Italian salad dressing

- Combine all vegetables in large bowl. (Add some chopped onion and chopped bell pepper if you have it in the refrigerator.)
- Pour Italian dressing over vegetables.
- Cover and refrigerate.

TIP: This is a great "make-ahead" salad and will stay fresh at least a week.

Marinated Brussels Sprouts

2 (10 ounce) packages Brussels sprouts, cooked
½ cup salad oil
¼ cup white wine vinegar
¼ cup sugar

- Combine all ingredients and marinate overnight.
- Serve cold.

Bell Pepper-Brussels Sprouts Salad

2 (10 ounce) boxes frozen Brussels sprouts
1 cup Italian salad dressing
1 cup chopped red bell pepper
½ cup chopped onion

- Pierce box of Brussels sprouts and cook in microwave for 7 minutes.
- Mix dressing, bell pepper and onion.
- Pour over Brussels sprouts and marinate for at least 24 hours.
- Drain to serve.

Broccoli-Cauliflower Salad

1 small head cauliflower
3 stalks broccoli
1 cup mayonnaise
1 tablespoon vinegar
1 tablespoon sugar
1 bunch fresh green onions with tops, chopped
8 ounces mozzarella cheese, cubed

- Cut cauliflower and broccoli into bite-size florets.
- Combine mayonnaise, vinegar and sugar.
- Combine cauliflower, broccoli, mayonnaise mixture, onions and cheese. (Add a little salt if you like.)
- Toss and refrigerate.

Green and White Salad

1 (16 ounce) package frozen green peas, thawed, uncooked
1 head cauliflower, cut into florets
1 (8 ounce) carton sour cream
1 (1 ounce) package dry ranch-style salad dressing mix

- In large bowl, combine peas and cauliflower.
- Combine sour cream and salad dressing, toss with vegetables and refrigerate.

Marinated Corn Salad

3 (15 ounce) cans whole kernel corn, drained
1 red bell pepper, chopped
1 cup chopped walnuts
¾ cup chopped celery
1 (8 ounce) bottle Italian salad dressing

- In bowl with lid, combine corn, bell pepper, walnuts and celery. (For a special little zip, add several dashes hot sauce.)
- Pour salad dressing over vegetables and refrigerate several hours before serving.

Cold Butter Bean Salad

2 (10 ounce) packages frozen baby limas
1 (15 ounce) can shoe-peg (or white) corn, drained
1 bunch fresh green onions with tops, chopped
1 cup mayonnaise
2 teaspoons dry ranch-style salad dressing mix

- Cook beans according to package directions and drain.
- Add corn, onions, mayonnaise and dressing mix, combine well and refrigerate.

Broccoli-Cheese Salad

4 cups broccoli, cut into small florets
1 red onion, chopped
1 (8 ounce) package cubed cheddar cheese
6 slices bacon, cooked, crumbled

- Combine all ingredients. (You could substitute mozzarella cheese if you prefer).
- Toss with Broccoli Dressing.

Broccoli Dressing:

1 cup mayonnaise
¼ cup sugar
2 tablespoons vinegar

- Combine all ingredients and mix well.
- Pour over Broccoli-Cheese Salad.

Cashew-Pea Salad

1 (16 ounce) package frozen green peas, thawed
¼ cup diced celery
1 bunch fresh green onions with tops, chopped
1 cup chopped cashews
½ cup mayonnaise

- Combine peas, celery, onions and cashews.
- Toss with mayonnaise seasoned with ½ teaspoon seasoned salt and black pepper.

Marinated Black-Eyed Peas

3 (16 ounce) can jalapeno black-eyed peas, drained
1 cup chopped celery
1 bunch fresh green onions with tops, chopped
1 (4 ounce) jar pimentos, drained
1 (8 ounce) bottle Italian salad dressing

- Mix all ingredients and refrigerate for several hours before serving.

Broccoli-Green Bean Salad

1 large bunch broccoli, cut into florets
2 (15 ounce) cans cut green beans, drained
1 bunch fresh green onions with tops, chopped
2 (6 ounce) jars marinated artichoke hearts, chopped, drained
1½ cups prepared ranch-style salad dressing with mayonnaise

- Combine broccoli, green beans, onions and artichokes and mix well.
- Add dressing and toss.
- Refrigerate 24 hours before serving.

Special Rice Salad

This rice salad has lots of flavor!

1 (6 ounce) package chicken-flavored rice and macaroni
¾ cup chopped green pepper
1 bunch fresh green onion with tops, chopped
2 (6 ounce) jars marinated artichoke hearts
½ to ⅔ cup mayonnaise

- Cook rice and macaroni according to directions (but without butter), drain and cool.
- Add green pepper, onions, artichoke hearts and mayonnaise, toss and refrigerate.

Mediterranean Potato Salad

2 pounds red-skinned new potatoes, quartered
¾ to 1 cup caesar dressing
½ cup grated parmesan cheese
¼ cup chopped fresh parsley
½ cup chopped roasted red peppers

- Cook potatoes in boiling water until fork-tender, drain and place in large bowl.
- Pour dressing over potatoes, add cheese, parsley and peppers and toss lightly.
- Serve warm or chilled.

Terrific Tortellini Salad

2 (14 ounce) packages frozen cheese tortellini
2 bell peppers: 1 green and 1 red, diced
1 cucumber, chopped
1 (14 ounce) can artichoke hearts, rinsed, drained
1 (8 ounce) bottle creamy caesar salad dressing

- Prepare tortellini according to package directions and drain.
- Rinse with cold water, drain and refrigerate.
- Combine tortellini, bell peppers, cucumber, artichoke hearts and dressing in large bowl.
- Cover and refrigerate at least 2 hours before serving.

Fusilli Pasta Salad

1 (16 ounce) package fusilli or corkscrew pasta
1 (16 ounce) package frozen broccoli-cauliflower combination
1 (8 ounce) package cubed mozzarella cheese
1 (8 ounce) bottle of catalina salad dressing

- Cook pasta according to package directions, drain and cool.
- Cook vegetables in microwave according to package directions, drain and cool.
- In large bowl, combine pasta, vegetables and cheese chunks.
- Toss with dressing and refrigerate for several hours before serving.

Color-Coded Salad

1 (16 ounce) package tri-colored macaroni, cooked, drained
1 red bell pepper, cut into julienne strips
1 cup chopped zucchini
1 cup broccoli florets
Caesar salad dressing

- Combine all ingredients.
- Toss with 1 cup caesar salad dressing and refrigerate.

Broccoli-Noodle Salad

1 cup slivered almonds
1 cup sunflower seeds
2 (3 ounce) packages chicken-flavored ramen noodles
1 (16 ounce) package broccoli slaw
1 (8 ounce) bottle Italian salad dressing

- Toast almonds and sunflower seeds in oven at 275° for about 10 minutes.
- Break up ramen noodles (discard seasoning packets) and mix with slaw, almonds and sunflower seeds.
- Toss with Italian salad dressing and refrigerate.

Sunflower Salad

2 apples, cored, chopped
1 cup seedless green grapes, halved
½ cup chopped celery
¾ cup chopped pecans
⅓ cup mayonnaise

- Combine all ingredients and refrigerate.

Nutty Cranberry Relish

1 pound fresh cranberries
2¼ cups sugar
1 cup chopped pecans, toasted
1 cup orange marmalade

- Wash and drain cranberries and mix with sugar.
- Place in 1-quart baking dish, cover and bake at 350° for 1 hour.
- Add marmalade and pecans to cranberry mixture.
- Mix well, pour into container and refrigerate before serving.

Pineapple Slaw

1 (8 ounce) can unsweetened pineapple tidbits with juice
3 cups finely shredded cabbage
1½ cups chopped red delicious apples with peel
½ cup chopped celery
¾ cup mayonnaise

- Drain pineapple and reserve 3 tablespoons juice.
- Combine pineapple, cabbage, apple, and celery in large bowl.
- Combine reserved juice and mayonnaise, add to cabbage mixture and toss gently. (Add dressing quickly after cutting apple so apple will not darken.)
- Cover and refrigerate.

Creamy Slaw

1 medium green cabbage, shredded
½ onion, chopped
⅓ cup sugar
1 cup mayonnaise
¼ cup vinegar

- Toss cabbage and onion together, add salt and pepper to taste and sprinkle sugar over mixture.
- Combine mayonnaise and vinegar and pour over cabbage and onion.
- Toss and refrigerate.

Red Cabbage Slaw

1 large head red cabbage
2 onions, chopped
½ cup coleslaw dressing
½ cup French salad dressing

- Slice cabbage and combine with onions.
- Combine dressings and toss with cabbage and onions.
- Refrigerate.

Calypso Coleslaw

1 (16 ounce) package shredded cabbage
1 bunch green onions with tops, sliced
2 cups cubed cheddar or mozzarella cheese
¼ cup sliced ripe olives
1 (15 ounce) can whole kernel corn with peppers, drained

- Combine all slaw ingredients and add a few sprinkles of salt.
- Serve with dressing

Dressing for Calypso Coleslaw:

1 cup mayonnaise
2 tablespoons sugar
1 tablespoon prepared mustard
2 tablespoons vinegar

- Combine dressing ingredients and mix well.
- Add dressing to slaw, toss, cover and refrigerate.

Tropical Mango Salad

2 (15 ounce) cans mangoes with juice
1 (6 ounce) package orange gelatin
1 (8 ounce) package cream cheese, softened
½ (8 ounce) carton whipped topping, thawed

- Place all mango slices on dinner plate and cut into bite-size pieces.
- Pour mango juice and, if necessary, enough water to make 1½ cups, into saucepan and bring to boiling point.
- Pour juice over gelatin in mixing bowl and mix well.
- Start mixer very slowly and add cream cheese. Gradually increase speed until cream cheese mixes with gelatin.
- Stir in mango pieces and place in refrigerator until mixture congeals slightly.
- Fold in whipped topping, pour into 7 x 11-inch dish and refrigerate.

Angel Salad

1 (8 ounce) package cream cheese, softened
½ cup sugar
1 (16 ounce) can chunky fruit cocktail, drained
1 (15 ounce) can pineapple chunks, drained
1 (8 ounce) carton whipped topping, thawed

- With mixer, beat cream cheese and sugar until creamy.
- Add fruit and mix gently.
- Fold in whipped topping.
- Pour into crystal bowl and refrigerate.

Fantastic Fruit Salad

2 (11 ounce) cans mandarin oranges
2 (15 ounce) cans pineapple chunks
1 (16 ounce) carton frozen strawberries, thawed
1 (20 ounce) can peach pie filling
1 (20 ounce) can apricot pie filling

- Drain oranges, pineapple and strawberries.
- Combine all ingredients and fold together gently.

Cherry Salad

1 (20 ounce) can cherry pie filling
1 (20 ounce) can crushed pineapple, drained
1 (14 ounce) can sweetened condensed milk
1 cup miniature marshmallows
1 cup chopped pecans
1 (8 ounce) carton whipped topping, thawed

- In large bowl, combine pie filling, pineapple, condensed milk, marshmallows and pecans.
- Fold in whipped topping, refrigerate and serve in pretty crystal bowl. (You may add a couple drops of red food coloring if you like a brighter color.)

Orange-Pear Salad

1 (15 ounce) can sliced pears with juice
1 (6 ounce) package orange gelatin
1 (8 ounce) package cream cheese, softened
1 (8 ounce) carton whipped topping, thawed

- Boil juice from pears with ½ cup water, add gelatin and stir until it dissolves.
- Refrigerate until partially set.
- Blend pears and cream cheese in blender.
- Fold pear mixture and whipped topping into gelatin mixture and blend well.
- Pour into 7 x 11-inch shallow dish.

Pistachio Salad or Dessert

1 (20 ounce) can crushed pineapple with juice
1 (3 ounce) package instant pistachio pudding mix
2 cups miniature marshmallows
1 cup chopped pecans
1 (8 ounce) carton whipped topping, thawed

- Place pineapple in large bowl and sprinkle with dry pudding mix.
- Add marshmallows and pecans and fold in whipped topping.
- Pour into crystal serving dish and refrigerate.

Snickers Salad

6 large apples with peel, chopped
6 (2 ounce) Snickers® candy bars, chopped
½ cup chopped pecans, optional
1 (12 ounce) carton whipped topping, thawed

- In large bowl, combine apples, candy bars and pecans and mix well.
- Fold in whipped topping and refrigerate.

Coconut Bananas

4 bananas
4 tablespoons lemon juice
1 (16 ounce) carton sour cream
1¼ cups flaked coconut

- Cut bananas into fourths.
- Place lemon juice, sour cream and coconut in separate bowls.
- Dip bananas into lemon juice, roll in sour cream and dredge in coconut until covered thoroughly.
- Place in covered bowl and refrigerate several hours or overnight.

Fluffy Fruit Salad

2 (20 ounce) cans pineapple tidbits, drained
1 (16 ounce) can whole cranberry sauce
2 (11 ounce) cans mandarin oranges, drained
½ cup chopped pecans
1 (8 ounce) carton whipped topping, thawed

- In bowl, combine pineapple, cranberry sauce, oranges, and pecans and fold in whipped topping.
- Serve in pretty crystal bowl.

Peachy Fruit Salad

2 (20 ounce) cans peach pie filling
1 (20 ounce) can pineapple chunks, drained
1 (11 ounce) can mandarin oranges, drained
1 (8 ounce) jar maraschino cherries, drained
1 cup miniature marshmallows

- Combine all ingredients in large bowl, fold together gently and refrigerate. (Bananas may be added if you like.)
- Serve in pretty crystal bowl.

Stained-Glass Fruit Salad

2 (20 ounce) cans peach pie filling
3 bananas, sliced
1 (16 ounce) package frozen unsweetened strawberries, drained
1 (20 ounce) can pineapple tidbits, drained

- Combine all ingredients and place in pretty crystal bowl.
- Refrigerate overnight.

TIP: *If you like, use 1 can peach pie filling and 1 can apricot pie filling.*

Strawberry-Rhubarb Salad

2 cups diced frozen rhubarb
¾ cup sugar
¼ cup water
1 (3 ounce) package strawberry gelatin
1½ cups whipped topping, thawed

- In saucepan, bring rhubarb, sugar and water to boil, reduce heat and simmer, uncovered, for 3 to 5 minutes or until rhubarb softens.
- Remove from heat and stir in gelatin until it dissolves.
- Pour into bowl and refrigerate for 30 minutes or until partially set.
- Fold in whipped topping.
- Pour into serving dish and refrigerate until firm.

Watergate Salad

1 (20 ounce) can crushed pineapple with juice
2 (3 ounce) packages pistachio instant pudding mix
¾ cup chopped pecans
1 (12 ounce) carton whipped topping, thawed

- Combine pineapple with instant pudding mix until slightly thick and add pecans.
- When combined well, fold in whipped topping.
- Pour into pretty crystal bowl and refrigerate.

Cashew Salad

1 (6 ounce) package lemon gelatin
1 quart vanilla ice cream
1 (15 ounce) can fruit cocktail, drained
1 cup chopped cashews

- Dissolve gelatin in 1 cup boiling water and stir in ice cream until it melts.
- Add fruit cocktail and cashews and mix well.
- Pour into 7 x 11-inch glass dish and refrigerate overnight.

Orange-Sherbet Salad

1 (3 ounce) package orange gelatin
1 (3 ounce) package lemon gelatin
1 pint orange sherbet
2 (11 ounce) cans mandarin oranges

- Place gelatin in bowl, pour 1 cup boiling water over gelatin and mix well.
- Fold in sherbet and stir until it blends thoroughly.
- Add oranges, pour into 8-inch ring mold or 7 x 11-inch dish and refrigerate.

Cottage Cheese-Fruit Salad

1 (16 ounce) carton small-curd cottage cheese
1 (6 ounce) package orange gelatin
2 (11 ounce) cans mandarin oranges, drained
1 (20 ounce) can chunk pineapple, drained
1 (8 ounce) carton whipped topping, thawed

- Sprinkle gelatin over cottage cheese and mix well.
- Add oranges and pineapple and mix well.
- Fold in whipped topping, refrigerate, and serve in pretty crystal bowl.

Cold Cola Salad

1 (6 ounce) package cherry gelatin
1 (10 ounce) bottle maraschino cherries, drained
1 cup cola soda
1 cup chopped pecans

- Dissolve gelatin in ¾ cup boiling water.
- Chop cherries into 4 slices each and add cherries, cola and pecans to gelatin.
- Pour into 8-cup gelatin mold and refrigerate until firm.

Mincemeat-Cherry Salad

1 (6 ounce) package cherry gelatin
1 cup prepared mincemeat
1 rib celery, chopped
⅔ cup chopped pecans

- Dissolve gelatin in ¾ cup boiling water and fold in mincemeat, celery and pecans.
- Pour into 8-inch mold and refrigerate.

Holiday Cheer

2 cups ginger ale
1 (6 ounce) package orange gelatin
1 cup wine
1 (9 ounce) package condensed mincemeat
1 cup chopped pecans

- Heat ginger ale, stir in gelatin and mix well.
- Add wine, mincemeat and pecans.
- Pour into 9 x 13-inch glass dish and refrigerate.

Serendipity Salad

1 (6 ounce) package raspberry gelatin
1 (16 ounce) can fruit cocktail with juice
1 (8 ounce) can crushed pineapple with juice
2 bananas, cut into small chunks
1 cup miniature marshmallows

- Dissolve gelatin in 1 cup boiling water and mix well.
- Add fruit cocktail and pineapple and refrigerate until gelatin begins to thicken.
- Add bananas and marshmallows and pour into sherbet dishes.
- Cover with plastic wrap and refrigerate. (You could also pour salad into 7 x 11-inch glass dish and cut into squares to serve.)

Lime-Cherry Salad

1 (6 ounce) package lime gelatin
1 (10 ounce) bottle maraschino cherries, halved, drained
1 cup diced apples, unpeeled
1 cup chopped pecans

- Dissolve gelatin in 1½ cups boiling water and mix well.
- Stir in cherries and place in refrigerator until mixture congeals slightly.
- Add apples and pecans and pour into 7 x 11-inch dish.
- Refrigerate until firm.

Purple Lady Salad

1 (6 ounce) box grape gelatin
1 (20 ounce) can blueberry pie filling
1 (20 ounce) can crushed pineapple with juice
1 cup miniature marshmallows
1 cup chopped pecans

- In large bowl, pour 1 cup boiling water over gelatin and mix well.
- Add blueberry pie filling and pineapple and place in refrigerator until gelatin begins to thicken.
- Stir in marshmallows and pecans.
- Pour into 9 x 13-inch glass dish and refrigerate.

TIP: To make a completely different salad, you can fold in an 8-ounce carton whipped topping, thawed, when mixture begins to congeal.

Luscious Strawberry Salad

1 (6 ounce) package strawberry gelatin
2 (10 ounce) boxes frozen strawberries, thawed
3 bananas, sliced
1 (8 ounce) carton sour cream

- Dissolve gelatin in 1¼ cups boiling water and mix well.
- Add strawberries and bananas.
- Pour half mixture in 7 x 11-inch dish (leave bananas in bottom layer) and refrigerate until firm.
- Spread sour cream over firm gelatin.
- Add remaining gelatin over sour cream and refrigerate until firm.

Cranberry Salad

1 (6 ounce) package cherry gelatin
1 (16 ounce) can whole cranberry sauce
1 pint sour cream
¾ cup chopped pecans

- Dissolve gelatin in 1¼ cups boiling water and mix well.
- Add cranberry sauce, stir mixture well and refrigerate until it congeals slightly.
- Add sour cream and pecans, mix well and pour into 7 x 11-inch casserole dish.
- Refrigerate for several hours before serving.

Salad Supreme

1 (6 ounce) package orange gelatin
1 (8 ounce) package cream cheese, softened
2 (15 ounce) cans mangoes with juice
2 (10 ounce) cans mandarin oranges, drained

- Place gelatin in mixing bowl, add ¾ cup boiling water and mix well.
- Let gelatin partially cool and, beginning at very slow speed, beat in cream cheese until it mixes.
- Fold in mangoes and mandarin oranges.
- Pour into 8-cup molds and refrigerate for several hours.

Cinnamon-Apple Salad

1 cup red cinnamon candies
1 (6 ounce) package cherry gelatin
1 (16 ounce) jar applesauce
1 cup chopped pecans
Sour cream

- Heat candies in 1¼ cups boiling water until they melt.
- While mixture is still hot, pour over gelatin and mix well.
- Add applesauce and chopped pecans and mix well.
- Pour into 7 x 11-inch glass dish and refrigerate until firm.
- To serve, cut in squares and place a dollop of sour cream on top of each serving.

Cherry Crush

1 (6 ounce) box cherry gelatin
1 (8 ounce) package cream cheese, softened
1 (20 ounce) can cherry pie filling
1 (15 ounce) can crushed pineapple with juice

- Dissolve gelatin with ¾ cup boiling water.
- With electric mixer, beat in cream cheese. (Beat very slowly at first.)
- Fold in pie filling and crushed pineapple.
- Pour into 9 x 13-inch casserole dish and refrigerate.

Pink Salad

1 (6 ounce) package raspberry gelatin
1 (20 ounce) can crushed pineapple with juice
1 cup cream-style cottage cheese
1 (8 ounce) carton whipped topping, thawed
¼ cup chopped pecans

- Place gelatin in large bowl.
- Combine juice from pineapple and, if necessary, enough water to make 1¼ cups. Heat, pour over gelatin and mix well.
- Cool in refrigerator just until gelatin begins to thicken.
- Fold in cottage cheese, whipped topping and pecans.
- Pour into molds or 9 x 13-inch dish and refrigerate.

Applesauce Salad

2 cups applesauce
1 (6 ounce) package lime gelatin
2 (12 ounce) cans lemon-lime carbonated drink
1 (8 ounce) can crushed pineapple, drained

- Heat applesauce in large saucepan.
- Add gelatin to hot applesauce and stir until it dissolves.
- Stir in lemon-lime drink and pineapple.
- Pour into 8-inch mold and refrigerate.

Pineapple Salad

1 (20 ounce) can crushed pineapple with juice
1 (6 ounce) package lemon gelatin
1 (8 ounce) package cream cheese, softened, cubed
1 (8 ounce) carton whipped topping, thawed

- Heat pineapple to a boil, pour over gelatin in mixing bowl and stir to dissolve.
- Combine pineapple mixture and cream cheese and whip slowly until mixture combines well.
- Refrigerate until partially set.
- Fold in whipped topping and pour into 8-cup mold.

Creamy Cranberry Salad

1 (6 ounce) package cherry gelatin
1 (8 ounce) carton sour cream
1 (16 ounce) can whole cranberry sauce
1 (15 ounce) can crushed pineapple with juice

- Dissolve gelatin in 1¼ cups boiling water and mix well.
- Stir in sour cream, cranberry sauce and pineapple and pour into 7 x 11-inch glass dish.
- Refrigerate until firm.

Peaches 'n Cream Salad

1 (6 ounce) package lemon gelatin
1 cup boiling water
1 (8 ounce) package cream cheese, softened
1 (8 ounce) carton whipped topping, thawed
1 (20 ounce) can peach pie filling
1 (15 ounce) can sliced peaches, drained

- In mixing bowl, combine gelatin and boiling water and mix well. Pour half into separate bowl and set aside.
- Add cream cheese to gelatin in mixing bowl and beat very slowly until smooth and creamy.
- Place in refrigerator just until it begins to thicken (but is not yet set).
- Fold in whipped topping, pour into 9 x 13-inch glass dish and refrigerate until set.
- Mix peach pie filling and sliced peaches into remaining gelatin, pour over first layer and refrigerate several hours.

Cream Cheese-Mango Salad

2 (15 ounce) cans mangoes with juice
1 (6 ounce) package lemon gelatin
2 (8 ounce) packages cream cheese, softened
1 (8 ounce) can crushed pineapple with juice

- Drain juice from mangoes and combine with enough water to make ¾ cup liquid.
- Bring liquid to a boil, add gelatin and stir until it dissolves.
- In mixing bowl, cream mangoes and cream cheese and fold in pineapple.
- Mix creamed mixture into hot gelatin and pour into muffin tins or mold.

Divinity Salad

1 (6 ounce) package lemon gelatin
1 (8 ounce) package cream cheese, softened
¾ cup chopped pecans
1 (15 ounce) can crushed pineapple with juice
1 (8 ounce) carton whipped topping, thawed

- With mixer, blend gelatin with 1 cup boiling water until it dissolves.
- Add cream cheese, beat slowly and increase speed until smooth.
- Stir in pecans and pineapple and cool in refrigerator until nearly set.
- Fold in whipped topping, pour into 9 x 13-inch dish and refrigerate.

Cherry-Cranberry Salad

1 (6 ounce) package cherry gelatin
1 cup boiling water
1 (20 ounce) can cherry pie filling
1 (16 ounce) can whole cranberry sauce

- In mixing bowl, combine cherry gelatin and boiling water and mix until gelatin dissolves.
- Mix pie filling and cranberry sauce into gelatin.
- Pour into 9 x 13-inch dish and refrigerate.

Berry Salad Dream

1 (15 ounce) can crushed pineapple with juice
1 (6 ounce) package blackberry gelatin
1 (15 ounce) can blueberries, drained
Whipped topping, thawed, optional

- Add enough water to pineapple juice to make 2 cups, put in saucepan and bring to a boil.
- Pour hot liquid over gelatin and mix until it dissolves.
- Refrigerate until mixture begins to thicken.
- Stir in pineapple and blueberries, pour into 7 x 11-inch dish and refrigerate.

Topping for Berry-Salad Dream:

1 (8 ounce) package cream cheese, softened
1 (8 ounce) carton sour cream
½ cup sugar
½ cup chopped pecans

- With mixer, beat cream cheese, sour cream and sugar until smooth and fluffy.
- Pour over congealed salad and refrigerate.
- Sprinkle with pecans before serving.

Creamy Orange Salad

1 (6 ounce) package orange gelatin
1 (8 ounce) package cream cheese, softened
1 (14 ounce) can sweetened condensed milk
1 (8 ounce) carton whipped topping, thawed
2 (11 ounce) cans mandarin orange slices, drained

- In bowl, dissolve gelatin in 1¼ cups boiling water.
- In mixing bowl, beat cream cheese until fluffy, gradually blend in hot gelatin and beat on low speed until smooth.
- Stir in condensed milk and refrigerate until mixture begins to thicken.
- Fold in whipped topping and orange slices.
- Spoon into 9 x 13-inch glass dish and refrigerate 4 hours before serving.

Apple-Pineapple Salad

1 (6 ounce) package lemon gelatin
1 (15 ounce) can pineapple tidbits with juice
1 cup diced apples with peel
1 cup chopped pecans

- Dissolve gelatin in 1 cup boiling water.
- Add pineapple and place in refrigerator until slightly thick.
- Fold in apples and pecans.
- Pour into solid mold or 7 x 11-inch dish and refrigerate until firm.

Frozen Cherry Salad

1 (8 ounce) package cream cheese, softened
1 (8 ounce) carton whipped topping, thawed
1 (20 ounce) can cherry pie filling
2 (11 ounce) cans mandarin oranges, drained
¾ cup coarsely chopped pecans

- With mixer, beat cream cheese until smooth and fold in whipped topping.
- Stir in pie filling, oranges and pecans.
- Transfer to 9 x 5-inch loaf pan, cover and freeze overnight.
- Remove from freezer 15 minutes before slicing and serve on a lettuce leaf.

Coconut-Orange Salad

1 (6 ounce) package orange gelatin
1 pint vanilla ice cream, softened
½ cup flaked coconut
1 (11 ounce) can mandarin oranges, drained

- Dissolve gelatin in 1 cup boiling water and cool slightly.
- Fold in ice cream, coconut and oranges.
- Pour into 7 x 11-inch dish and freeze.

Butter-Mint Salad

1 (6 ounce) box lime gelatin
1 (20 ounce) can crushed pineapple with juice
½ (10 ounce) bag miniature marshmallows
1 (8 ounce) carton whipped topping, thawed
1 (8 ounce) bag butter mints, crushed

- Pour dry gelatin over pineapple, stir in marshmallows and set overnight.
- Fold in whipped topping and butter mints.
- Pour into 9 x 13-inch dish and freeze.

Frozen Cranberry-Pineapple Salad

1 (20 ounce) can crushed pineapple, drained
2 (16 ounce) cans whole cranberry sauce
1 (8 ounce) carton sour cream
¾ cup chopped pecans

- In large bowl, combine all ingredients and pour into sprayed 8 x 11-inch glass dish.
- Freeze several hours before serving.

Holiday Salad

1 (15 ounce) can whole cranberry sauce
1 (15 ounce) can crushed pineapple, drained
2 (15 ounce) cans fruit cocktail, drained
1 (8 ounce) carton sour cream

- Combine all ingredients and freeze in cranberry and pineapple cans.
- When ready to serve, cut upper end of cans and push salad out.
- Slice and serve on lettuce leaf.

Frozen Dessert Salad

1 (8 ounce) package cream cheese, softened
1 cup powdered sugar
1 (10 ounce) box frozen strawberries, thawed
1 (15 ounce) can crushed pineapple, drained
1 (8 ounce) carton whipped topping, thawed

- In mixing bowl, beat cream cheese and sugar and fold in strawberries, pineapple and whipped topping. (This will be even better if you stir in ¾ cup chopped pecans.)
- Pour into 9 x 9-inch pan and freeze.
- Cut into squares to serve.

Chicken Salad

3 cups chicken breast halves, cooked, finely chopped
1½ cups chopped celery
½ cup sweet pickle relish
2 hard-boiled eggs, chopped
¾ cup mayonnaise

- Combine all ingredients and several sprinkles salt and pepper.

TIP: Adding ½ cup chopped pecans gives the chicken salad a special taste.

Savory Chicken Salad

4 boneless, skinless chicken breast halves, cooked
1 cup chopped celery
1 red bell pepper, seeded, chopped
⅔ cup slivered almonds, toasted

- Slice chicken breasts into long, thin strips.
- Combine chicken, celery, bell pepper and almonds.
- Toss and refrigerate.

TIP: For dressing, use flavored mayonnaise: ½ cup mayonnaise with 1 tablespoon lemon juice.

Mexican Chicken Salad

3 to 4 boneless, skinless chicken breast halves, cooked, cubed
1 (15 ounce) can chick-peas, drained
1 red bell pepper, seeded, diced
1 green bell pepper, seeded, diced
1 cup chopped celery

- Combine all ingredients and serve with dressing below.

Dressing for Mexican Chicken Salad:

1½ cups sour cream
2 tablespoons chili sauce
2 teaspoons ground cumin
1 small bunch cilantro, minced

- Combine all ingredients for dressing and add a little salt and pepper.
- Pour over chicken salad and toss.
- Refrigerate before serving.

Tarragon-Chicken Salad

1 cup chopped pecans
3 to 4 boneless, skinless chicken breast halves, cooked, cubed
1 cup chopped celery
¾ cup peeled, chopped cucumbers

- Place pecans in shallow pan and toast at 300° for 10 minutes.
- Combine chicken, celery and cucumbers.

Dressing for Tarragon-Chicken Salad:

⅔ cup mayonnaise
1 tablespoon lemon juice
2 tablespoons tarragon vinegar
1¼ teaspoons crumbled, dried tarragon

- Combine all dressing ingredients and mix well.
- When ready to serve, toss with chicken mixture and add pecans.

Broccoli-Chicken Salad

3 to 4 boneless, skinless chicken breast halves, cooked, cubed
2 cups fresh broccoli florets
1 sweet red bell pepper, seeded, chopped
1 cup chopped celery

- Combine all ingredients.
- Toss mixture with honey-mustard salad dressing and refrigerate.

Spinach Sandwiches

1 (10 ounce) package chopped spinach, thawed,
    well drained
1 cup mayonnaise
1 (8 ounce) carton sour cream
½ cup finely minced onion
1 (1 ounce) package dry vegetable soup mix

- Squeeze spinach between paper towels to completely remove excess moisture.
- Combine all ingredients and mix well. (If you like, ¾ cup finely chopped pecans may be added.)
- Refrigerate for 3 to 4 hours before making sandwiches.
- To make sandwiches, use thin white bread.

Lady Cream Cheese Sandwiches

2 (8 ounce) packages cream cheese, softened
1 (4 ounce) can black olives, chopped
¾ cups finely chopped pecans
Pumpernickel rye bread

- Beat cream cheese until creamy and fold in olives and pecans.
- Trim crusts from bread and spread cream cheese on bread.
- Slice sandwich into 3 finger strips.

Party Sandwiches

1 (8 ounce) package cream cheese, softened
⅓ cup chopped stuffed olives
2 tablespoons olive juice
⅓ cup chopped pecans
6 slices bacon, cooked, crumbled

- Beat cream cheese with mixer until smooth and stir in olives, olive juice, pecans and bacon.
- Spread on party rye bread.

Confetti Sandwiches

1 tablespoon lemon juice
1 (8 ounce) package cream cheese, softened
Mayonnaise
½ cup grated carrots
¼ cup grated cucumber
¼ cup grated red onion
¼ cup grated bell pepper

- Combine lemon juice with cream cheese and add enough mayonnaise to make cheese into spreading consistency.
- Fold in grated vegetables, spread on bread for sandwiches and refrigerate.

Turkey-Asparagus Sandwiches

4 (1 ounce) slices cheddar cheese
2 English muffins, split, toasted
½ pound thinly sliced turkey
1 (15 ounce) can asparagus spears, drained
1 (1 ounce) package hollandaise sauce blend

- Place 1 cheese slice on each muffin half and top evenly with turkey.
- Cut asparagus spears to fit muffin halves and top each with 3 or 4 asparagus spears. (Save remaining asparagus for another use.)
- Prepare sauce mix according to package directions, pour evenly over sandwiches and sprinkle with paprika, if desired.

Reuben Sandwiches

For each sandwich:
  2 slices rye bread
  1 slice Swiss cheese
  Generous slices corned beef
  2 tablespoons sauerkraut
  Dijon mustard

- Butter 1 slice bread on 1 side and place butter side down in skillet over low heat.
- Layer cheese, corned beef and sauerkraut on bread.
- Spread mustard on 1 side of other slice, butter opposite side of bread and place butter side up on sauerkraut.
- Cook until bottom browns, turn carefully and brown other side.

Grilled Bacon-Banana Sandwiches

  Peanut butter
  8 slices English muffins
  2 bananas
  8 slices bacon, cooked crispy
  Butter, softened

- Spread peanut butter over 8 slices of muffin.
- Slice bananas and arrange on top of 4 muffin halves.
- Place 2 strips bacon on each of 4 muffin halves on top of banana slices.
- Top with remaining muffin slices and spread butter over top slice.
- Brown sandwiches butter side down.
- Spread butter other side, turn and cook until golden brown. Serve hot.

Pizza Flash

  1 (14 ounce) package English muffins
  1½ cups pizza sauce
  1 pound bulk sausage, cooked, drained
  1 (4 ounce) can mushrooms, drained
  1 (8 ounce) package shredded mozzarella cheese

- Split muffins and layer ingredients on each muffin half ending with cheese.
- Broil until cheese melts.

Ham and Cheese Hot Pockets

1 (8 ounce) can refrigerated crescent rolls
2 tablespoons mayonnaise
2 teaspoons prepared mustard
1 cup finely chopped ham
½ cup shredded Swiss cheese

- Unroll dough, separate into 4 rectangles and press seams to seal.
- Combine mayonnaise and mustard and spread over rectangles, leaving a ½ inch border.
- Sprinkle ham and cheese evenly over half of each rectangle.
- Moisten edges with water, fold dough over and pinch edges to seal.
- Bake at 375° for 10 minutes or until puffed and golden.

Reubens on a Bun

1 (1 pound) package smoked frankfurter
8 hot dog buns
1 (8 ounce) can sauerkraut, well drained
Caraway seeds
Thousand island salad dressing

- Preheat oven to 325°.
- Pierce each frankfurter and place into split buns.
- Arrange 2 tablespoons sauerkraut over each frank and sprinkle with caraway seeds.
- Place in 9 x 13-inch shallow pan and drizzle with thousand island salad dressing.
- Heat 10 minutes or just until franks are thoroughly hot.

Hot Bunwiches

8 hamburger buns
8 slices Swiss cheese
8 slices ham
8 slices turkey
8 slices American cheese

- Place slices of Swiss cheese, ham, turkey and American cheese on bottom buns.
- Place top bun over American cheese, wrap each bunwich individually in foil and place in freezer.
- Remove from freezer 2 to 3 hours before serving.
- Heat at 325° for about 30 minutes and serve hot.

Everyday Sloppy Joes

1 pound lean ground beef
1 (10 ounce) can Italian tomato soup
2 teaspoons Worcestershire sauce
⅛ teaspoon black pepper
6 hamburger buns, split, toasted

- In skillet, cook beef until brown, stir to separate meat and spoon off fat.
- Add soup, Worcestershire, pepper and ¼ cup water.
- Heat thoroughly and stir often.
- Serve on buns.

Peppered Meatball Hoagies

1 small onion, diced
1 small green bell pepper, diced
1 (15 ounce) can sloppy joe sauce
30 to 32 frozen cooked meatballs
4 hoagie buns

- Sauté onion and pepper in 1 tablespoon oil.
- Add sauce and meatballs and cook 10 minutes or until thoroughly heated, stirring often.
- Spoon evenly onto hoagie buns.

Easy Dog Wraps

8 wieners
8 slices cheese
1 (8 ounce) package refrigerated crescent rolls

- Split wieners lengthwise and fill with folded cheese slice.
- Wrap wiener in crescent dough roll and bake at 375° for 12 minutes.
- Serve with mustard.

Turkey-Cranberry Croissant

1 (8 ounce) package cream cheese, softened
¼ cup orange marmalade
6 large croissants, split
Lettuce leaves
1 pound thinly sliced, cooked turkey
¾ cup whole cranberry sauce

- Beat cream cheese and orange marmalade and spread evenly on cut sides of croissants.
- Place lettuce leaves and turkey on croissant bottoms and spread with cranberry sauce.
- Cover with croissant tops.

Reuben Dogs

1 (20 ounce) can sauerkraut, rinsed, drained
2 teaspoons caraway seeds
8 hot dogs, halved lengthwise
1 cup shredded Swiss cheese
Thousand island salad dressing

- Place sauerkraut in greased 2-quart baking dish, sprinkle with caraway seeds and top with hot dogs.
- Bake uncovered at 350° for 20 minutes or until heated through.
- Sprinkle with cheese and bake 3 to 5 minutes longer or until cheese melts.
- Serve with salad dressing.

Sandwiches Extraordinaire

Here are some new or different combinations for sandwiches you may not have tried before. You'll get some "ooh's" and "aah's" and maybe even a raised eyebrow or two.

Sandwich Inspiration I
Pumpernickel bread
Mayonnaise
Deli sliced corned beef
Slices of Swiss cheese
Lettuce

Sandwich Inspiration II
Dark rye bread
2 slices corned beef
2 slices Swiss cheese
4 tablespoons sauerkraut
Russian dressing

Sandwich Inspiration III
Hoagie rolls
Dijon-style mustard
Slices of pastrami
Slices of mozzarella cheese
Deli coleslaw

Sandwich Inspiration IV
Pita bread
Ham slices
Mozzarella cheese slices
Slices of sweet pickles
Bean sprouts
Mayonnaise

Sandwich Inspiration V
Rye bread
Slices mozzarella cheese
Deli ham salad
Avocado slices
Lettuce

Sandwich Inspiration VI
French bread slices
Turkey and deli beef slices
Slices of American cheese
Slices of Monterey Jack cheese
Lettuce
Mayonnaise

Sandwich Inspiration VII
Whole wheat bread
Slices of American cheese
Deli shrimp or crab salad
Avocado slices
Lettuce

Sandwich Inspiration VIII
Kaiser rolls
Spread with softened cream cheese
Deli egg salad
Slices of dill pickles
Fresh bean sprouts

Sandwich Inspiration IX
Multi-grain bread
Deli sliced turkey breasts
Slices havarti cheese
Fresh spinach
Garlic Mayonnaise (page 148)

Sandwich Inspiration X
Pumpernickle bread
Deli roast beef
Fresh spinach
 Tomato slices
Quick Guacamole (page 148)

Sandwich Inspiration XI
French rolls
Thin slices brie cheese
Deli sliced turkey breast
Chutney spread
Mayonnaise

Sandwich Inspiration XII
Kaiser rolls
Grilled chicken breasts
Canned pineapple slices
Leaf lettuce
Sesame-Ginger Mayonnaise (page 148)

Sandwich Inspiration XIII
Slices marble rye bread
Deli sliced peppered roast beef
Slices sweet onion, separated
    into rings
Leaf lettuce
Horseradish Mayonnaise (page 148)

Sandwich Inspiration XIV
Honey nut bread
Crisp cooked bacon slices
Tomato slices
Bibb lettuce
Remoulade Mayonnaise (page 148)

Cheese 'n Wiener Crescents

8 large wieners
4 slices American cheese, cut into 6 strips each
1 (8 ounce) can refrigerated crescent dinner rolls

- Slit wieners to within ½-inch of end and insert 3 strips cheese in each slit.
- Separate crescent dough into 8 triangles and wrap dough around wiener.
- Keep cheese side up and place on baking sheet.
- Bake at 375° for 12 to 15 minutes or until golden brown.

Chihuahua Dogs

1 (10 ounce) can chili hot dog sauce
1 (10 count) package beef franks
1 (10 count) package pre-formed taco shells
Shredded cheddar cheese

- Place chili sauce in saucepan and heat to warm.
- Place 1 frank in each taco shell and top with warm chili sauce and cheese. (Add onions and tomatoes if you like.)
- Place in microwave and heat for 30 seconds or until frankfurters are warm.

Ranch Cheeseburger Mix

1 (1 ounce) package dry ranch-style salad dressing mix
1 pound lean ground beef
1 cup shredded cheddar cheese
4 large hamburger buns, toasted

- Combine dressing mix with beef and cheese.
- Shape into 4 patties, cook covered on grill until patties are brown and fully done.

Provolone-Pepper Burgers

⅓ cup finely cubed provolone cheese
¼ cup diced roasted red peppers
¼ cup finely chopped onion
1 pound lean ground beef
4 hamburger buns, split

- In bowl, combine cheese, red peppers, onion and a little salt and pepper.
- Add beef, mix well and shape into 4 patties.
- Grill covered over medium-hot heat for 5 minutes on each side or until meat is no longer pink.
- Add your favorite lettuce, tomatoes, etc. and serve on hamburger buns.

Pizza Burgers

1 pound lean ground beef
½ teaspoon salt
½ cup pizza sauce, divided
4 slices mozzarella cheese

- Combine beef, salt and half pizza sauce.
- Mold into 4 patties and pan-fry over medium heat for 5 to 6 minutes on each side.
- Just before burgers are done, top each with 1 spoonful pizza sauce and 1 slice cheese.
- Serve on hamburger buns.

Burgers with Flair

Basic Burgers:

1¼ pounds ground chuck
1 egg, optional
2 teaspoons Worcestershire sauce
½ teaspoon salt
¼ teaspoon black pepper

- Mix ground chuck with egg, Worcestershire, salt and pepper.
- Form into 4 or 5 patties about ½-inch thick and about 4 inches in diameter.
- Cook on grill for about 5 to 6 minutes on each side or in skillet for about 4 to 5 minutes on each side.
- Toast 4 buns and spread with mayonnaise or mustard.
- Add lettuce, tomatoes and slice of onion and serve.

Here are some suggested additions to your basic hamburger for a little change of taste.

Tex-Mex Burgers: Spread with some prepared guacamole and place sliced jalapeno peppers on each bun.

Garden Burgers: Instead of lettuce, place about 3 tablespoons deli coleslaw and some sunflower seeds on each bun.

Nutty Harvest Burgers: Add thin slices of apples and some chopped peanuts.

Farmer-in-the-Dell Burgers: Add thin slices of cucumber and sliced olives.

South-of-the-Border Burgers: Instead of American cheese, use Monterey Jack cheese, and instead of mayonnaise or mustard, use prepared guacamole as spread.

Pastrami-Cheese Burgers: Add slices of pastrami and slices of mozzarella cheese.

Salami-Swiss Burgers: Add slices of salami and slices of Swiss cheese.

Bacon-Mex Burgers: Add slices of avocado, mayonnaise (not mustard) and slices of crisp, cooked bacon.

Hot and Sweet Mustard for Burgers and Sandwiches

4 ounces dry mustard
1 cup vinegar
3 eggs
1 cup sugar

- Soak dry mustard in vinegar overnight.
- Beat eggs and sugar and add to vinegar-mustard mixture.
- In top of double boiler, cook over low heat for approximately 15 minutes, stirring constantly. (Mixture will resemble custard consistency.)
- Pour immediately into jars and store in refrigerator.

TIP: Great to keep in the refrigerator for ham sandwiches.

Sandwich Spreads:

Just combine all the ingredients and refrigerate.

Horseradish Mayonnaise:
½ cup mayonnaise
1 tablespoon chopped fresh chives
1 tablespoon prepared horseradish
⅛ teaspoon seasoned salt

Garlic Mayonnaise:
⅔ cup mayonnaise
1 tablespoon chopped roasted garlic
1 teaspoon finely chopped onion
⅛ teaspoon salt

Remoulade Mayonnaise:
½ cup mayonnaise
2 tablespoons chunky salsa
1 teaspoon chopped fresh parsley
1 teaspoon sweet pickle relish
1 teaspoon dijon-style mustard

Spicy Remoulade Mayonnaise:
1 cup mayonnaise
½ cup chunky salsa
¼ cup sweet pickle relish
1 teaspoon dijon-style mustard
1 tablespoon horseradish

Chutney Spread:
⅓ cup peach preserves
½ cup chopped fresh peaches
2 teaspoons finely chopped
    green onion
½ teaspoon balsamic vinegar
¼ teaspoon crushed red pepper flakes

Sesame-Ginger Mayonnaise:
⅔ cup mayonnaise
1 tablespoon honey
1 tablespoon toasted sesame seeds
2 teaspoon grated fresh gingerroot

Quick Guacamole:
1 (1 ounce) package dry onion
    soup mix
2 (8 ounce) cartons avocado dip
2 green onions with tops, chopped
½ teaspoon crushed dillweed

Avocado Butter:
2 large avocados, peeled, seeded
2 tablespoons lime juice
1 pound butter, softened
¼ teaspoon ginger

Side Dishes
&
Vegetables

Cheddar Potatoes

1 (10 ounce) can cheddar cheese soup
⅓ cup sour cream
2 fresh green onions with tops, chopped
3 cups instant seasoned mashed potatoes, prepared

- In saucepan, heat soup and add sour cream, onion and a little black pepper.
- Stir in potatoes until they blend well.
- Pour into buttered 2-quart casserole dish and cook at 350° for 25 minutes.

Potato Souffle

2⅔ cups instant mashed potatoes
2 eggs, beaten
1 cup shredded cheddar cheese
1 (3 ounce) can french-fried onions

- Prepare mashed potatoes according to package directions.
- Add eggs and cheese and mix well.
- Spoon mixture into lightly greased 2-quart baking dish.
- Sprinkle with onions and bake uncovered at 325° for 25 minutes.

Ranch Mashed Potatoes

4 cups prepared, unsalted instant mashed potatoes
1 (1 ounce) package ranch-style salad dressing mix
¼ cup (½ stick) butter
½ cup sour cream

- Combine all ingredients in saucepan and mix well.
- Heat on low until potatoes are thoroughly heated.

Chive-Potato Souffle

3 eggs, separated
2 cups hot instant mashed potatoes
½ cup sour cream
2 heaping tablespoons chopped chives
1 teaspoon seasoned salt

- Beat egg whites until stiff and set aside.
- Beat yolks until smooth and add to potatoes.
- Fold beaten egg whites, sour cream, chives and salt into potato-egg yolk mixture and pour into buttered 2-quart baking dish.
- Bake at 350° for 45 minutes.

Mashed Potatoes Supreme

1 (8 ounce) package cream cheese, softened
½ cup sour cream
2 tablespoons (¼ stick) butter, softened
1 (1 ounce) package ranch-style salad dressing mix
6 to 8 cups warm, prepared instant mashed potatoes

- With mixer, combine cream cheese, sour cream, butter and dressing mix and mix well.
- Add potatoes and stir well.
- Transfer to 2-quart casserole dish and bake at 350° for 25 minutes or until heated through.

Creamy Mashed Potatoes

6 large potatoes
1 (8 ounce) carton sour cream
1 (8 ounce) package cream cheese, softened
1 teaspoon salt
½ teaspoon white pepper

- Peel, cut up and boil potatoes. Drain.
- Add sour cream, cream cheese, salt and pepper and whip until cream cheese melts. Pour into greased 3-quart baking dish.
- Cover with foil and bake at 325° for about 20 minutes. (Bake about 10 minutes longer if reheating.)

Potato Puff

3 eggs, separated
2 cups instant mashed potatoes, prepared, hot
½ cup sour cream
2 teaspoons dried parsley

- Beat egg whites until stiff but still moist and set aside.
- Beat yolks until smooth and add to potatoes.
- Fold in beaten egg whites, sour cream, parsley, plus ½ teaspoon seasoned salt and white pepper.
- Pour mixture into buttered 2-quart casserole dish and bake uncovered at 350° for 45 minutes.

Creamy Cheesy Potatoes

1 (32 ounce) bag frozen hash brown potatoes, thawed
1 (16 ounce) package cubed processed cheese
1 (10 ounce) can cream of chicken soup
1 (8 ounce) carton sour cream

- In large bowl, combine hash browns, cheese, soup and sour cream. (Add ½ teaspoon salt if desired.)
- Spoon mixture into buttered 9 x 13-inch baking dish and cover.
- Bake at 325° for 1 hour and stir twice during baking to prevent burning.

Potatoes Supreme

1 (32 ounce) package frozen hash-brown potatoes, thawed
1 onion, chopped
2 (10 ounce) cans cream of chicken soup
1 (8 ounce) carton sour cream

- In large bowl, combine all ingredients and mix well.
- Pour into greased 9 x 13-inch baking dish.
- Bake covered at 350° for 1 hour.

TIP: *This recipe is also good with ½ cup parmesan or cheddar cheese sprinkled on top for the last 5 minutes of baking.*

Golden Potato Casserole

1 (32 ounce) bag frozen hash brown potatoes, thawed
1 (16 ounce) carton sour cream
1 (8 ounce) package shredded cheddar cheese
1 bunch fresh green onions with tops, chopped

- Combine potatoes, sour cream, cheese and onion in large bowl and thoroughly mix.
- Pour into 9 x 13-inch buttered casserole dish and sprinkle a little paprika over top.
- Cover and bake at 325° for 55 minutes.

Potatoes au Gratin

1 (8 ounce) package cubed processed cheese
1 (16 ounce) carton half-and-half cream
1 cup shredded cheddar cheese
½ cup (1 stick) butter
1 (32 ounce) package frozen hash brown potatoes, thawed

- In double boiler, melt processed cheese, cream, cheddar cheese and butter.
- Place hash browns in greased 9 x 13-inch baking dish and pour cheese mixture over potatoes.
- Bake uncovered at 350° for 1 hour.

Oven Fries

5 medium baking potatoes
⅓ cup oil
¼ teaspoon black pepper
¾ teaspoon seasoned salt
Paprika

- Scrub potatoes, cut each in 6 lengthwise wedges and place in shallow baking dish.
- Combine oil, pepper and seasoned salt and brush potatoes with mixture.
- Sprinkle potatoes lightly with paprika.
- Bake at 375° for about 50 minutes or until potatoes are tender and light brown. Baste twice with remaining oil mixture while baking.

Terrific 'Taters

5 to 6 medium potatoes
1 (8 ounce) carton sour cream
1 (1 ounce) package dry ranch-style salad dressing mix
1½ cups shredded cheddar cheese
3 pieces bacon, fried, drained, crumbled

- Peel, slice and boil potatoes and drain.
- Place potatoes in 2-quart baking dish.
- Combine sour cream, salad dressing mix and a little pepper.
- Toss until potatoes are coated with sour cream mixture and sprinkle cheese on top.
- Bake at 350° for about 20 minutes.
- Sprinkle bacon on top and serve hot.

Scalloped Potatoes

6 medium potatoes
½ cup (1 stick) butter
1 tablespoon flour
2 cups grated cheddar cheese
¾ cup milk

- Peel and slice potatoes.
- Place half potatoes in greased 3-quart baking dish.
- Slice half butter over potatoes, sprinkle with flour and cover with half cheese.
- Repeat layers with cheese on top.
- Pour milk over casserole and sprinkle with a little pepper. (Prepare potatoes as fast as you can so they will not turn dark.)
- Cover and bake at 350° for 1 hour.

Cheddar-Potato Strips

3 large potatoes, cut into ½-inch strips
½ cup milk
2 tablespoons (¼ stick) butter
½ cup shredded cheddar cheese
1 tablespoon minced fresh parsley

- In greased 9 x 13-inch baking dish, arrange potatoes in single layer.
- Pour milk over potatoes, dot with butter and sprinkle with a little salt and pepper.
- Cover and bake at 400° for 30 minutes or until potatoes are tender.
- Sprinkle with cheese and parsley and bake uncovered for 5 minutes longer.

Creamy Potato Bake

6 to 8 baked potatoes
1 (8 ounce) carton sour cream
1 (8 ounce) package cream cheese, softened
1½ cups shredded cheddar cheese

- Cut potatoes in half lengthwise, scoop meat from potatoes and place meat in mixing bowl.
- Add sour cream, cream cheese and salt to taste and whip until all blend.
- Spoon mashed potatoes back into potato skins and place in oven until potatoes reheat.
- Sprinkle cheddar cheese over potatoes.

Oven-Roasted Potatoes

2 pounds potatoes with peel
1 (1 ounce) package dry onion soup mix
⅓ cup oil
½ teaspoon black pepper

- Wash potatoes and cut into medium-size chunks.
- In large plastic bag, combine all ingredients and shake until potatoes coat evenly.
- Empty coated potatoes into greased 9 x 13-inch baking pan.
- Bake uncovered at 425° for 40 minutes or until golden brown and stir mixture twice during cooking.

Potato Pancakes

3 pounds white potatoes, peeled, grated
1 onion, finely minced
3 eggs, beaten
½ cup dry seasoned breadcrumbs

- In large bowl, combine potatoes, onion, eggs, breadcrumbs and a little salt and pepper and mix well.
- Drop mixture by spoonfuls into skillet with hot oil and brown on both sides.

Twice-Baked Potatoes

8 medium baking potatoes
2 tablespoons (¼ stick) butter
½ teaspoon salt
1 (10 ounce) can cheddar cheese soup
1 tablespoon chopped dried chives

- Bake potatoes at 350° for 1 hour or until done.
- Cut potatoes in half lengthwise and scoop pulp from potatoes leaving thin shell.
- With mixer, whip pulp with butter and salt.
- Gradually add soup and chives and beat until light and fluffy.
- Spoon mixture into potato skin shells and sprinkle with paprika.
- Bake at 425° for 15 minutes.

TIP: *If you want a little "zip" to these potatoes, add 1 (10 ounce) can fiesta nacho cheese soup instead of cheddar cheese soup.*

Loaded Baked Potatoes

6 medium to large potatoes
1 pound hot sausage
1 (16 ounce) package cubed, processed cheese
1 (10 ounce) can diced tomatoes and green chiles, drained

- Wrap potatoes in foil and bake at 375° for 1 hour or until done.
- Brown sausage and drain.
- Add cheese to sausage, heat until cheese melts and add tomatoes and green chiles.
- Serve sausage-cheese mixture over baked potatoes.

Ham Baked Potatoes

4 potatoes, baked
1 cup diced, cooked ham
1 (10 ounce) can cream of mushroom soup
1 cup shredded cheddar cheese

- Place hot potatoes in microwave-safe dish and cut each potato in half lengthwise.
- Fluff up potatoes with fork and top each potato with one-quarter ham.
- In saucepan, heat soup with ¼ cup water just until mixture is easy to spread.
- Spoon soup over potatoes and top with cheese.
- Microwave on HIGH for 4 minutes or until hot.

Broccoli-Topped Potatoes

4 hot baked potatoes, halved
1 cup diced, cooked ham
1 (10 ounce) can cream of broccoli soup
½ cup shredded cheddar cheese

- Place hot baked potatoes in microwave-safe dish.
- Carefully fluff up potatoes with fork and top each potato with ham.
- Stir soup in can until smooth and spoon over potatoes.
- Top with cheese and microwave on HIGH for 4 minutes.

Herbed New Potatoes

1½ pounds new potatoes
6 tablespoons (¾ stick) butter, sliced
¼ teaspoon thyme
½ cup chopped fresh parsley
½ teaspoon rosemary

- Scrub potatoes and cut in halves but do not peel.
- In medium saucepan, boil potatoes in lightly salted water for about 20 minutes or until tender and drain.
- Add butter, thyme, parsley and rosemary and toss gently until butter melts.
- Serve hot.

Sweet Potato Wedges

3 pounds sweet potatoes, peeled, quartered
6 tablespoons (¾ stick) butter, melted
6 tablespoons orange juice
¾ teaspoon salt
¾ teaspoon ground cinnamon

- Arrange sweet potatoes in greased 9 x 13-inch baking pan.
- Combine butter, orange juice, salt and cinnamon and drizzle over sweet potatoes.
- Cover and bake at 350° for 60 minutes or until tender.

Sweet Potato Casserole

1 (28 ounce) can sweet potatoes
½ cup chopped pecans
1½ cups packed light brown sugar
½ cup (1 stick) butter

- Slice sweet potatoes into 2-quart casserole dish and sprinkle with pecans.
- Combine brown sugar and butter with just enough water to make syrup and bring mixture to a boil.
- Pour syrup over sweet potatoes and bake at 350° for 30 minutes until potatoes brown.

Marshmallow Sweet Potatoes

2 (15 ounce) cans sweet potatoes
¼ cup (½ stick) butter, melted
¼ cup orange juice
1 cup miniature marshmallows

- Combine sweet potatoes, butter, orange juice and ½ teaspoon salt in mixing bowl.
- Beat until fluffy and fold in marshmallows.
- Spoon mixture into buttered 2-quart casserole dish.
- Bake uncovered at 350° for 25 minutes.

TIP: You might want to sprinkle top with additional marshmallows and broil until light brown.

Whipped Sweet Potatoes

1 (28 ounce) can sweet potatoes
1 cup (2 sticks) butter, melted, divided
1 cup packed light brown sugar
1½ cups crushed corn flakes

- Drain most of liquid from sweet potatoes.
- Place sweet potatoes in mixing bowl and cut large pieces of potatoes into several pieces.
- Beat sweet potatoes until creamy and fold in ¾ cup (1½ sticks) melted butter and brown sugar.
- Beat until butter and sugar thoroughly combine with sweet potatoes and pour into buttered 2-quart baking dish.
- Combine crushed corn flakes and remaining ¼ cup (½ stick) melted butter and sprinkle over sweet potato casserole. (If you like, add ⅓ cup chopped pecans to corn flake mixture.)
- Bake uncovered at 350° for 40 minutes.

Baked Sweet Potato Topping

4 sweet potatoes
6 tablespoons (¾ stick) butter, melted
½ cup granulated sugar
½ cup packed brown sugar
1 teaspoon cinnamon
½ cup flaked coconut

- Prick each sweet potato several times with fork, wrap individually in foil and bake at 375° for about 1 hour.
- Check for doneness. Unwrap sweet potatoes, make slit down center of each potato, and use fork to fluff up potato meat.
- In small bowl, combine melted butter, both sugars, cinnamon and coconut and mix well.
- Spoon ¼ mixture over each potato and, again, fluff with fork to make sure sugar mixture goes into each potato.

Speedy Sweet Potatoes

2 (16 ounce) cans sweet potatoes, drained
1 (8 ounce) can crushed pineapple with juice
½ cup chopped pecans
⅓ cup packed brown sugar
1 cup miniature marshmallows, divided

- In 2-quart microwave-safe dish, layer sweet potatoes, a little salt, pineapple, pecans, brown sugar and ½ cup marshmallows.
- Cover and microwave on HIGH for 6 minutes or until bubbly around edges.
- Top with remaining marshmallows and heat uncovered on HIGH for 30 seconds or until marshmallows puff. (If you like, sprinkle sweet potatoes with a little nutmeg.)

Maple-Ginger Sweet Potatoes

4 medium sweet potatoes
½ cup sour cream
⅓ cup maple syrup
¼ teaspoon ground ginger
¼ cup chopped pecans

- Pierce sweet potatoes several times with fork, place on baking sheet and bake at 375° for 1 hour.
- Combine sour cream, syrup and ginger, spoon over split potatoes and sprinkle with pecans.

Sweet Potatoes and Pecans

2 (17 ounce) cans sweet potatoes, drained, divided
1½ cups packed brown sugar
¼ cup (½ stick) butter, melted
1 cup chopped pecans

- Slice half sweet potatoes and place in buttered 2-quart baking dish.
- Combine brown sugar, butter and pecans and sprinkle half mixture over sweet potatoes.
- Repeat layers and bake uncovered at 350° for 30 minutes.

Creamy Seasoned Noodles

1 (8 ounce) package wide egg noodles
1 (1 ounce) envelope dry Italian salad dressing mix
½ cup whipping cream
¼ cup (½ stick) butter
¼ cup grated parmesan cheese

- Cook noodles according to package directions and drain.
- Add dressing mix, cream, butter and cheese and toss lightly to blend thoroughly. (Cut butter in chunks so it will melt more easily.)
- Serve hot.

Spinach Fettuccine

1 (12 ounce) package spinach fettuccine
1 (6 ounce) can tomato paste
1 (5 ounce) can evaporated milk
½ cup (1 stick) butter

- Cook fettuccine according to package directions.
- In saucepan, combine tomato paste, milk and butter and heat until butter melts.
- Season with a little salt and pepper.
- Serve sauce over fettuccine.

Favorite Creamy Pasta

4 ounces spinach linguine, uncooked
1 cup whipping cream
1 cup chicken broth
½ cup freshly grated parmesan cheese
½ cup frozen English peas

- Cook linguine according to package directions, drain and keep warm.
- Combine whipping cream and chicken broth in saucepan and bring to a boil.
- Reduce heat and simmer mixture 25 minutes or until it thickens and reduces to 1 cup.
- Remove from heat, add cheese and peas and stir until cheese melts.
- Toss with linguine and serve immediately.

Pasta with Basil

2½ cups uncooked small tube pasta
1 small onion, chopped
2 tablespoons oil
2½ tablespoons dried basil
1 cup shredded mozzarella cheese

- Cook pasta according to package directions.
- In skillet, sauté onion in oil.
- Stir in basil, 1 teaspoon salt and ¼ teaspoon pepper, cook and stir 1 minute.
- Drain pasta and add to basil mixture. (Leave about ½ cup water so pasta won't be too dry.)
- Remove from heat and stir in cheese just until it begins to melt.
- Serve immediately.

Creamy Fettuccine

1 (8 ounce) package fettuccine
1 pound Italian sausage
1 (10 ounce) can cream of mushroom soup
1 (16 ounce) carton sour cream

- Cook fettuccine according to package directions and drain.
- Cut sausage into 1-inch pieces, brown over medium heat, cook for 8 minutes and drain.
- Combine all ingredients and pour into 2-quart greased baking dish.
- Bake at 325° for 30 minutes.

Creamy Pasta Sauce

1 (8 ounce) jar roasted red peppers, drained
1 (15 ounce) can chicken broth
1 (3 ounce) package cream cheese
8 ounces pasta

- Combine red peppers and broth in blender and mix well.
- Pour mixture into saucepan and heat to a boil.
- Reduce heat and whisk in cream cheese.
- Serve over your favorite pasta.

Macaroni and Cheese

1 cup uncooked macaroni
1½ cups small-curd cottage cheese
1½ cup shredded cheddar or American cheese
¼ cup grated parmesan cheese

- Cook macaroni according to package directions and drain.
- Combine all 3 cheeses and add macaroni to cheese mixture.
- Spoon into greased 2-quart baking dish.
- Bake covered at 350° for 35 minutes.

Macaroni, Cheese and Tomatoes

2 cups elbow macaroni
1 (14 ounce) can stewed tomatoes with liquid
1 (8 ounce) package shredded cheddar cheese
2 tablespoons sugar
1 (6 ounce) package cheese slices

- Cook macaroni according to package directions and drain.
- In large mixing bowl, combine macaroni, tomatoes, shredded cheese, sugar, ¼ cup water and a little salt and mix well.
- Pour into 9 x 13-inch baking dish and place cheese slices on top.
- Bake at 350° for 30 minutes or until bubbly.

Special Shells and Cheese

1 (8 ounce) package small pasta shells
1 (15 ounce) can stewed tomatoes
1 (8 ounce) package cubed processed cheese
3 tablespoons butter, melted

- Cook shells according to package directions and drain.
- In large bowl, combine all ingredients.
- Pour into buttered 2-quart baking dish.
- Bake covered at 350° for 35 minutes.

Carnival Couscous

This is a delicious, colorful dish that easily replaces rice or a vegetable.

1 (6 ounce) box herbed chicken couscous
¼ cup (½ stick) butter
1 red bell pepper, minced
1 yellow squash, seeded, minced
¾ cup fresh broccoli florets, finely chopped

- Cook couscous according to package directions but leave out butter.
- With butter in saucepan, saute bell pepper, squash and broccoli and cook about 10 minutes or until vegetables are almost tender.
- Combine couscous and vegetables and serve. (If you want to do this a little ahead of time, place couscous and vegetables in sprayed baking dish and heat at 325° for about 20 minutes.)

Red Rice

1 (16 ounce) package smoked sausage, sliced
2 (10 ounce) cans diced tomato and green chiles
3 cups chicken broth
2 teaspoons Creole seasoning
1½ cups uncooked, long-grain rice

- Sauté sausage in Dutch oven until brown.
- Stir in tomato and green chiles, broth and seasoning and bring to a boil.
- Stir in rice, cover and reduce heat.
- Simmer 25 minutes, uncover and cook until liquid absorbs.

Green Chile-Rice

1 cup instant rice, cooked
1 (12 ounce) package shredded Monterey Jack cheese
1 (7 ounce) can diced green chiles
2 (8 ounce) cartons sour cream
½ teaspoon garlic powder

- In large bowl, combine and mix all ingredients and add a little salt if you like.
- Spoon into greased 9 x 13-inch baking dish and bake at 350° for 30 minutes.

Brown Rice

1 cup rice (not instant)
1 (10 ounce) can French onion soup
1 (15 ounce) can beef broth
3 tablespoons butter, melted

- Place rice in casserole dish and pour soups and butter over top.
- Bake covered at 350° for 45 minutes.

Mushroom Rice

1 (6 ounce) package chicken-flavored rice and macaroni
1 (4 ounce) can sliced mushrooms, drained
⅓ cup slivered almonds
1 (8 ounce) carton sour cream

- Prepare rice and macaroni according to package directions.
- Fold in mushrooms, almonds and sour cream and place in greased 3-quart casserole dish.
- Bake covered at 350° for 25 to 30 minutes.

Baked Rice

2 cups uncooked rice
½ cup (1 stick) butter, melted
1 (10 ounce) can cream of celery soup
1 (10 ounce) can cream of onion soup

- Combine all ingredients plus 1½ cups water and mix well.
- Pour into buttered 3-quart baking dish and bake covered at 350° for 1 hour.

Tasty Rice

¼ cup (½ stick) butter
1 cup uncooked white rice
2 (15 ounce) cans beef broth
½ cup parmesan cheese

- Melt butter in 3-quart casserole dish.
- Add rice, pour beef broth over rice and sprinkle with parmesan cheese.
- Cover and bake at 350° for 45 minutes.

Green Rice and Spinach

1 cup uncooked instant rice
1 (10 ounce) package frozen chopped spinach
1 onion, finely chopped
3 tablespoons butter
¾ cup grated cheddar cheese

- Cook rice in large saucepan.
- Punch holes in box of spinach and cook in microwave for about 3 minutes.
- Reserve 3 tablespoons cheese for topping and add spinach, onion, butter, cheese and ¼ teaspoon salt to rice. (If rice mixture seems a little dry, add several tablespoons water.)
- Pour into greased 2-quart baking dish and bake at 350° for 25 minutes.

Old South Hoppin' John

2 (16 ounce) cans jalapeno black-eyed peas
¾ pound ham, chopped
1 cup chopped onion
2 cups hot cooked rice
½ cup chopped green onions

- In saucepan, combine peas, ham and onion.
- Bring to a boil, reduce heat and simmer 15 minutes.
- Stir in rice and green onions and serve hot.

Roasted Vegetables

1½ pounds assorted fresh vegetables
1 (11 ounce) can water chestnuts, drained
1 (1 ounce) dry savory herb with garlic soup mix
2 tablespoons (¼ stick) butter, melted

- Cut all vegetables in uniform 2-inch pieces and place in greased 2-quart casserole dish with water chestnuts.
- Combine melted butter and soup mix, drizzle mixture over vegetables and stir well.
- Cover, bake vegetables at 400° for 20 to 25 minutes or until tender and stir once.

TIP: Use your favorite vegetables such as squash, carrots, red bell peppers, zucchini, cauliflower or broccoli.

Mixed Vegetable-Cheese Casserole

1 (16 ounce) package frozen mixed vegetables
1¾ cups shredded American cheese
¾ cup mayonnaise
1 tube round, buttery crackers, crushed
6 tablespoons (¾ stick) butter, melted

- Cook vegetables according to package directions, drain and place in buttered 2-quart casserole dish.
- Mix cheese and mayonnaise and spread over vegetables.
- Combine cracker crumbs and butter and sprinkle on top.
- Bake at 350° for 35 minutes.

TIP: *These vegetables are worthy of Sunday dinner and a way to get kids to eat vegetables.*

Herb-Seasoned Vegetables

1 (14 ounce) can seasoned chicken broth with Italian herbs
½ teaspoon garlic powder
1 (16 ounce) package frozen vegetables
½ cup grated parmesan cheese

- Heat broth, garlic powder and vegetables to a boil.
- Cover and cook over low heat for 5 minutes or until tender-crisp and drain.
- Place vegetables in serving dish and sprinkle with cheese.

Buttered Vegetables

½ cup (1 stick) butter
2 yellow squash, sliced
1 (16 ounce) package broccoli florets
1 (10 ounce) box frozen corn

- Melt butter in large skillet and combine all vegetables.
- Sauté vegetables for 10 to 15 minutes or until tender-crisp.
- Add a little salt if you like and serve warm.

Shoe-Peg Corn

½ cup (1 stick) butter, softened
1 (8 ounce) package cream cheese, softened
3 (15 ounce) cans shoe-peg (or white) corn
1 (4 ounce) can diced green chiles

- Use mixer or fork to combine butter and cream cheese.
- Add corn and green chiles and mix well.
- Spoon into greased 7 x 11-inch casserole dish.
- Bake covered at 350° for 30 minutes.

Shoe-Peg Corn Casserole

½ cup (1 stick) butter
1 (8 ounce) package cream cheese
3 (16 ounce) cans shoe-peg (or white) corn, drained
1 (4 ounce) can diced green chiles
1½ cups cracker crumbs

- Melt butter in saucepan, stir in cream cheese and mix until cream cheese melts.
- Add corn and chiles (and some salt and pepper if you like), mix and pour into greased baking dish.
- Sprinkle cracker crumbs over casserole and bake at 350° for 25 minutes.

Corny Green Chile Casserole

2 (10 ounce) packages frozen whole kernel corn
2 tablespoons (¼ stick) butter
1 (8 ounce) package cream cheese
1 tablespoon sugar
1 (4 ounce) can diced green chiles

- Cook corn according to package directions, drain and set aside.
- Melt butter in saucepan over low heat, add cream cheese and stir until it melts.
- Stir in corn, sugar and green chiles and spoon into greased 2-quart baking dish.
- Cover and bake at 350° for 25 minutes.

Corn Olé

2 (16 ounce) cans whole corn, drained
1 (8 ounce) package cream cheese
1 (4 ounce) can diced green chiles
1 (2 ounce) jar pimentos

- Combine all ingredients in saucepan and mix well.
- Simmer over low heat until cheese melts.

Fantastic Fried Corn

2 (16 ounce) packages frozen whole kernel corn
½ cup (1 stick) butter
1 cup whipping cream
1 tablespoon sugar

- Place corn in large skillet over medium heat and add butter, whipping cream, sugar and 1 teaspoon salt.
- Stirring constantly, heat until most of whipping cream and butter absorbs into corn.

TIP: Yes, I know this has too many calories, but it's my grandkids' favorite vegetable. And who can turn down grandkids?

Corn Pudding

1 (8 ounce) package corn muffin mix
1 (15 ounce) can cream-style corn
½ cup sour cream
3 eggs, slightly beaten

- Combine all ingredients and pour into buttered 2-quart baking dish.
- Bake uncovered at 350° for 35 minutes.

Corn au Gratin

3 (15 ounce) cans Mexicorn®, drained
1 (4 ounce) can sliced mushrooms, drained
1 (10 ounce) can cream of mushroom soup
1 cup shredded cheddar cheese

- Combine all ingredients in saucepan and heat slowly until cheese melts.
- Serve hot.

Italian Corn

1 (16 ounce) package frozen whole kernel corn
2 slices bacon, cooked, diced
1 onion, chopped
1 (16 ounce) can Italian-style stewed tomatoes with liquid

- Combine all ingredients in 2-quart pan and cook until most of tomato liquid is gone.
- Add a little salt and pepper and serve hot.

Hominy

1 (8 ounce) jar jalapeno processed cheese spread
2 (15 ounce) cans golden yellow hominy
1 (8 ounce) carton sour cream
1 teaspoon seasoned salt

- Remove lid from jar and heat processed cheese spread in microwave until cheese is soft enough to mix with hominy.
- Combine processed cheese spread, hominy, sour cream and salt.
- Pour into 2-quart casserole dish and bake at 350° for 30 minutes or until bubbly and brown on top.

Corn-Okra Jambalaya

¼ pound bacon
1 pound fresh okra, sliced
2 onions, chopped
1 (16 ounce) can stewed tomatoes with liquid
1 (16 ounce) can whole kernel corn, drained

- Fry bacon in large skillet until crisp and drain.
- In skillet with bacon drippings, sauté okra and onions but do not brown.
- Add tomatoes and corn and bring to a boil.
- Simmer about 5 to 10 minutes. (Jambalaya must not be runny.)
- Serve over hot rice and sprinkle bacon on top of each serving.

Okra Gumbo

1 large onion, chopped
1 pound fresh okra, sliced
¼ cup (½ stick) butter
2 (15 ounce) cans tomatoes
1 potato, chopped

- Brown onion and okra in butter.
- Add tomatoes and potato and bring to a boil.
- Simmer until potatoes are done about 30 minutes.

Black-Eyed Peas and Okra

3 (15 ounce) cans black-eyed peas, drained
¾ cup shredded ham
1 onion, chopped
1 pound small, fresh whole okra pods

- In large saucepan, combine peas, ham and onion and bring to a boil.
- Place all okra over pea-onion mixture but DO NOT STIR.
- Bring to a boil again, lower heat and simmer for 5 to 10 minutes or until okra is tender.
- Serve hot.

Tasty Black-Eyed Peas

2 (10 ounce) packages frozen black-eyed peas
1¼ cups chopped green pepper
¾ cup chopped onion
3 tablespoons butter
1 (15 ounce) can stewed tomatoes with liquid

- Cook black-eyed peas according to package directions and drain.
- Saute green pepper and onion in butter.
- Add peas, tomatoes and a little salt and pepper.
- Cook over low heat until thoroughly heated and stir often.

Butter Beans and Green Onions

1 (10 ounce) package frozen butter beans
1 bunch fresh green onions with tops, chopped
½ teaspoon garlic powder
½ cup chopped fresh parsley
6 bacon slices, cooked, drained, crumbled

- Cook butter beans according to package directions and set aside.
- Sauté green onions in bacon drippings.
- Stir in butter beans, garlic powder, parsley and a little salt and pepper and cook just until thoroughly heated.
- Pour into serving bowl and sprinkle with bacon.

Better Butter Beans

1 cup sliced celery
1 onion, chopped
¼ cup (½ stick) butter
1 (10 ounce) can diced tomatoes and green chiles
½ teaspoon sugar
2 (15 ounce) cans butter beans

- Sauté celery and onion in butter for about 3 minutes
- Add tomatoes and chiles, several sprinkles of salt and sugar.
- Add butter beans, cover and simmer about 20 minutes.
- Serve hot.

Sautéed Celery

1 bunch celery, chopped diagonally
1 (8 ounce) can water chestnuts, drained, chopped
¼ cup slivered almonds, toasted
¼ cup (½ stick) butter, melted

- Boil celery in salted water just until tender-crisp and drain.
- Sauté water chestnuts and almonds in melted butter.
- Toss celery with water chestnut-almond mixture.
- Serve hot.

Creamed Green Peas

1 (16 ounce) package frozen English peas
2 tablespoons (¼ stick) butter
1 (10 ounce) can cream of celery soup
1 (3 ounce) package cream cheese
1 (8 ounce) can water chestnuts, drained

- Cook peas in microwave for 8 minutes and turn dish after 4 minutes.
- In large saucepan, combine butter, soup and cream cheese, cook on medium heat and stir until butter and cream cheese melt.
- Add peas and water chestnuts and mix.
- Serve hot.

Cheesy Peas Please

1 (10 ounce) can cream of mushroom soup
1 (6 ounce) roll garlic cheese
2 (15 ounce) cans green peas, drained
⅛ teaspoon red pepper

- In saucepan, heat soup and cheese until cheese melts.
- Add peas and red pepper and heat thoroughly.

Swiss Cheesy Peas

3 (15 ounce) cans green peas and onions, drained
1 (8 ounce) carton sour cream
1 (8 ounce) package grated Swiss cheese
2 cups crushed corn flakes

- In large bowl, combine peas and onions, sour cream, cheese and salt to taste.
- Spoon into buttered 3-quart baking dish and sprinkle corn flakes over top.
- Bake uncovered at 350° for 35 minutes.

Baked Onions

4 large onions, thinly sliced
1½ cups crushed potato chips
1 cup shredded cheddar cheese
1 (10 ounce) can cream of chicken soup

- In 9 x 13-inch baking dish, alternate layers of onion, potato chips and cheese.
- Spoon soup over last layer and pour ¼ cup milk or water over top.
- Sprinkle with a little red or black pepper and bake at 300° for 1 hour.

Cheesy Baked Onions

4 yellow onions, peeled, sliced
½ cup (1 stick) butter
25 round, buttery crackers, crushed
⅓ cup grated parmesan cheese

- Sauté onions in butter until transparent.
- Spread half onions in buttered 2-quart casserole dish and top with half crackers and half cheese.
- Repeat layers and bake uncovered at 325° for 30 minutes.

Onion Casserole

5 to 6 medium mild onions, thinly sliced
3 tablespoons butter
1 cup milk
4 eggs

- Sauté onions in butter in covered skillet for 30 minutes and cool.
- In bowl, beat milk and eggs, stir in onions and transfer to greased baking dish.
- Bake at 325° for 45 to 50 minutes or until light brown.

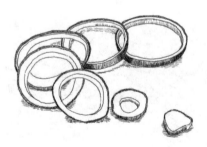

Sour Cream Cabbage

1 medium head cabbage, cooked tender-crisp, drained
2 tablespoons (¼ stick) butter
1 tablespoon sugar
¼ teaspoon nutmeg
1 (4 ounce) jar pimentos, drained
1 (8 ounce) package cream cheese

- Combine cabbage, butter, sugar, nutmeg and pimentos in saucepan.
- Add cream cheese while on low heat and stir until cream cheese melts.

Creamy Cabbage Bake

1 head cabbage, shredded
1 (10 ounce) can cream of celery soup
⅔ cup milk
1 (8 ounce) package shredded cheddar cheese

- Place cabbage in 2-quart buttered baking dish.
- Dilute celery soup with milk and pour over cabbage.
- Bake covered at 325° for 30 minutes.
- Remove from oven, sprinkle with cheese and bake uncovered another 5 minutes.

Brown Sugar Carrots

2 (15 ounce) cans carrots
¼ cup (½ stick) butter
3 tablespoons brown sugar
1 teaspoon ground ginger

- Drain carrots but reserve 2 tablespoons liquid.
- Combine reserved liquid with butter, brown sugar and ginger and heat thoroughly.
- Add carrots, stir gently and cook for 3 minutes.
- Serve hot.

Glazed Carrots

1 (16 ounce) package frozen baby carrots
¼ cup apple cider
¼ cup apple jelly
1½ teaspoons dijon-style mustard

- Place carrots and apple cider in saucepan and bring to a boil.
- Reduce heat, cover and simmer for 8 minutes or until carrots are tender.
- Remove cover and cook on medium heat until liquid evaporates.
- Stir in jelly and mustard and cook until jelly melts and carrots glaze.

Creamy Carrots with Toasted Almonds

2 (15 ounce) cans sliced carrots
1 (10 ounce) can cream of celery soup
½ cup milk
⅓ cup chopped almonds, toasted

- In saucepan, combine carrots, soup and milk.
- Over medium heat stir to mix and heat thoroughly.
- Stir in almonds just before serving.
- Serve hot.

Almond Green Beans

⅓ cup almonds, slivered
¼ cup (½ stick) butter
¾ teaspoon garlic salt
3 tablespoons lemon juice
2 (16 ounce) cans french-cut green beans

- In saucepan, cook almonds in butter, garlic salt and lemon juice until slightly golden brown.
- Add drained green beans to almonds and heat.

Green Beans and Almonds

2 (16 ounce) packages frozen french-cut green beans
2 tablespoons (¼ stick) butter
2 (8 ounce) cans water chestnuts, chopped
½ cup slivered almonds, toasted

- Cook beans according to package directions.
- Drain beans, add butter and heat just until butter melts.
- Fold in water chestnuts.
- Place in serving dish and sprinkle almonds over top.

Pine Nut Green Beans

1 (16 ounce) package frozen green beans
¼ cup (½ stick) butter
¾ cup pine nuts
¼ teaspoon garlic powder
Salt and pepper

- Cook beans in water in covered 3-quart saucepan for 10 to 15 minutes or until tender-crisp and drain.
- Melt butter in skillet over medium heat, add pine nuts and cook, stirring frequently, until golden.
- Add pine nuts to green beans and add seasonings.
- Serve hot.

Crunchy Green Beans

3 (15 ounce) cans whole green beans
2 (10 ounce) cans cream of mushroom soup
2 (11 ounce) cans water chestnuts, drained, chopped
2 (2.8 ounce) cans french-fried onion rings

- Combine green beans, soup, water chestnuts, ½ teaspoon salt and a little pepper.
- Pour mixture into 2-quart casserole dish and bake covered at 350° for 30 minutes.
- Remove casserole from oven, sprinkle onion rings over top and bake for 10 more minutes.

Cheesy Green Beans

¾ cup milk
1 (8 ounce) package cream cheese
½ teaspoon garlic powder
½ cup fresh parmesan cheese
2 (16 ounce) cans green beans

- In saucepan, combine milk, cream cheese, garlic powder and parmesan cheese and heat until cheeses melt.
- Heat green beans in pan, drain and cover with cream cheese mixture.
- Toss to coat evenly and serve hot.

Parmesan Broccoli

1 (16 ounce) package frozen broccoli spears
½ teaspoon garlic powder
½ cup breadcrumbs
¼ cup (½ stick) butter, melted
½ cup parmesan cheese

- Cook broccoli as directed on package and drain.
- Add garlic powder, breadcrumbs, butter and cheese (and some salt if you like) and toss.
- Heat and serve.

Lemon Broccoli

2 (16 ounce) packages of broccoli florets
¼ cup (½ stick) butter
1 tablespoon lemon juice
½ teaspoon seasoned salt

- Cook broccoli according to package directions and drain.
- Melt butter and stir in lemon juice and seasoned salt.
- Pour butter mixture over broccoli and toss to coat.

Crunchy Broccoli

2 (10 ounce) packages frozen broccoli florets
1 (8 ounce) can sliced water chestnuts, drained, chopped
½ cup (1 stick) butter, melted
1 (1 ounce) package dry onion soup mix

- Place broccoli in microwave-safe dish, cover and microwave for 5 minutes.
- Turn dish and cook another 4 minutes.
- Add water chestnuts.
- Combine melted butter and soup mix, blend well and toss with broccoli.

Baked Broccoli

2 (10 ounce) packages frozen broccoli spears
1 (10 ounce) can cream of chicken soup
⅔ cup mayonnaise
¾ cup breadcrumbs
Paprika

- Place broccoli spears in baking dish.
- In saucepan, heat soup and mayonnaise.
- Pour soup mixture over broccoli and sprinkle with breadcrumbs and paprika.
- Bake at 325° for 45 minutes.

Pine Nut Broccoli

1 bunch fresh broccoli
¼ cup (½ stick) butter
½ cup pine nuts
⅓ cup golden raisins
2 tablespoons lemon juice

- Steam broccoli until tender-crisp.
- In saucepan, sauté butter, nuts and raisins for about 3 minutes.
- When ready to serve, add lemon juice to nut mixture and pour over broccoli.

Heavenly Broccoli

2 (16 ounce) packages frozen broccoli spears
1 (8 ounce) container cream cheese and chives
2 (10 ounce) cans cream of shrimp soup
2 teaspoons lemon juice
¼ cup (½ stick) butter, melted

- Trim some stems off broccoli and discard stems.
- Cook broccoli in microwave according to package directions and place in 2-quart baking dish.
- In saucepan, combine cream cheese, soup, lemon juice and butter, heat just enough to mix thoroughly and pour over broccoli.
- Bake at 350° just until hot and bubbly.

Broccoli Supreme

2 (10 ounce) packages broccoli spears
1 (6 ounce) roll garlic cheese
1 (10 ounce) can cream of mushroom soup
1 (3 ounce) can mushrooms, drained
¾ cup herb dressing, crushed

- Boil broccoli for 3 minutes and drain.
- In saucepan, melt cheese on medium heat in mushroom soup.
- Add mushrooms and combine with broccoli.
- Pour broccoli mixture into greased 2-quart baking dish and top with crushed herb dressing.
- Bake uncovered at 350° for 30 minutes.

TIP: *For a change of pace, use cream of chicken soup instead of cream of mushroom and leave out the mushrooms.*

Tomatoes and Broccoli

1 (10 ounce) package frozen chopped broccoli
1½ cups grated Monterey Jack cheese, divided
¼ cup finely chopped onion
3 large tomatoes, halved horizontally

- Cook broccoli according to package directions, drain and combine with 1 cup cheese and onion.
- Place tomato halves in greased baking dish and cover each tomato half with broccoli mixture.
- Top with remaining cheese and broil at 350° for 10 to 12 minutes.

Broccoli-Stuffed Tomatoes

4 medium tomatoes
1 (10 ounce) package frozen chopped broccoli
1 (6 ounce) roll garlic cheese, softened
½ teaspoon garlic salt

- Cut tops off tomatoes and scoop out pulp.
- Cook broccoli according to package directions and drain well.
- Combine broccoli, cheese and garlic salt and heat just until cheese melts.
- Stuff broccoli mixture into tomatoes and place on baking sheet.
- Bake at 375° for about 10 minutes.

Stewed Tomato Casserole

2 (15 ounce) cans Mexican-style stewed tomatoes
2 onions, sliced
1¼ cups cracker crumbs
1 cup shredded cheddar cheese

- In 2-quart casserole dish layer tomatoes, onions, cracker crumbs and cheese and repeat layers.
- Sprinkle with a little salt and pepper.
- Bake at 350° for 45 minutes.

Baked Tomatoes

2 (16 ounce) cans diced tomatoes, drained
1½ cups breadcrumbs, toasted, divided
Scant ¼ cup sugar
½ onion, chopped
¼ cup (½ stick) butter, melted

- Combine tomatoes, 1 cup breadcrumbs, sugar, onion and butter.
- Pour into buttered baking dish and cover with remaining breadcrumbs.
- Bake at 325° for 25 to 30 minutes or until crumbs are light brown.

Eggplant Casserole

1 large eggplant
1 cup cracker crumbs
1 cup shredded cheddar cheese, divided
1 (10 ounce) can tomatoes and green chiles

- Peel and slice eggplant.
- Place eggplant in saucepan, cover with water and cook for 10 minutes or until tender.
- Drain eggplant well on paper towels and mash.
- Stir in crackers, ¾ cup cheese and tomatoes and chiles and mix well.
- Spoon eggplant mixture in 1-quart buttered baking dish and sprinkle with remaining cheese.
- Bake at 350° for 30 minutes.

Baked Eggplant

1 medium eggplant
¼ cup (½ stick) butter, melted
1 (5 ounce) can evaporated milk
1½ cups cracker crumbs

- Peel, slice and boil eggplant until easily mashed and drain.
- Season with a little salt and pepper and add butter, evaporated milk and crumbs.
- Pour into 2-quart buttered baking dish and bake at 350° for 25 minutes.

Cheesy Baked Eggplant

1 eggplant
½ cup mayonnaise
⅔ cup seasoned breadcrumbs
¼ cup grated parmesan cheese

- Peel eggplant and slice ½-inch thick.
- Spread both sides of eggplant slices with mayonnaise and dip in mixture of crumbs and cheese until coated well.
- Place in single layer in shallow baking dish and bake at 400° for 20 minutes.

Eggplant Fritters

1 medium eggplant
1 egg, beaten
3 tablespoons flour
½ teaspoon salt
½ teaspoon baking powder

- Peel and slice eggplant, steam until tender and drain.
- Mash eggplant until smooth.
- Add egg, flour, salt and baking powder and mix well.
- Form into patties and deep fry in hot oil.

Zucchini Patties

1½ cups grated zucchini
1 egg, beaten
2 tablespoons flour
⅓ cup finely minced onion
½ teaspoon seasoned salt

- Heat about 3 tablespoons oil in skillet.
- Mix all ingredients and drop by tablespoons into skillet on medium high heat.
- Turn and brown both sides.
- Remove and drain on paper towels.

Fried Zucchini

3 large zucchini, grated
5 eggs
1 pack round, buttery crackers (⅓ of 12-ounce box), crushed
½ cup grated parmesan cheese

- Combine zucchini, eggs and cracker crumbs and mix well.
- Add cheese and a little salt and pepper.
- Drop by spoonfuls into skillet with a little oil.
- Fry for 15 minutes and brown on each side.

Zucchini au Gratin

6 medium zucchini, sliced
1 onion, chopped
1 (8 ounce) carton sour cream
1¼ cups grated cheddar cheese
2 teaspoons sesame seeds, toasted

- Cook zucchini and onion in a little salted water and drain well. (Be careful not to overcook.)
- Place half zucchini mixture in buttered 2-quart casserole and sprinkle with salt and pepper.
- Spread with half sour cream and half cheese and repeat all layers.
- Top with sesame seeds.
- Bake uncovered at 350° for 35 minutes.

Cheesy Zucchini

5 to 6 medium zucchini, sliced in round
1 cup grated Monterey Jack cheese
⅔ cup dry, seasoned breadcrumbs
1 (15 ounce) can Mexican-style stewed tomatoes

- Boil zucchini for 8 minutes until tender-crisp and drain.
- Place half zucchini in greased 2-quart casserole dish and sprinkle with cheese and crumbs.
- Top with remaining zucchini and cover with stewed tomatoes.
- Bake at 350° for 30 minutes.

Zucchini Bake

4 cups grated zucchini
1½ cups grated Monterey Jack cheese
4 eggs, beaten
2 cups cheese cracker crumbs

- In bowl, combine zucchini, cheese and eggs and mix well.
- Spoon into buttered 3-quart baking dish and sprinkle cracker crumbs over top.
- Bake uncovered at 350° for 35 minutes.

Baked Squash

5 cups squash, cooked, drained
¾ cup grated Monterey Jack cheese
1 (10 ounce) can cream of chicken soup
1 (16 ounce) box herb dressing mix

- Place cooked squash in mixing bowl and season with salt to taste.
- Add cheese and soup and blend well.
- Mix dressing according to package directions and place half dressing in greased 9 x 13-inch baking dish.
- Spoon in squash mixture and sprinkle remaining dressing on top.
- Bake uncovered at 375° for 30 minutes.

Squash on the Run

5 medium yellow squash, sliced
2 thinly sliced potatoes
1 onion, chopped
2 (10 ounce) cans cream of chicken soup

- In buttered 2-quart casserole dish, layer squash, potatoes and onion.
- In saucepan, combine soup and ¾ can water and heat just enough to mix well. Pour over vegetables.
- Cover and bake at 350° for 45 minutes.

Chile-Cheese Squash

1 pound yellow squash
⅔ cup mayonnaise
1 (4 ounce) can diced green chiles, drained
⅔ cup grated longhorn cheese
⅔ cup breadcrumbs

- Cook squash in salted water just until tender-crisp and drain.
- Return squash to saucepan and stir in mayonnaise, chiles, cheese and breadcrumbs.
- Serve hot.

Squash Casserole

6 medium yellow squash, sliced
1 yellow onion, chopped
1 (8 ounce) jar processed cheese spread
1 (4 ounce) can diced green chiles

- Boil squash and onion until tender and drain well.
- Mix with cheese and chiles.
- Pour into buttered 7 x 11-inch baking dish and bake at 375° for 15 minutes.

Sunny Yellow Squash

6 to 8 medium yellow squash
1 (8 ounce) package cream cheese, softened, cubed
2 tablespoons (¼ stick) butter
1 teaspoon sugar

- Cut up squash, place in saucepan with a little water, boil until tender and drain.
- Add cream cheese, butter, sugar and a little salt and pepper.
- Cook over low heat and stir until cream cheese melts.

Stuffed Yellow Squash

5 large yellow squash
1 (16 ounce) package frozen chopped spinach
1 (8 ounce) package cream cheese, cubed
1 (1 ounce) package dry onion soup mix
Shredded cheddar cheese

- Steam squash whole until tender.
- Slit squash lengthwise and remove seeds with spoon.
- Cook spinach according to package directions and drain well.
- Add cream cheese to cooked spinach and stir until cheese melts. (Do not let boil.)
- Add soup mix and blend well.
- Fill scooped out squash shells with spinach mixture and top with few sprinkles cheddar cheese.
- Place on baking sheet and bake at 325° for 15 minutes.

Spinach to Like

2 (10 ounce) packages frozen, chopped spinach
1 (8 ounce) carton sour cream
½ (1 ounce) package dry onion soup mix
⅔ cup dry, seasoned breadcrumbs

- Cook spinach according to package directions and drain well.
- Add sour cream and onion soup mix to spinach.
- Pour into 2-quart casserole and sprinkle breadcrumbs on top.
- Bake at 350° for 35 minutes.

Creamed-Spinach Bake

2 (10 ounce) packages frozen chopped spinach
2 (3 ounce) packages cream cheese, softened
3 tablespoons butter
1 cup seasoned breadcrumbs

- Cook spinach according to package directions and drain.
- Combine cream cheese and butter with spinach and heat until they melt and mix well with spinach.
- Pour into greased baking dish and sprinkle a little salt over spinach.
- Cover with breadcrumbs and bake at 350° for 15 to 20 minutes.

Herbed Spinach

2 (16 ounce) packages frozen chopped spinach
1 (8 ounce) package cream cheese, softened
¼ cup (½ stick) butter, melted, divided
1 (6 ounce) package herbed stuffing

- Cook spinach according to package directions and drain.
- Add cream cheese and half butter to spinach and season with a little salt and pepper.
- Pour into buttered casserole dish and spread herb stuffing over top.
- Drizzle with remaining butter and bake at 350° for 25 minutes.

Spinach Casserole

1 (16 ounce) package frozen chopped spinach
1 (8 ounce) package cream cheese and chives
1 (10 ounce) can cream of mushroom soup
1 egg, beaten
Cracker crumbs

- Cook spinach according to package directions and drain.
- Blend cream cheese and soup with egg, mix with spinach and pour into buttered casserole dish.
- Top with cracker crumbs and bake at 350° for 35 minutes.

Cheese Please Spinach

1 (16 ounce) package frozen chopped spinach
3 eggs
½ cup flour
1 (16 ounce) carton small-curd cottage cheese
2 cups shredded cheddar cheese

- Cook spinach, drain and set aside.
- Beat eggs and add flour, cottage cheese and a little salt and pepper.
- Stir in spinach and cheddar cheese and pour into 1½-quart baking dish.
- Bake uncovered at 350° for 35 minutes.

Easy Spinach Bake

2 (8 ounce) packages cream cheese, softened
1 (10 ounce) can cream of chicken soup
2 (16 ounce) packages frozen chopped spinach, thawed, well drained
1 cup crushed round, buttery crackers

- In mixing bowl, beat cream cheese until smooth, add soup and mix well.
- Stir in spinach and spoon mixture into greased 3-quart baking dish.
- Sprinkle cracker crumbs over casserole and bake uncovered at 325° for 35 minutes.

Favorite Spinach

2 (10 ounce) packages frozen chopped spinach, thawed, well drained
1 (1 ounce) package dry onion soup mix
1 (8 ounce) carton sour cream
⅔ cup shredded Monterey Jack cheese

- Combine spinach, onion soup mix and sour cream and pour into buttered 2-quart baking dish.
- Bake at 350° for 20 minutes.
- Remove from oven, sprinkle cheese over top and return casserole to oven for 5 more minutes.

Cauliflower au Gratin

1 large head cauliflower
Salt and pepper
1 (8 ounce) carton sour cream
1 ¼ cups grated cheddar cheese
2 teaspoons toasted sesame seeds

- Break cauliflower into florets, cook until tender-crisp, about 10 minutes, and drain.
- Place half of cauliflower in buttered 2-quart casserole, sprinkle with salt and pepper and spread with half sour cream and half cheese.
- Repeat layers and top with sesame seeds.
- Bake uncovered at 350° about 15 minutes.

Souper Cauliflower

1 (16 ounce) package frozen cauliflower, cooked, drained
1 (10 ounce) can cream of celery soup
¼ cup milk
1 cup shredded cheddar cheese

- Place cauliflower in greased 2-quart baking dish.
- In saucepan, combine soup, milk and cheese and heat just enough to mix well.
- Pour mixture over cauliflower and bake at 350° for 15 minutes.

Cauliflower Medley

1 head cauliflower, cut into florets
1 (15 ounce) can Italian-style stewed tomatoes with juice
1 bell pepper, chopped
1 onion, chopped
¼ cup (½ stick) butter
1 cup shredded cheddar cheese

- In large saucepan, place cauliflower, stewed tomatoes, bell pepper, onion and butter with about 2 tablespoons water and some salt and pepper.
- Cook in saucepan with lid until cauliflower is done, about 10 to 15 minutes. (Do not let cauliflower get mushy.)
- Place in 2-quart casserole and sprinkle cheese on top.
- Bake at 350° just until cheese melts.

Savory Cauliflower

1 head cauliflower
1 (1 ounce) package hollandaise sauce mix
Fresh parsley
Lemon slices, optional

- Cut cauliflower into small florets and cook in salted water until barely tender. (Be VERY careful not to overcook cauliflower.)
- Mix sauce according to package directions.
- Drain cauliflower, top with sauce and sprinkle with parsley.
- Garnish with lemon slices if you like.

Best Cauliflower

1 (16 ounce) package frozen cauliflower
Salt and pepper
1 (8 ounce) carton sour cream
1½ cups grated American or cheddar cheese
4 teaspoons sesame seeds, toasted

- Cook cauliflower according to package directions, drain and place half cauliflower in 2-quart baking dish.
- Sprinkle a little salt and pepper on cauliflower and spread with half sour cream and half cheese.
- Top with 2 teaspoons sesame seeds and repeat layers.
- Bake at 350° for about 15 to 20 minutes.

Asparagus Bake

4 (10 ounce) cans asparagus
3 eggs, hard-boiled, sliced
⅓ cup milk
1½ cups grated cheddar cheese
1¼ cups cheese cracker crumbs

- Place asparagus in 7 x 11-inch baking dish, layer hard-boiled eggs on top and pour milk over casserole.
- Sprinkle cheese on top and add cracker crumbs.
- Bake uncovered at 350° for 30 minutes.

Asparagus-Ham Roll-Ups

4 slices Swiss cheese
2 (10 ounce) cans asparagus spears
4 slices ham
1 (10 ounce) can cream of celery soup

- Place 1 slice cheese and 3 asparagus spears on each ham slice. Roll up and secure with toothpick.
- Place each roll-up in casserole dish, seam side down.
- In saucepan, dilute soup with ⅓ cup water and heat just enough to mix well.
- Pour over roll-ups and bake at 350° for 15 to 20 minutes.

Sesame Asparagus

6 fresh asparagus spears, trimmed
1 tablespoon butter
1 teaspoon lemon juice
1 teaspoon sesame seeds

- Place asparagus in skillet (sprinkle with salt if desired), add ¼ cup water and bring to a boil.
- Reduce heat, cover and simmer for 4 minutes.
- Melt butter and add lemon juice and sesame seeds.
- Drain asparagus and drizzle with butter mixture.

Creamy Asparagus Bake

2 (15 ounce) cans cut asparagus spears
3 hard-boiled eggs, chopped
½ cup chopped pecans
1 (10 ounce) can cream of asparagus soup

- Drain asparagus spears and set aside liquid.
- Arrange asparagus spears in buttered 2-quart baking dish and top with eggs and pecans.
- Heat asparagus soup and add liquid from asparagus spears.
- Spoon soup mixture over eggs and pecans and bake covered at 350° for 25 minutes.

Country Baked Beans

4 (16 ounce) cans baked beans, drained
1 (12 ounce) bottle chili sauce
1 large onion, chopped
½ pound bacon, cooked, crumbled
2 cups packed brown sugar

- In ungreased 3-quart baking dish, combine all ingredients and stir until blended.
- Bake uncovered at 325° for 55 minutes or until heated through.

Classic Baked Beans

3 (18 ounce) cans baked beans
½ cup chili sauce
⅓ cup packed brown sugar
4 slices bacon, cooked, crumbled

- In buttered 3-quart baking dish, combine baked beans, chili sauce and brown sugar.
- Bake at 325° for 40 minutes.
- When ready to serve, sprinkle bacon over top.

Chili-Baked Beans

2 (16 ounce) cans pork and beans
1 (15 ounce) can chili with beans
¼ cup molasses
1 teaspoon chili powder

- Drain just visible liquid from can of pork and beans.
- In 2-quart casserole, combine all ingredients and heat until bubbly.

Baked Beans

2 (15 ounce) cans pork and beans, slightly drained
½ onion, finely chopped
⅔ cup packed brown sugar
¼ cup chili sauce
1 tablespoon Worcestershire sauce
2 strips bacon

- In bowl, combine beans, onion, brown sugar, chili sauce and Worcestershire.
- Pour into buttered 2-quart casserole dish and place bacon strips over bean mixture.
- Bake uncovered at 325° for 50 minutes.

Veggies to Love

1 (16 ounce) package frozen broccoli, cauliflower and carrots
1 (10 ounce) can cream of celery soup
⅓ cup milk
1 (3 ounce) can french-fried onions

- Cook vegetables according to package directions.
- Add soup and milk and mix well.
- Pour into buttered 2-quart baking dish and sprinkle french-fried onions over top.
- Bake at 350° for 30 minutes or until bubbly.

Creamy Vegetable Casserole

1 (16 ounce) package frozen broccoli, carrots and cauliflower
1 (10 ounce) can cream of mushroom soup
1 (8 ounce) carton garden vegetable cream cheese
1 cup seasoned croutons

- Cook vegetables according to package directions, drain and place in large bowl.
- Place soup and cream cheese in saucepan and heat just enough to mix easily.
- Pour soup mixture into vegetable mixture, stir well and pour into 2-quart baking dish.
- Sprinkle with croutons and bake uncovered at 375° for 25 minutes or until bubbly.

Corn Vegetable Medley

1 (8 ounce) can whole kernel corn, drained
⅔ cup milk
2 cups fresh broccoli florets
2 cups cauliflower florets
1 cup shredded cheddar cheese

- In saucepan over medium heat, heat corn and milk to boiling and stir often.
- Stir in broccoli and cauliflower florets and return to boiling.
- Reduce heat to low and cover.
- Cook 20 minutes or until vegetables are tender and stir occasionally.
- Stir in cheese and heat until cheese melts.

Vegetable Medley

1 (16 ounce) package frozen broccoli, cauliflower and carrots
1 (16 ounce) package frozen corn
2 (10 ounce) cans nacho cheese soup
½ cup milk

- Combine vegetable mixture and corn in greased 2-quart baking dish.
- Combine nacho cheese soup and milk in saucepan and heat just enough to mix well.
- Pour soup mixture over vegetables, cover and bake at 350° for 30 minutes.

Calico Corn

1 (16 ounce) package frozen whole kernel corn
1 bell pepper, chopped
⅓ cup chopped celery
1 (10 ounce) can cheddar cheese soup

- Cook corn in microwave according to package directions and drain well.
- Add bell pepper and celery.
- Stir in soup and mix well.
- Pour into buttered 2-quart casserole dish and bake covered at 350° for 30 minutes.

Wild West Corn

3 (15 ounce) cans whole kernel corn, drained
1 (10 ounce) can tomatoes and green chiles, drained
1 (8 ounce) package shredded Monterey Jack cheese
1 cup cheese cracker crumbs

- In large bowl, combine corn, tomatoes and green chiles, and cheese and mix well.
- Pour into buttered 2½-quart baking dish.
- Sprinkle cracker crumbs over casserole.
- Bake uncovered at 350° for 25 minutes.

Mushrooms and Corn

4 ounces fresh mushrooms, sliced
3 fresh green onions with tops, chopped
¼ cup (½ stick) butter
1 (15 ounce) package frozen whole kernel corn

- Place all ingredients in 2-quart saucepan and cook over medium heat for 5 to 10 minutes.
- Add salt and pepper to taste.

Corn Maize

¼ cup (½ stick) butter, melted
1 (3 ounce) package cream cheese, softened
2 (15 ounce) cans whole kernel corn, drained
⅓ cup salsa

- Combine butter and cream cheese and add corn and salsa.
- Pour mixture into buttered 2-quart baking dish.
- Bake covered at 350° for 25 minutes.
- Serve hot.

Hot Corn Bake

3 (15 ounce) cans whole kernel corn, drained
1 (10 ounce) can cream of celery soup
1 cup salsa
1 (8 ounce) package shredded Mexican cheese blend, divided

- Combine corn, soup, salsa and half cheese and mix well.
- Pour into buttered 3-quart baking dish and sprinkle remaining cheese on top.
- Bake at 350° for 20 to 30 minutes.

Main Dishes
Chicken, Beef, Pork, Seafood & Leftovers

Cranberry Chicken

6 skinless, boneless chicken breast halves
1 (16 ounce) can whole cranberry sauce
1 large tart apple, peeled, chopped
⅓ cup chopped walnuts
1 teaspoon curry powder

- Place chicken in sprayed 9 x 13-inch baking pan and bake uncovered at 350° for 20 minutes.
- Combine cranberry sauce, apple, walnuts and curry powder and spoon over chicken.
- Bake uncovered for 25 minutes longer or until chicken juices run clear.

Onion-Sweet Chicken

2 chickens, quartered
1 (15 ounce) can whole cranberry sauce
1 (8 ounce) bottle catalina salad dressing
1 (1 ounce) package dry onion soup mix

- Place chicken quarters in a well-greased large shallow baking dish.
- Combine cranberry sauce, dressing and soup mix, combine well and pour over chicken.
- Cover and bake at 350° for 1 hour 10 minutes.
- During last 10 minutes, uncover chicken and place back in oven to brown.

Hawaiian Chicken

2 small whole chickens, quartered
Flour to coat chicken
Oil
1 (20 ounce) can sliced pineapple
2 bell peppers, cut in strips

- Wash and pat chicken dry with paper towels.
- Coat chicken with salt, pepper and flour, brown in oil and place in shallow pan.
- Drain pineapple into 2-cup measure, add enough water (or orange juice if you have it) to make 1½ cups liquid and reserve liquid for sauce.

Sauce for Hawaiian Chicken:

1 cup sugar
3 tablespoons cornstarch
¾ cup vinegar
1 tablespoon lemon juice
1 tablespoon soy sauce
2 teaspoons chicken bouillon

- In medium saucepan, combine reserved 1½ cups liquid, sugar, cornstarch, vinegar, lemon juice, soy sauce and chicken bouillon.
- Bring to a boil and stir constantly until thick and clear and pour over chicken.
- Bake at 350° covered for 40 minutes.
- Place pineapple slices and bell pepper on top of chicken and bake another 10 minutes. Serve on fluffy white rice.

Pineapple-Teriyaki Chicken

6 boneless, skinless chicken breast halves
½ red onion, sliced
1 green bell pepper, seeded, sliced
1 cup teriyaki marinade with pineapple juice, divided
1 (15 ounce) can pineapple rings, drained

- Place chicken in sprayed 9 x 13-inch baking dish and arrange vegetables over chicken.
- Pour marinade over vegetables and chicken.
- Bake uncovered at 350° for 45 minutes. Spoon juices over chicken once during baking.
- About 10 minutes before chicken is done, place pineapple slices over chicken and return to oven.

Lemonade Chicken

6 boneless, skinless chicken breast halves
1 (6 ounce) can frozen lemonade, thawed
⅓ cup soy sauce
1 teaspoon garlic powder

- Place chicken in greased 9 x 13-inch baking dish.
- Combine lemonade, soy sauce and garlic powder and pour over chicken.
- Cover with foil and bake at 350° for 45 minutes.
- Uncover, pour juices over chicken and cook for another 10 minutes uncovered.

Sweet and Sour Chicken

6 to 8 boneless, skinless chicken breast halves
Oil
1 (1 ounce) package dry onion soup mix
1 (6 ounce) can frozen orange juice concentrate, thawed
⅔ cup water

- Brown chicken in a little oil or butter and place chicken in greased 9 x 13-inch baking dish.
- In small bowl, combine onion soup mix, orange juice and water, mix well and pour over chicken.
- Bake uncovered at 350° for 45 to 50 minutes.

Sweet 'n Spicy Chicken

1 pound boneless, skinless chicken breast halves
3 tablespoons taco seasoning
1 (11 ounce) jar chunky salsa
1 cup peach preserves

- Cut chicken into ½-inch cubes.
- Place chicken in large, resealable plastic bag, add taco seasoning and toss to coat.
- In skillet, brown chicken in a little oil.
- Combine salsa and preserves, stir into skillet and bring mixture to a boil.
- Reduce heat, cover and simmer until juices run clear. Serve over rice or noodles.

Spicy Chicken and Rice

3 cups cooked, sliced chicken
2 cups cooked brown rice
1 (10 ounce) can fiesta nacho cheese soup
1 (10 ounce) can diced tomatoes and green chiles

- Combine all ingredients and mix well.
- Spoon mixture into buttered 3-quart baking dish.
- Cook covered at 350° for 45 minutes.

Saucy Chicken

5 to 6 boneless, skinless chicken breast halves
2 cups thick and chunky salsa
⅓ cup packed light brown sugar
1½ tablespoons dijon-style mustard

- Place chicken breasts in greased 9 x 13-inch baking dish.
- Combine salsa, sugar and mustard and pour over chicken.
- Cover and bake at 350° for 45 minutes.
- Serve over rice.

Classy Chicken

4 boneless, skinless chicken breast halves
¼ cup lime juice
1 (1 ounce) package dry Italian salad dressing mix
¼ cup (½ stick) butter, melted

- Season chicken with salt and pepper and place in shallow baking dish.
- Combine lime juice, salad dressing mix and melted butter and pour over chicken.
- Cover and bake at 325° for 1 hour. Remove cover for last 15 minutes of cooking time.

Chile Pepper Chicken

5 boneless, skinless chicken breast halves
1 (1 ounce) package hot and spicy coating mixture
1 (4 ounce) can diced green chiles
Chunky salsa

- Dredge chicken in coating mixture and place in greased 9 x 13-inch baking dish.
- Bake at 375° for 25 minutes.
- Remove from oven, spread green chiles over chicken breasts and return to oven for 5 minutes.
- Serve with salsa over each chicken breast.

Adobe Chicken

2 cups cooked brown rice
1 (10 ounce) can diced tomatoes and green chiles, drained
3 cups chopped, cooked chicken
1 (8 ounce) package shredded Monterey Jack cheese, divided

- Combine rice, tomatoes and green chiles, chicken, and half cheese.
- Spoon into buttered 7 x 11-inch baking dish and cook covered at 325° for 30 minutes.
- Uncover, sprinkle with remaining cheese and return to oven for 5 minutes.

Picante Chicken

4 boneless, skinless chicken breast halves
1 (16 ounce) jar salsa
4 tablespoons brown sugar
1 tablespoon prepared mustard
Hot cooked rice

- Place chicken in shallow sprayed baking dish.
- In small bowl, combine salsa, brown sugar and mustard and pour over chicken.
- Bake uncovered at 375° for 45 minutes or until chicken juices run clear and serve over rice.

Oregano Chicken

¼ cup (½ stick) butter, melted
1 (1 ounce) package dry Italian salad dressing mix
2 tablespoons lemon juice
4 skinless, boneless chicken breast halves
2 tablespoons dried oregano

- Combine butter, salad dressing mix and lemon juice.
- Place chicken in ungreased 9 x 13-inch baking pan and spoon butter mixture over chicken.
- Cover and bake at 350° for 45 minutes. Uncover, baste with pan drippings and sprinkle with oregano.
- Bake another 15 minutes or until chicken juices run clear.

Ranch Chicken

½ cup grated parmesan cheese
1½ cups corn flakes
1 (1 ounce) package dry ranch-style salad dressing mix
8 to 9 (2 pounds) chicken drumsticks
½ cup (1 stick) butter, melted

- Combine cheese, corn flakes and dressing mix
- Dip washed, dried chicken in melted butter and dredge in corn flake mixture.
- Bake uncovered at 350° for 50 minutes or until golden brown.

Chicken Olé

6 boneless, skinless chicken breast halves
1 (8 ounce) package cream cheese, softened
1 (16 ounce) jar salsa
2 teaspoons cumin
1 bunch fresh green onions with tops, chopped

- Pound chicken breasts flat.
- In mixing bowl, beat cream cheese until smooth and add salsa, cumin and onions.
- Place 1 heaping spoonful of mixture on each chicken breast, roll and place seam side down in shallow baking pan.
- Pour remaining sauce over top of chicken rolls and bake uncovered at 350° for 50 minutes.

Apricot Chicken

1 cup apricot preserves
1 (8 ounce) bottle catalina salad dressing
1 (1 ounce) package dry onion soup mix
6 to 8 boneless, skinless chicken breast halves

- Combine apricot preserves, dressing and soup mix.
- Place chicken breasts in large, buttered baking dish and pour apricot mixture over chicken. (For a change of pace, use Russian dressing instead of catalina).
- Bake uncovered at 325° for 1 hour 20 minutes and serve over hot rice.

Catalina Chicken

6 to 8 boneless, skinless chicken breast halves
1 (8 ounce) bottle catalina salad dressing
1 teaspoon black pepper
1½ cups crushed cracker crumbs

- Marinate chicken breasts in dressing for 3 to 4 hours and discard marinade.
- Combine pepper and cracker crumbs.
- Dip each chicken breast in crumbs and place in large, greased baking dish.
- Bake uncovered at 350° for 1 hour.

Oven-Fried Chicken

⅔ cup fine dry breadcrumbs
⅓ cup grated parmesan cheese
½ teaspoon garlic salt
6 boneless, skinless chicken breast halves
¼ cup Italian salad dressing

- In small bowl, combine breadcrumbs, cheese and garlic salt.
- Dip chicken in salad dressing, dredge in crumb mixture and place in 9 x 13-inch sprayed pan.
- Bake uncovered at 350° for 50 minutes.

Chicken Crunch

4 to 6 boneless, skinless chicken breast halves
½ cup Italian salad dressing
½ cup sour cream
2½ cups crushed corn flakes

- Place chicken in resealable plastic bag, add dressing and sour cream and refrigerate for 1 hour.
- Remove chicken from marinade and discard marinade.
- Dredge chicken in corn flakes and place in sprayed 9 x 13-inch non-stick baking dish.
- Bake uncovered at 375° for 45 minutes.

Crispy Nutty Chicken

⅓ cup dry-roasted peanuts, minced
1 cup corn flake crumbs
½ cup ranch-style buttermilk salad dressing
6 boneless, skinless chicken breast halves

- Combine peanuts and corn flake crumbs on wax paper.
- Pour dressing into pie plate, dip each piece chicken in dressing and roll chicken in crumb mixture to coat.
- Arrange chicken in shallow 9 x 13-inch baking dish.
- Bake uncovered at 350° for 50 minutes or until light brown.

One-Dish Chicken Bake

1 (1 ounce) package dry vegetable soup/dip mix
1 (6 ounce) package chicken stuffing mix
1⅔ cups water
4 boneless, skinless chicken breast halves
1 (10 ounce) can cream of mushroom soup
⅓ cup sour cream

- Toss soup mix, stuffing mix and water and set aside.
- Place chicken in greased 9 x 13-inch baking dish.
- Mix soup and sour cream in saucepan over low heat just enough to pour over chicken and spoon stuffing mixture evenly over top.
- Bake uncovered at 375° for 40 minutes.

Favorite Chicken Breasts

6 to 8 boneless, skinless chicken breast halves
1 (10 ounce) can golden mushroom soup
1 cup white wine or white cooking wine
1 (8 ounce) carton sour cream

- Place chicken breasts in large, shallow baking pan, sprinkle with a little salt and pepper and bake uncovered at 350° for 30 minutes.
- In saucepan, combine soup, wine and sour cream and heat enough to mix well.
- Remove chicken from oven and cover with sour cream mixture.
- Reduce heat to 300° and return to oven for another 30 minutes. Baste twice.
- Serve over rice.

Wine and Chicken

6 to 8 boneless, skinless chicken breast halves
1 (10 ounce) can cream of mushroom soup
1 (10 ounce) can cream of onion soup
1 cup white wine

- In skillet, brown chicken in a little oil and place in 9 x 13-inch baking dish.
- Combine soups and wine and pour over chicken.
- Bake covered at 325° for 35 minutes.
- Uncover and bake another 25 minutes.

E Z Chicken

6 to 8 boneless, skinless chicken breast halves
1 (10 ounce) can cream of chicken soup
1 (3 ounce) package cream cheese
1 (8 ounce) carton sour cream
Lemon pepper

- Place chicken breasts in shallow 9 x 13-inch baking dish.
- In saucepan, combine soup, cream cheese and sour cream and heat on low just until cream cheese melts and ingredients mix well.
- Pour mixture over chicken breasts and sprinkle with lemon pepper.
- Cover and bake at 300° for 60 minutes.
- Uncover, bake another 15 minutes and serve over cooked rice.

Chicken Bake

8 boneless, skinless chicken breast halves
8 slices Swiss cheese
1 (10 ounce) can cream of chicken soup
1 (8 ounce) box chicken stuffing mix

- Flatten each chicken breast with rolling pin and place in greased 9 x 13-inch baking dish.
- Place cheese slices over chicken.
- Combine chicken soup and ½ cup water and pour over chicken.
- Prepare stuffing mix according to package directions and sprinkle over chicken.
- Bake uncovered at 325° for 1 hour.

Nacho Chicken

2 chickens, quartered
2 (10 ounce) cans fiesta nacho cheese soup
¾ cup milk
3 tablespoons marinade for chicken

- Place chicken quarters in large baking pan with sides.
- In saucepan, combine nacho cheese soup, milk and marinade for chicken and heat just enough spread over chicken.
- Cover and bake at 350° for 1 hour.

Sesame Chicken

½ cup (1 stick) butter, melted
¾ tablespoon chili powder
4 skinless, boneless chicken breast halves
1 cup sesame seeds, lightly toasted

- Combine butter and chili powder.
- Dip chicken in butter mixture and roll in sesame seeds.
- Place in buttered 9 x 13-inch baking dish, bake uncovered at 325° for 1 hour and turn at 30 minutes.

Chicken Cutlets

6 boneless, skinless chicken breast halves
1½ cups dry breadcrumbs
½ cup grated parmesan cheese
1 teaspoon dried basil
½ teaspoon garlic powder
1 (8 ounce) carton sour cream

- Flatten chicken to ½-inch thickness.
- In shallow dish, combine breadcrumbs, parmesan cheese, basil and garlic powder.
- Dip chicken in sour cream, coat with crumb mixture and place (make sure chicken breasts do not touch) in 10 x 15-inch greased baking dish.
- Bake uncovered at 325° for 50 to 60 minutes or until golden brown.

Chicken Parmesan

1½ cups biscuit mix
⅔ cup grated parmesan cheese
6 to 8 boneless, skinless chicken breast halves
½ cup (1 stick) butter, melted

- In shallow bowl, combine biscuit mix and parmesan cheese.
- Dip chicken in butter and then biscuit-cheese mixture.
- Place chicken in large, buttered baking dish and bake uncovered at 325° for 1 hour or until light brown.

Mozzarella Cutlets

4 boneless, skinless chicken breast halves
1 cup dry Italian-seasoned breadcrumbs
1 cup prepared spaghetti sauce
4 slices mozzarella cheese

- Pound each chicken breast to flatten slightly.
- Coat chicken well in breadcrumbs and arrange in greased 9 x 13-inch baking dish.
- Spread quarter of sauce over each portion.
- Place 1 slice cheese over each and garnish with remaining breadcrumbs.
- Bake uncovered at 350° for 45 minutes.

El Pronto Chicken

⅔ cup dry, seasoned breadcrumbs
½ cup grated parmesan cheese
4 boneless, skinless chicken breast halves
½ cup (1 stick) butter, melted

- Combine crumbs, cheese, some garlic powder, salt and pepper and mix well.
- Dip chicken in butter, roll in crumb-cheese mixture and place in greased 9 x 13-inch baking dish.
- Cover and bake at 350° for 55 minutes.
- Serve over rice.

Chip Chicken

2 cups crushed potato chips
¼ teaspoon garlic powder
5 to 6 boneless, skinless chicken breast halves
½ cup (1 stick) butter, melted

- Combine potato chips and garlic powder and mix well.
- Dip chicken breasts in butter and roll in potato chip mixture.
- Place in greased, shallow baking dish and bake uncovered at 350° for 55 minutes.

Baked Chicken Poupon

2 tablespoons dijon-style mustard
2 tablespoons oil
1 teaspoon garlic powder
½ teaspoon Italian seasoning
4 boneless, skinless chicken breast halves

- Mix dijon-style mustard, oil, garlic powder and seasoning in plastic bag, add chicken breasts and set for 15 minutes.
- Place chicken in sprayed shallow baking pan.
- Bake uncovered at 375° for 35 minutes.

Cola Chicken

4 to 6 boneless, skinless chicken breast halves
1 cup ketchup
1 cup cola
2 tablespoons Worcestershire sauce

- Place chicken in 9 x 13-inch casserole dish and sprinkle with salt and pepper.
- Mix ketchup, cola and Worcestershire sauce and pour over chicken.
- Cover and bake at 350° for 50 minutes.

Jiffy Chicken

8 boneless, skinless chicken breast halves
¾ cup mayonnaise
2 cups crushed corn flakes
½ cup grated parmesan cheese

- Sprinkle chicken breasts with salt and pepper.
- Dip chicken in mayonnaise and spread mayonnaise over chicken with brush.
- Combine corn flakes and parmesan cheese and dip mayonnaise-covered chicken in corn flake mixture until completely coated.
- Place on sprayed 9 x 13-inch glass baking dish and bake uncovered at 325° for 1 hour.

Curry-Glazed Chicken

3 tablespoons butter
⅓ cup honey
2 tablespoons dijon-style mustard
1½ teaspoons curry powder
4 boneless, skinless chicken breast halves

- Place butter in 9 x 13-inch baking pan, preheat oven to 375° and melt butter.
- Mix honey, mustard and curry powder in pan with butter.
- Add chicken to pan and turn until chicken is coated with butter mixture.
- Bake uncovered for 50 minutes, baste twice and serve over rice.

Tangy Chicken

1 (2 pound) broiler-fryer chicken, cut up
3 tablespoons butter
½ cup steak sauce
½ cup water

- Brown chicken pieces in skillet with butter and place in shallow pan.
- Combine sauce and water and pour over chicken.
- Cover with foil and bake at 350° for 45 minutes. Remove foil for last 10 minutes of cooking time so chicken can brown.

Honey-Baked Chicken

2 whole chickens, quartered
½ cup (1 stick) butter, melted
⅔ cup honey
¼ cup dijon-style mustard
1 teaspoon curry powder

- Place chicken pieces skin side up in large, shallow baking dish and sprinkle with a little salt.
- Combine butter, honey, mustard and curry powder and pour over chicken.
- Bake uncovered at 350° for 1 hour 5 minutes and baste every 20 minutes.

Chicken and Beef

1 (4 ounce) jar sliced dried beef, separated
6 strips bacon
6 boneless, skinless chicken breast halves
1 (10 ounce) can cream of chicken soup

- Place dried beef in greased 9 x 13-inch baking dish.
- Wrap bacon strip around each chicken breast and place over beef.
- In saucepan, heat chicken soup and ¼ cup water just enough to pour over chicken.
- Bake covered at 325° for 1 hour 10 minutes.

Party Chicken Breasts

6 to 8 boneless, skinless chicken breast halves
8 strips bacon
1 (2.5 ounce) jar dried beef
1 (10 ounce) can cream of chicken soup
1 (8 ounce) carton sour cream

- Wrap each chicken breast with 1 strip bacon and secure with toothpicks.
- Place dried beef in bottom of large, shallow baking pan and place chicken on top.
- Heat soup and sour cream just enough to pour over chicken.
- Cover chicken with sour cream mixture and bake uncovered at 325° for 1 hour.

Bacon-Wrapped Chicken

6 boneless, skinless chicken breast halves
1 (8 ounce) carton whipped cream cheese with onion and chives
Butter
6 bacon strips

- Flatten chicken to ½-inch thickness and spread 3 tablespoons cream cheese over each piece.
- Dot with butter and a little salt, roll up and wrap each with 1 bacon strip.
- Place seam side down in greased 9 x 13-inch baking dish and bake uncovered at 375° for 40 to 45 minutes or until juices run clear.
- To brown, broil 6 inches from heat for about 3 minutes or until bacon is crisp.

Italian Chicken and Rice

3 boneless, chicken breasts halves, cut into strips
1 (14 ounce) can chicken broth seasoned with Italian herbs
¾ cup uncooked rice
¼ cup grated parmesan cheese

- Cook chicken in non-stick skillet until brown, stirring often, and remove.
- Add broth and rice to skillet and heat to a boil.
- Cover and simmer over low heat for 25 minutes. (Add more water if necessary.)
- Stir in cheese and return chicken to pan.
- Cover and cook for 5 minutes or until done.

Glazed Chicken and Rice

4 boneless, skinless chicken breast halves, cubed
1 (20 ounce) can pineapple chunks with juice
½ cup honey mustard grill-and-glaze sauce
1 red bell pepper, chopped

- In skillet with a little oil, brown chicken and cook on low heat for 15 minutes.
- Add pineapple, honey mustard and bell pepper and bring to a boil.
- Reduce heat to low and simmer for 10 to 15 minutes or until sauce thickens slightly.
- Serve over hot cooked rice.

Broccoli-Cheese Chicken

4 boneless, skinless chicken breast halves
1 tablespoon butter
1 (10 ounce) can condensed broccoli-cheese soup
1 (10 ounce) package frozen broccoli spears
⅓ cup milk

- In skillet, cook chicken in butter for 15 minutes or until brown on both sides, remove and set aside.
- In same skillet, combine soup, broccoli, milk and a little black pepper and heat to boiling, return chicken to skillet and reduce heat to low.
- Cover and cook another 25 minutes or until chicken is no longer pink and broccoli is tender and serve over rice.

Dijon Chicken in a Skillet

¼ cup prepared ranch salad dressing
1 tablespoon dijon-style mustard
4 boneless, skinless chicken breast halves
2 tablespoons (¼ stick) butter
3 tablespoons white wine or chicken broth

- In bowl, combine salad dressing and mustard and set aside.
- In skillet, cook chicken in butter and let simmer for 10 to 15 minutes.
- Add wine or broth and simmer another 20 minutes.
- Whisk in mustard mixture, cook and stir until blended and heated through.
- Serve over instant long grain and wild rice.

Asparagus-Cheese Chicken

1 tablespoon butter
4 boneless, skinless chicken breast halves
1 (10 ounce) can condensed broccoli-cheese soup
1 (10 ounce) package frozen asparagus cuts
⅓ cup milk

- In skillet, heat butter and cook chicken 10 to 15 minutes or until brown on both sides.
- Remove chicken and set aside.
- In same skillet, combine soup, asparagus and milk and heat to boiling.
- Return chicken to skillet, reduce heat to low, cover and cook another 25 minutes until chicken is no longer pink and asparagus is tender.

Chicken Marseilles

3 tablespoons butter
5 to 6 boneless, skinless chicken breast halves
1 (1 ounce) package dry vegetable soup/dip mix
½ teaspoon dillweed
½ cup sour cream

- Melt butter in skillet, brown chicken about 10 to 15 minutes and turn occasionally.
- Stir 2 cups water, soup mix and dill into skillet and bring to a boil.
- Reduce heat, cover and simmer, stirring occasionally, for 25 to 30 minutes or until chicken is tender.
- Remove chicken to heated plate, add sour cream to skillet and stir until creamy.
- Place chicken on hot brown rice and spoon sauce over chicken.

Fried Chicken Breasts

4 boneless, skinless chicken breast halves
20 saltine crackers, crushed
2 eggs, beaten
¼ teaspoon black pepper

- Pound chicken breasts to ¼-inch thickness.
- Combine eggs, pepper and 2 tablespoons water.
- Dip chicken in egg mixture and crushed crackers and coat well.
- Deep fry until golden brown and drain well.

Grilled Chicken Cordon Bleu

6 boneless, skinless chicken breast halves
6 slices Swiss cheese, divided
6 thin slices deli ham
3 tablespoons oil
1 cup seasoned breadcrumbs

- Flatten chicken to ¼-inch thickness and place 1 slice each of cheese and ham on each piece of chicken to within ¼ inch of edges.
- Fold in half and secure with toothpicks.
- Brush chicken with oil and roll in breadcrumbs.
- Grill, covered, over medium-high heat for 15 to 18 minutes or until juices run clear.

Chicken and Noodles

1 (3 ounce) package chicken-flavored instant ramen noodles
1 (16 ounce) package frozen broccoli, cauliflower and carrots
⅔ cup sweet and sour sauce
3 boneless, skinless chicken breast halves, cooked

- Reserve seasoning packet from noodles.
- In saucepan, cook noodles and vegetables in 2 cups boiling water for 3 minutes, stir occasionally and drain.
- Combine noodle-vegetable mixture with seasoning packet, sweet and sour sauce and a little salt and pepper. (You may want to add 1 tablespoon soy sauce.)
- Cut chicken in strips, add chicken to noodle mixture and heat thoroughly.

Chicken Quesadillas

6 boneless, skinless chicken breast halves, cubed
1 (10 ounce) can cheddar cheese soup
⅔ cup chunky salsa
10 flour tortillas

- Cook chicken in skillet until juices evaporate and stir often.
- Add soup and salsa and heat thoroughly.
- Spread about ⅓ cup soup mixture on half tortilla to within ½-inch of edge.
- Moisten edges of tortillas with water, fold over and seal.
- Place tortillas on 2 baking sheets (5 tortillas each) and bake at 400° for 5 to 6 minutes.

Hurry-Up Chicken Enchiladas

2½ to 3 cups cooked, cubed chicken breast
1 (10 ounce) can cream of chicken soup
1½ cups chunky salsa, divided
8 (6 inch) flour tortillas
1 (10 ounce) can fiesta nacho cheese soup

- In saucepan, combine chicken, cream of chicken soup and ½ cup salsa and heat.
- Spoon about ⅓ cup chicken mixture down center of each tortilla and roll tortilla around filling.
- Place rolled tortillas seam-side down in sprayed 9 x 13-inch baking dish.
- Mix nacho cheese soup, remaining salsa and ¼ cup water and pour over enchiladas.
- Cover with wax paper and microwave on HIGH, turning several times, for 5 minutes or until bubbly.

Festive Cranberry Stuffing

1 (14 ounce) can chicken broth
1 rib celery, chopped
½ cup fresh or frozen cranberries
1 small onion, chopped
4 cups herb-seasoned stuffing

- Mix broth, celery, cranberries, onion and a dash of black pepper in saucepan and heat to boil.
- Cover and cook over low heat for 5 minutes.
- Add stuffing, mix lightly and spoon into baking dish.
- Bake at 325° just until thoroughly heated.

Skillet Chicken and Stuffing

1 (16 ounce) box stuffing mix for chicken
1 (16 ounce) package frozen whole kernel corn
¼ cup (½ stick) butter
4 boneless, skinless chicken breast halves, cooked

- In large skillet, combine corn, butter and 1⅔ cups water and bring to a boil.
- Reduce heat, cover and simmer for 5 minutes.
- Stir in stuffing mix just until moist.
- Cut chicken into thin slices and mix with stuffing-corn mixture.
- Cook on low heat just until mixture heats well.

Chicken for Lunch

4 cooked chicken breast slices from deli (thick sliced)
1 (3 ounce) package cream cheese, softened
3 tablespoons salsa
2 tablespoons mayonnaise

- Place chicken slices on serving platter.
- Use mixer to blend cream cheese, salsa and mayonnaise until smooth and creamy.
- Place heaping tablespoon cream cheese mixture on top of each chicken slice and serve cold.

Chicken Oriental

1 (6 ounce) jar sweet and sour sauce
1 (1 ounce) package dry onion soup mix
1 (16 ounce) can whole cranberry sauce
6 to 8 boneless, skinless chicken breast halves

- In bowl, combine sweet and sour sauce, soup mix and cranberry sauce.
- Place chicken breasts in sprayed, shallow 9 x 13-inch baking dish and pour cranberry mixture over chicken breasts.
- Bake covered at 325° for 30 minutes.
- Uncover and bake for 25 minutes longer.

Chunky Fruited Chicken

6 large boneless, skinless chicken breast halves
½ cup (1 stick) butter, melted
⅔ cup flour
Salt, pepper and paprika
1 (15 ounce) can chunky fruit cocktail with juice

- Dip chicken in butter and flour, place in shallow 9 x 13-inch baking dish and sprinkle with a little salt, pepper and paprika.
- Bake uncovered at 350° for 45 minutes.
- Pour fruit and half juice over chicken and bake for another 20 minutes.

Maple-Plum Glazed Turkey Breast

2 cups red plum jam
1 cup maple syrup
1 teaspoon dry mustard
¼ cup lemon juice
1 (5 pound) bone-in turkey breast

- In saucepan, combine plum jam, syrup, mustard and lemon juice and bring to a boil.
- Turn down heat and simmer for about 20 minutes or until thick. Set aside 1 cup.
- Place turkey breast in roasting pan, pour remaining glaze over turkey and bake according to directions on turkey breast package.
- Slice turkey and serve with heated reserved glaze.

Best Ever Meatloaf

2 pounds ground turkey
1 (6 ounce) package stuffing mix for beef
2 eggs, beaten
½ cup ketchup, divided

- Combine ground turkey, stuffing mix, eggs and ¼ cup ketchup and mix well.
- Shape meat into oval loaf in 9 x 13-inch baking dish and spread remaining ¼ cup ketchup over top of loaf.
- Bake at 350° for 1 hour.

Turkey and Noodles

1 (8 ounce) package noodles
2½ cups diced, cooked turkey
1 (10 ounce) package chicken gravy, prepared
2 cups round, buttery cracker crumbs

- Boil noodles according to package directions and drain.
- Arrange alternating layers of noodles, turkey and gravy in greased 2-quart baking dish and cover with crumbs.
- Bake uncovered at 350° for 35 minutes.

Asian Beef and Noodles

1¼ pounds ground beef
2 (3 ounce) packages oriental-flavored ramen noodles
1 (16 ounce) package frozen oriental stir-fry vegetable mixture
½ teaspoon ground ginger
3 tablespoons thinly sliced green onions

- In large skillet, brown ground beef and drain.
- Add ½ cup water, salt and pepper, simmer 10 minutes, and transfer to separate bowl.
- In same skillet, combine 2 cups water, vegetables, noodles (broken up), cginger and both seasoning packets.
- Bring to a boil and reduce heat.
- Cover, simmer 3 minutes or until noodles are tender and stir occasionally.
- Return beef to skillet and stir in green onions. Serve right from skillet.

Potato-Beef Casserole

4 medium potatoes, peeled, sliced
1¼ pounds lean ground beef, browned, drained
1 (10 ounce) can cream of mushroom soup
1 (10 ounce) can condensed vegetable beef soup
½ teaspoon salt
½ teaspoon pepper

- In large bowl, combine all ingredients and transfer to greased 3-quart baking dish.
- Bake covered at 350° for 1 hour 30 minutes or until potatoes are tender.

Tater Tots and Beef

2 pounds extra lean ground beef
1 (10 ounce) can golden mushroom soup
1 cup grated cheddar cheese
1 (2 pound) package frozen tater tots

- Pat ground beef into greased 9 x 13-inch pan.
- Spread soup over meat, cover with grated cheese and top with tater tots.
- Bake covered at 350° for 1 hour. Uncover for last 15 minutes.

Shepherds' Pie

1 pound lean ground beef
1 (1 ounce) envelope taco seasoning mix
1 cup shredded cheddar cheese
1 (11 ounce) can whole kernel corn, drained
2 cups instant mashed potatoes, prepared

- In skillet, brown beef, cook 10 minutes and drain.
- Add taco seasoning and ¾ cup water and cook another 5 minutes.
- Spoon beef mixture into 8-inch baking pan and sprinkle cheese on top.
- Sprinkle with corn and spread mashed potatoes over top.
- Bake at 350° for 25 minutes or until top is golden.

Potato-Beef Bake

1 pound ground beef
1 (10 ounce) can sloppy Joe sauce
1 (10 ounce) can fiesta nacho cheese soup
1 (32 ounce) package frozen hash-brown potatoes, thawed

- In skillet, cook beef over medium heat until no longer pink, and drain.
- Add sloppy Joe sauce and fiesta nacho cheese soup to beef and mix well.
- Place hash browns in greased 9 x 13-inch baking dish and top with beef mixture.
- Cover and bake at 400° for 25 minutes.
- Uncover and bake 10 minutes longer.

TIP: *This is really good sprinkled with 1 cup grated cheddar cheese.*

Casserole Supper

1 pound lean ground beef
¼ cup uncooked white rice
1 (10 ounce) can French onion soup
1 (2.8 ounce) can french-fried onion rings

- Brown ground beef, drain and place in buttered 7 x 11-inch baking dish.
- Add rice, onion soup and ½ cup water.
- Cover and bake at 325° for 40 minutes.
- Uncover, sprinkle onion rings over top and return to oven for 10 minutes.

Onion-Beef Bake

3 pounds lean ground beef
1 (1 ounce) package dry onion soup mix
½ cup water
2 (10 ounce) cans condensed French onion soup

- Combine beef, soup mix and water and stir well.
- Shape into patties about ½-inch thick, cook in large skillet and brown on both sides.
- Place patties in 9 x 13-inch baking dish and pour soup over patties.
- Cover and bake at 350° for 35 minutes.

Beef Patties in Creamy Onion Sauce

1½ pounds lean ground beef
⅓ cup salsa
⅓ cup butter cracker crumbs
1 (10 ounce) can cream of onion soup

- Combine beef, salsa and cracker crumbs and form into 5 to 6 patties.
- Brown patties in skillet and reduce heat.
- Add ¼ cup water and simmer for 15 minutes.
- In saucepan, combine onion soup and ½ cup water or milk, heat and mix.
- Pour mixture over beef patties and serve over hot, cooked noodles.

Easy Salisbury Steak

1¼ pounds lean ground beef
½ cup flour
1 egg
1 (10 ounce) can beef gravy

- In large bowl, combine beef, flour and egg.
- Add a little seasoned salt and pepper and mix well.
- Shape into 5 patties and place in shallow 7 x 11-inch baking dish.
- Bake uncovered at 350° for 20 minutes and drain off any fat.
- Pour beef gravy over patties and bake another 20 minutes. Serve over rice or noodles.

Delicious Meatloaf

1½ pounds lean ground beef
⅔ cup dry Italian-seasoned breadcrumbs
1 (10 ounce) can golden mushroom soup, divided
2 eggs, beaten
2 tablespoons (¼ stick) butter

- Mix beef, breadcrumbs, half mushroom soup and eggs thoroughly.
- In baking pan, shape firmly into 8 x 4-inch loaf and bake at 350° for 45 minutes.
- In small saucepan, mix butter, remaining soup and ¼ cup water, heat thoroughly and serve sauce over meat loaf.

Savory Herb Meatloaf

1 pound ground round beef, browned
1 (10 ounce) can cream of mushroom soup
1 (10 ounce) can cream of celery soup
1 (1 ounce) package savory herb with garlic soup mix
1 cup cooked rice

- Combine all ingredients and mix well.
- Place in 9 x 13-inch baking dish and form loaf.
- Bake at 350° for 50 minutes.

Spanish Meatloaf

1½ pounds lean ground beef
1 (16 ounce) can Spanish rice
1 egg, beaten
¾ cup round, buttery cracker crumbs
Chunky salsa

- Combine beef, rice, egg and crumbs and shape into loaf in greased pan.
- Bake at 350° for 1 hour.
- Serve meatloaf topped with salsa.

A Wicked Meatloaf

1 (7 ounce) package stuffing mix with seasoning packet
1 egg
½ cup salsa
1½ pounds lean ground beef

- In bowl combine stuffing mix, seasoning packet, egg, salsa and ⅓ cup water and mix well.
- Add ground beef to stuffing mixture and mix well.
- Spoon into 9 x 5-inch loaf pan and bake at 350° for 1 hour.

Beef Picante Skillet

A good family dish!

1 pound lean ground beef
1 (10 ounce) can tomato soup
1 cup chunky salsa or picante sauce
6 (6 inch) flour tortillas, cut into 1-inch pieces
1¼ cups shredded cheddar cheese, divided

- Brown beef in skillet and drain.
- Add soup, salsa, ¾ cup water, tortilla pieces, ½ teaspoon salt and half of cheese.
- Bring to a boil, cover and cook over low heat 5 minutes.
- Top with remaining cheese and serve right from skillet.

Smothered Beef Patties

1½ pounds ground beef
½ cup chili sauce
½ cup buttery cracker crumbs
1 (14 ounce) can beef bouillon

- Combine beef, chili sauce and cracker crumbs and form into 5 or 6 patties.
- In skillet, brown patties, pour beef bouillon over patties and bring to a boil.
- Reduce heat, cover and simmer for 40 minutes.

Spiced Beef

1 pound lean ground beef
1 (1 ounce) package taco seasoning mix
1 (16 ounce) can Mexican-style stewed tomatoes
1 (16 ounce) can kidney beans
1 (1 pound) package egg noodles

- Cook beef in skillet and drain.
- Add taco seasoning and ½ cup water and simmer 15 minutes.
- Add stewed tomatoes and kidney beans. (You may need to add ¼ teaspoon salt.)
- Cook egg noodles according to package directions and serve beef over noodles.

Pinto Bean Pie

1 pound lean ground beef
1 onion, chopped
2 (16 ounce) cans pinto beans
1 (10 ounce) can tomatoes and green chiles
1 (6 ounce) can french-fried onion rings

- In skillet, brown beef and onion and drain.
- In 2-quart casserole dish, layer 1 can beans, half beef-onion mixture and half can tomatoes and green chiles and repeat layers.
- Top with onion rings and bake uncovered at 350° for 30 minutes.

Chili Casserole

1 (40 ounce) can chili with beans
2 (4 ounce) cans diced green chiles
1 (2¼ ounce) can sliced ripe olives, drained
1 (8 ounce) package shredded cheddar cheese
2 cups crushed, ranch-flavored tortilla chips

- Combine all ingredients and transfer to greased 3-quart casserole dish.
- Bake uncovered at 350° for 35 minutes or until bubbly.

Texas Chili Pie

2 (20 ounce) cans chili without beans
1 (16 ounce) package small corn chips
1 onion, chopped
1 (16 ounce) package shredded cheddar cheese

- Heat chili in saucepan.
- In 9 x 13-inch baking dish, layer corn chips, chili, onion and cheese one-third at a time. Repeat layers with cheese on top.
- Bake at 325° for 20 minutes or until cheese bubbles.

Southwestern Steak

½ pound tenderized round steak
1 (15 ounce) can Mexican-style stewed tomatoes
¾ cup salsa
2 teaspoons beef bouillon

- Cut beef into serving-size pieces and dredge in flour.
- In skillet, brown steak in a little oil.
- Mix tomatoes, salsa and beef bouillon and pour over steak.
- Cover and bake at 325° for 1 hour.

Steak-Bake Italiano

2 pounds lean round steak
2 teaspoons Italian herb seasoning
1 teaspoon garlic salt
2 (15 ounce) cans stewed tomatoes

- Cut steak into serving-size pieces, brown in skillet and place in 9 x 13-inch baking dish.
- Combine herb seasoning, garlic salt and stewed tomatoes, mix well and pour over steak pieces.
- Cover and bake at 325° for 1 hour.

Baked Onion-Mushroom Steak

1½ pounds (½-inch thick) round steak
Salt and pepper
1 (10 ounce) can cream of mushroom soup
1 (1 ounce) package dry onion soup mix

- Place steak in greased 9 x 13-inch baking dish and sprinkle with salt and pepper.
- Pour mushroom soup and ½ cup water over steak and sprinkle with onion soup mix.
- Cover and bake at 325° for 2 hours.

Smothered Beef Steak

2 pounds lean round steak
1 cup uncooked rice
1 (14 ounce) can beef broth
1 green bell pepper, chopped

- Cut steak into serving-size pieces and brown in very large skillet.
- Add rice, beef broth, bell peppers and 1 cup water to skillet and bring to a boil.
- Reduce heat and cover and simmer for 1 hour.

Smothered Steak

1 (2 pound) round steak
1 (10 ounce) can golden mushroom soup
1 (1 ounce) package dry onion soup mix
⅔ cup milk

- Cut steak into serving-size pieces and place in greased 9 x 13-inch baking pan.
- In saucepan, combine mushroom soup, soup mix and milk.
- Heat just enough to mix well and pour over steak.
- Seal with foil and bake at 325° for 1 hour.

Red Wine Round Steak

2 pounds (¾-inch thick) round steak
1 (1 ounce) package dry onion soup mix
1 cup dry red wine
1 (4 ounce) can sliced mushrooms

- Remove all fat from steak and cut in serving-size pieces.
- Brown meat in skillet with a little oil. When browned on both sides, place in buttered 9 x 13-inch casserole dish.
- In frying pan, combine onion soup mix, wine, 1 cup hot water and mushrooms and pour over browned steak.
- Cover and bake for 1 hour 20 minutes or until steak is tender.

Roasted Garlic Steak

2 (15 ounce) cans tomato soup with roasted garlic
**   and herbs**
½ cup Italian salad dressing
⅓ cup water
1½ pounds (¾-inch) boneless beef sirloin steak

- In saucepan, combine soups, dressing and water.
- Broil steaks to desired doneness. (Allow 15 minutes for medium.)
- Turn once and brush often with sauce.
- Heat remaining sauce to serve with steak.

Pepper Steak

1 (1¼ pound) sirloin steak, cut in strips
Seasoned salt
1 (16 ounce) package frozen bell pepper and onion strips, thawed
1 (16 ounce) package cubed Mexican processed cheese

- Sprinkle steak with seasoned salt.
- Coat large skillet with non-stick vegetable spray and cook steak strips for 10 minutes or until no longer pink.
- Remove steak from skillet and set aside.
- Stir in vegetables and ½ cup water and simmer vegetables for 5 minutes or until all liquid cooks out.
- Add processed cheese and turn heat to medium-low.
- When cheese melts, stir in steak and serve over hot, cooked rice.

Rump Roast

1 (3 to 4 pound) boneless rump roast
4 medium potatoes, peeled, cut into pieces
2 onions, quartered
1 (10 ounce) can golden mushroom soup

- Place meat in roasting pan, season with seasoned salt and pepper and cover.
- Bake at 350° for 1 hour.
- Uncover, add potatoes and onions and continue cooking for 1 more hour.
- In saucepan, combine soup and ½ cup water and heat enough to pour over roast and vegetables.
- Place roasting pan back in oven just until soup is hot.

Supper-Ready Beef

1 (3 to 4) pound rump roast
1 (10 ounce) can French onion soup
1 (14 ounce) can beef broth
1 teaspoon garlic powder

- Place roast in roasting pan, pour soup and bouillon over roast and sprinkle with garlic powder.
- Place lid on roasting pan and bake at 350° for 3 hours 30 minutes.
- Gravy will be in pan.

Easy Roast

1 (4 pound) rump roast
1 (10 ounce) can cream of mushroom soup
1 (1 ounce) package dry onion soup mix
½ cup white wine

- Place roast in roasting pan.
- Combine mushroom soup, soup mix, white wine and ⅓ cup water.
- Pour over roast, cover with foil and bake at 325° for 3 to 4 hours.

Pot Roast

4 to 6 pound chuck roast
1 (10 ounce) can French onion soup
1 (1 ounce) package dry onion soup mix
4 to 6 potatoes, peeled, quartered

- Place roast on large sheet of heavy-duty foil.
- Combine soup and soup mix and cover roast with soup mixture.
- Add potatoes and secure edges of foil tightly.
- Bake at 350° for 3 to 4 hours.

Lemon-Herb Pot Roast

1 teaspoon garlic powder
2 teaspoons lemon-pepper seasoning
1 teaspoon dried basil
1 (3 to 3½ pound) boneless beef chuck roast
1 tablespoon oil

- Combine garlic, lemon pepper and basil and press evenly into surface of beef.
- In Dutch oven, heat oil over medium-high heat and brown roast.
- Add 1 cup water, bring to a boil, reduce heat to low, cover tightly and simmer for 3 hours. (Vegetables may be added to roast the last hour of cooking.)

Prime Rib of Beef

⅓ cup each chopped onion and chopped celery
1 teaspoon salt
½ teaspoon garlic powder
1 (6 to 8 pound) beef rib roast
1 (14 ounce) can beef broth

- Combine onion and celery and place in greased roasting pan.
- Combine salt, garlic powder and a little black pepper and rub over the roast.
- Place roast over vegetables with fat side up and bake uncovered at 350° for 2½ to 3½ hours or until meat reaches desired doneness. (medium-rare is 145°; medium is 160°; well-done is 170°)
- Let stand for about 15 minutes before carving.
- Skim fat from pan drippings and add beef broth.
- Stir to remove browned bits and heat.
- Strain and discard vegetables and serve roast with au jus.

Corned Beef Supper

1 (4 to 5 pound) corned beef brisket
4 large potatoes, peeled, quartered
6 carrots, peeled, halved
4 onions
1 head cabbage

- Place corned beef in roasting pan, cover with water and bring to a boil.
- Reduce heat and simmer 3 hours. (Add water if necessary.)
- Add potatoes, carrots and onions, cut cabbage into eighths and lay over top of other vegetables.
- Bring to a boil, reduce heat and cook another 30 to 40 minutes until vegetables are done.
- When slightly cool, slice corned beef across grain.

Slow Cookin', Good Tastin' Brisket

½ cup hickory-flavored liquid smoke
1 (4 to 5 pound) beef brisket
1 (5 ounce) bottle Worcestershire sauce
¾ cup barbecue sauce

- Pour liquid smoke over brisket, cover and refrigerate overnight.
- Drain and pour Worcestershire sauce over brisket.
- Cover and bake at 275° for 6 to 7 hours.
- Cover with barbecue sauce and bake uncovered for another 30 minutes.
- Slice very thin across grain.

Easy Breezy Brisket

1 (4 to 5 pound) brisket
1 (1 ounce) package dry onion soup mix
2 tablespoons Worcestershire sauce
1 cup red wine

- Place brisket in shallow baking pan and sprinkle onion soup mix over brisket.
- Pour Worcestershire sauce and red wine in baking pan.
- Cover and bake at 325° for 5 to 6 hours.

Oven Brisket

1 (5 to 6 pound) trimmed brisket
1 (1 ounce) package dry onion soup mix
1 (12 ounce) can cola
1 (10 ounce) bottle steak sauce

- Place brisket, fat side up, in roasting pan.
- Combine onion soup mix, cola and steak sauce and pour over brisket.
- Cover and bake at 325° for 4 to 5 hours or until tender.
- Remove brisket from pan, pour off drippings and refrigerate both, separately, overnight.
- Trim all fat from meat, slice and reheat.
- Skim fat off drippings, reheat and serve sauce over brisket.

Sweet and Savory Brisket

1 (3 to 4 pound) trimmed beef brisket, halved
⅓ cup grape or plum jelly
1 cup ketchup
1 (1 ounce) packet dry onion soup mix
¾ teaspoon black pepper

- Place half brisket in slow cooker.
- In bowl, combine jelly, ketchup, soup mix and pepper and spread half over meat.
- Top with remaining brisket and pour ketchup mixture over top. Cover and cook on low for 8 to 10 hours or until meat is tender.
- Slice brisket and serve with cooking juices.

Next-Day Beef

1 (5 to 6 pound) trimmed beef brisket
1 (1 ounce) package dry onion soup mix
1 (10 ounce) bottle steak sauce
1 (12 ounce) bottle barbecue sauce

- Place brisket, cut side up, in roasting pan.
- In bowl, combine onion soup mix, steak and barbecue sauces and pour over brisket.
- Cover and cook at 325° for 4 to 5 hours or until tender.
- Remove brisket from pan, pour off drippings and refrigerate both, separately, overnight.
- Trim all fat from meat, slice and reheat.
- Skim fat off drippings, reheat and serve sauce over brisket.

Smoked Brisket

1 (5 to 6 pound) trimmed brisket
1 (6 ounce) bottle liquid smoke
Garlic and celery salts
1 onion, chopped
Worcestershire sauce
1 (6 ounce) bottle barbecue sauce

- Place brisket in roasting pan and pour liquid smoke over brisket.
- Sprinkle with garlic salt and celery salt and top with onion.
- Cover and refrigerate overnight.
- Before cooking, pour off liquid smoke and douse with Worcestershire sauce.
- Cover with foil and bake at 300° for 5 hours.
- Uncover, pour barbecue sauce over brisket and bake for 1 more hour.

Great Brisket

2 onions, sliced
Paprika
Seasoned salt
1 (5 to 6 pound) trimmed brisket
1 (12 ounce) cola

- Place onions in bottom of roasting pan and sprinkle with paprika and seasoned salt.
- Lay brisket on top of onions, sprinkle with more seasoned salt and bake uncovered at 450° for 30 minutes.
- Pour cola over roast and reduce heat to 325°.
- Cover with foil and bake until tender, about 4 hours
- Baste occasionally with cola and juices from brisket.

Heavenly Smoked Brisket

½ cup packed dark brown sugar
2 tablespoons Cajun seasoning
1 tablespoon lemon pepper
1 tablespoon Worcestershire sauce
1 (5 to 6 pound) beef brisket, untrimmed

- Combine sugar, Cajun seasoning, pepper and Worcestershire in shallow baking dish, add brisket and turn to coat both sides.
- Cover and refrigerate 8 hours.
- Soak hickory wood chunks in water for 1 hour.
- Prepare charcoal fire in smoker and burn 20 minutes, drain chunks and place on coals.
- Place water pan in smoker and add water to depth of fill line.
- Remove brisket from marinade and place on lower food rack.
- Pour remaining marinade over meat and cover with smoker lid.
- Cook 5 hours or until meat thermometer inserted in thickest portion registers 170°.

Cheesy Beefy Gnocchi

1 pound lean ground beef
1 (10 ounce) can cheddar cheese soup
1 (10 ounce) can tomato bisque soup
2 cups uncooked gnocchi or shell pasta

- In skillet, cook beef until brown and drain.
- Add soups, 1½ cups water and pasta and bring mixture to a boil.
- Cover and cook over medium heat for 10 to 12 minutes or until pasta is done. Stir often.

Ham Patties

This is a great way to use leftover ham.

2 cups cooked, ground ham
2 eggs, slightly beaten
1 cup cracker crumbs

- Combine ham, eggs, cracker crumbs and a little pepper and shape into patties.
- Place a little oil in heavy skillet and sauté patties until golden brown.

Supper in a Dish

2 (7 ounce) bags instant boil-in-bag rice
1½ cups cubed, cooked ham
1½ cups shredded cheddar cheese
1 (8 ounce) can green peas

- Prepare rice according to package directions.
- In large bowl, combine rice, ham, cheese and peas.
- Pour into 3-quart baking dish and bake at 350° for 15 to 20 minutes.

Sunday Ham

2 to 3 pounds boneless, smoked ham
¼ cup prepared mustard
¼ cup packed brown sugar
4 potatoes, peeled, quartered

- Place ham in roasting pan.
- Combine mustard and sugar and spread mixture over ham.
- Place potatoes around ham, cover and bake at 300° for 2 hours 30 minutes to 3 hours.

Apricot-Baked Ham

1 (12 to 20 pound) whole ham, fully cooked
Whole cloves
2 tablespoons dry mustard
1¼ cups apricot jam
1¼ cups packed light brown sugar

- Preheat oven to 450°.
- Place ham on rack in large roasting pan and insert cloves into ham every inch or so.
- Combine dry mustard and jam and spread over entire surface of ham.
- Pat brown sugar over jam mixture.
- Reduce heat to 325° and bake uncovered for 15 minutes per pound.

Praline Ham

2 (½-inch thick) ham slices, cooked (about 2½ pounds)
½ cup maple syrup
3 tablespoons brown sugar
1 tablespoon butter
⅓ cup chopped pecans

- Heat ham slices in shallow pan at 325° for 10 minutes.
- Bring syrup, sugar and butter to boil in small saucepan and stir often.
- Stir in pecans and spoon syrup mixture over ham.
- Warm another 20 minutes.

Peachy Glazed Ham

1 (15 ounce) can sliced peaches in light syrup with juice
2 tablespoons dark brown sugar
2 teaspoons dijon-style mustard
1 (1 pound) center-cut ham slice
⅓ cup sliced green onions

- Drain peaches, reserve ½ cup syrup in large skillet and set peaches aside.
- Add sugar and mustard to skillet, bring to a boil over medium-high heat and cook 2 minutes or until slightly reduced.
- Add ham and cook 2 minutes on each side.
- Add peaches and green onions, cover and cook over low heat for 3 minutes or until peaches are thoroughly heated.

Ham with Orange Sauce

1 (½-inch thick) slice fully cooked ham
1 cup orange juice
2 tablespoons brown sugar
1½ tablespoons cornstarch
⅓ cup white raisins

- Place ham slice in shallow baking dish.
- In saucepan, combine orange juice, brown sugar, cornstarch and raisins.
- Bring to boil, stirring constantly, until mixture thickens and pour over ham slice.
- Warm at 350° for about 20 minutes.

Excellent Orange Sauce for Ham

⅔ cup orange juice
⅓ cup water
2 tablespoons brown sugar
1½ tablespoons cornstarch
⅓ cup golden raisins

- Mix all ingredients in saucepan.
- Heat and cook, stirring constantly, until sauce thickens and is clear and bubbly.
- Serve with pre-cooked ham.

Baked Ham and Pineapple

1 (6 to 8 pound) fully cooked, bone-in ham
Whole cloves
½ cup packed brown sugar
1 (8 ounce) can sliced pineapple with juice
5 maraschino cherries

- Place ham in roasting pan, score surface with shallow diagonal cuts making diamond shapes and insert cloves into diamonds.
- Cover and bake at 325° for 1 hour 30 minutes.
- Combine brown sugar and juice from pineapple and pour over ham.
- Arrange pineapple slices and cherries on ham. Bake uncovered another 40 minutes.

Pineapple Sauce for Ham

Pre-sliced, cooked honey-baked ham slices
1 (15 ounce) can pineapple chunks with juice
1 cup apricot preserves
1¼ cups packed brown sugar
¼ teaspoon cinnamon

- Place ham slices in shallow baking pan.
- In saucepan, combine pineapple, preserves, brown sugar and cinnamon and heat.
- Pour sauce over ham slices and heat.

Grilled Ham and Apples

½ cup orange marmalade
2 teaspoons butter
¼ teaspoon ground ginger
2 (½-inch thick) ham slices (about 2½ pounds)
4 apples, quartered

- Combine marmalade, butter and ginger in 1-cup glass measuring cup.
- Microwave on HIGH for 1 minute or until mixture melts and stir once.
- Cook ham covered with apples. Cover with grill lid and cook over medium-hot coals.
- Turn occasionally and baste with marmalade mixture, about 20 minutes.

Apple Pork Chops

4 butterflied pork chops
2 apples, peeled
2 teaspoons butter
2 tablespoons brown sugar

- Place pork chops in sprayed shallow baking dish and season with salt and pepper.
- Cover and bake at 350° for 30 minutes.
- Uncover and place peeled and cored apple halves on top of pork chops.
- Add a little butter and brown sugar on top of each apple and bake for another 15 minutes.

Pork Chops and Apples

Simple and delicious!

6 thick-cut pork chops
Flour
Oil
3 baking apples

- Dip pork chops in flour and coat well.
- In skillet, brown pork chops in oil and place in 9 x 13-inch greased casserole dish.
- Add ⅓ cup water to casserole and bake covered at 325° for 50 minutes.
- Peel, half and seed apples and place ½ apple over each pork chop.
- Return to oven for 10 minutes. (Don't overcook apples.)

Pineapple Pork Chops

6 to 8 thick, boneless pork chops
1 (6 ounce) can frozen pineapple juice concentrate, thawed
3 tablespoons brown sugar
⅓ cup wine vinegar or tarragon vinegar
⅓ cup honey

- In skillet, brown pork chops in a little oil and remove to shallow baking dish.
- Combine pineapple juice, sugar, vinegar and honey and pour over pork chops.
- Cook covered at 325° for about 50 minutes and serve over hot rice.

Orange-Pork Chops

6 to 8 medium thick pork chops
¼ cup (½ stick) butter
2¼ cups orange juice
2 tablespoons orange marmalade

- In hot skillet, brown both sides of pork chops in butter and add salt and pepper.
- Pour orange juice over chops.
- Cover and simmer for 1 hour or until done. (Time will vary with thickness of pork chops, and it may be necessary to add more orange juice.)
- During last few minutes of cooking, add 2 tablespoons orange marmalade.

TIP: *This makes delicious gravy to serve over rice.*

Onion-Smothered Pork Chops

6 (½-inch thick) pork chops
1 tablespoon oil
2 tablespoons (¼ stick) butter
1 onion, chopped
1 (10 ounce) can cream of onion soup

- In skillet, brown pork chops in oil, simmer about 10 minutes and place pork chops in greased shallow baking pan.
- In same skillet, add butter and saute chopped onion. (Pan juices are brown from pork chops so onions will be brown from juices already in skillet.)
- Add onion soup and ½ cup water and stir well. (Sauce will have a pretty, light brown color.)
- Pour onion-soup mixture over pork chops. Cover, bake at 325° for 40 minutes and serve over brown rice.

Oven Pork Chops

6 to 8 medium-thick pork chops
1 (10 ounce) can cream of chicken soup
3 tablespoons ketchup
1 tablespoon Worcestershire sauce
1 medium onion, chopped

- Brown pork chops in a little oil, season with salt and pepper and place drained pork chops in shallow baking dish.
- In saucepan, combine soup, ketchup, Worcestershire and onion, heat just enough to mix and pour over pork chops.
- Bake covered at 350° for 50 minutes. Uncover for the last 15 minutes.

Giddy-Up Pork Chops

6 boneless pork chops
½ cup salsa
½ cup honey or packed brown sugar
1 teaspoon soy sauce

- Brown pork chops in oven-proof pan.
- Combine salsa, honey or brown sugar and soy sauce and heat for 20 to 30 seconds in microwave.
- Pour salsa mixture over pork chops, cover and bake at 325° for 45 minutes or until pork chops are tender.

Baked Pork Chops

¾ cup ketchup
¾ cup packed brown sugar
¼ cup lemon juice
4 butterflied pork chops

- Combine ketchup, brown sugar, lemon juice and ½ cup water.
- Place pork chops in buttered 7 x 11-inch baking dish and pour sauce over pork chops.
- Bake covered at 325° for 50 minutes.

Mexicali Pork Chops

1 (1 ounce) packet taco seasoning
4 (½-inch thick) boneless pork loin chops
1 tablespoon oil
Salsa

- Rub taco seasoning over pork chops. In skillet, brown pork chops in oil over medium heat.
- Add 2 tablespoons water, turn heat to low and simmer pork chops about 40 minutes. (Add more water if needed.)
- Spoon salsa over pork chops to serve.

Spicy Pork Chops

4 to 6 pork chops
1 large onion
1 bell pepper
1 (10 ounce) can diced tomatoes and green chiles

- Brown pork chops in skillet with a little oil.
- Spray casserole dish with non-stick spray and place chops in dish.
- Cut onion and bell pepper into large chunks and place on chops.
- Pour tomato and green chiles over chops and sprinkle with 1 teaspoon salt.
- Bake covered at 350° for 45 minutes.

Saucy Pork Chops

4 (½-inch thick) pork chops
1 tablespoon oil
1 (10 ounce) can cream of onion soup
2 tablespoons soy sauce

- In skillet, brown pork chops in oil.
- Cook chops for 15 minutes, drain and set aside.
- In same skillet, combine soup and soy sauce and heat to a boil.
- Return chops to pan, reduce heat to low and cover.
- Simmer for 20 minutes.

Tangy Pork Chops

4 to 6 pork chops
¼ cup Worcestershire sauce
¼ cup ketchup
½ cup honey

- In skillet, brown pork chops and remove to shallow baking dish.
- Combine Worcestershire, ketchup and honey and pour over pork chops.
- Cover and bake at 325° for 45 minutes.

Sweet and Savory Pork Chops

6 to 8 (¾ to 1-inch thick) boneless pork chops, trimmed
½ cup grape, apple or plum jelly
½ cup chili sauce or hot ketchup
Soy sauce

- Brown pork chops and season to taste with salt and pepper.
- Transfer browned pork chops to shallow baking dish, place in oven and bake at 325° for 30 minutes.
- Combine jelly and chili sauce or ketchup and spread over pork chops.
- Bake for 15 minutes, baste with sauce and cook another 15 minutes or until pork chops are tender.
- Serve with soy sauce.

Pork Casserole

4 to 5 potatoes, peeled, sliced
6 pork chops
1 (10 ounce) can fiesta nacho cheese soup
½ soup can milk

- Place 2 layers potatoes in greased casserole dish and place pork chops on top.
- Combine cheese and milk and heat just enough to pour over chops.
- Bake covered at 350° for 45 minutes. Uncover and bake another 15 minutes.

Pork Chops in Cream Gravy

4 (¼-inch thick) pork chops
Flour
Oil
2¼ cups milk

- Trim all fat off pork chops and dip chops in flour with a little salt and pepper.
- Brown pork chops on both sides in a little oil and remove chops from skillet.
- Add about 2 tablespoons flour to skillet, brown lightly and stir in a little salt and pepper.
- Slowly stir in milk to make gravy.
- Return chops to skillet with gravy, cover and simmer on low heat for about 40 minutes.
- Serve over rice or noodles.

Pork-Potato Chop

6 boneless or loin pork chops
1 (14 ounce) can chicken broth
2 (1 ounce) packages dry onion gravy mix
4 red potatoes, sliced

- Season chops with salt and pepper and brown in large skillet with a little oil.
- Combine chicken broth and gravy mix, add potatoes to skillet with pork chops and cover with gravy mixture.
- Heat to a boil, cover and simmer 45 minutes or until pork chops and potatoes are fork-tender.

Pork Chops, Potatoes and Green Beans

6 to 8 boneless or loin pork chops
2 (1 ounce) packets gravy mix or 2 (12 ounce) jars prepared gravy
2 (15 ounce) cans white potatoes, drained
2 (15 ounce) cans cut green beans, drained

- Season pork chops with salt and pepper if desired and brown pork chops over medium heat in large, sprayed, non-stick Dutch oven.
- Mix gravy with water according to package directions (or use prepared gravy) and pour over pork chops.
- Cover and simmer for 30 minutes.
- Add potatoes and green beans and simmer about 10 minutes or until pork chops are tender and green beans and potatoes are hot.

Grilled Pork Loin

1 (4 pound) boneless pork loin roast
1 (8 ounce) bottle Italian salad dressing
1 cup dry white wine
3 cloves garlic, minced
10 black peppercorns

- Pierce roast at 1-inch intervals with fork and set aside.
- Combine salad dressing, white wine, garlic and peppercorns. Reserve ½ cup mixture for basting during grilling.
- Place roast in large, resealable plastic bag with remaining mixture, refrigerate 8 hours and turn occasionally.
- Remove roast from marinade and discard marinade.
- Place roast on rack in grill.
- Cook, covered with grill lid, for 35 minutes or until meat thermometer inserted into thickest portion reaches 160°. Turn occasionally and baste with ½ cup reserved dressing mixture.

Plum Peachy Pork Roast

1 (4 to 5 pound) boneless pork loin roast
1 (12 ounce) jar plum jelly
½ cup peach preserves
½ teaspoon ginger

- Place roast in shallow baking pan and bake at 325° for 35 minutes.
- Turn roast to brown other side and bake for another 35 minutes.
- In saucepan, heat jelly, peach preserves and ginger and brush roast generously with preserve mixture after it is done.
- Bake another 15 minutes and baste again.

Tenderloin with Apricot Sauce

3 pounds pork tenderloins
1 cup apricot preserves
⅓ cup lemon juice
⅓ cup ketchup
1 tablespoon soy sauce

- Place tenderloins in roasting pan.
- Combine preserves, lemon juice, ketchup and soy sauce.
- Pour preserve mixture over pork and bake covered at 325° for 1 hour 20 minutes.
- Baste once during cooking.
- Serve over white rice.

Hawaiian Aloha Pork

This is great served over rice.

1 (2 pound) lean pork tenderloin, cut into 1-inch cubes
1 (15 ounce) can pineapple chunks with juice
1 (12 ounce) bottle chili sauce
1 teaspoon ground ginger

- In skillet, season pork with salt and pepper.
- Combine meat, pineapple with juice, chili sauce and ginger.
- Simmer covered for 1 hour 30 minutes.

Apple-Topped Tenderloin

1 (3 to 4 pound) pork tenderloin
1½ cups hickory marinade, divided
1 (20 ounce) can apple pie filling
¾ teaspoon cinnamon

- Place tenderloin and 1 cup marinade in large, resealable plastic bag and marinate in refrigerator for at least 1 hour.
- Remove tenderloin and discard used marinade.
- Cook tenderloin, uncovered, at 325° for 1 hour and baste twice with ¼ cup marinade.
- Let stand for 10 or 15 minutes before slicing.
- In saucepan, combine pie filling, remaining ¼ cup marinade and cinnamon, heat and serve over tenderloin.

Pork Picante

1 pound pork tenderloin, cubed
2 tablespoons taco seasoning
1 cup chunky salsa
⅓ cup peach preserves

- Toss pork with taco seasoning and brown with a little oil in skillet.
- Stir in salsa and preserves and bring to a boil.
- Lower heat and simmer for 10 minutes.
- Pour over hot cooked rice to serve.

Cranberries and Apples

Great served with pork.

2 (21 ounce) cans pie apples
1 (16 ounce) can whole cranberry sauce
2 cups sugar
1 teaspoon ground cinnamon
Red food coloring, optional

- In large saucepan, mix apples, cranberry sauce, sugar and cinnamon and, if you like, add a few drops of red coloring.
- Simmer for about 45 minutes, stir occasionally and refrigerate.

Baked Applesauce

5 pounds tart green apples, peeled, cored, sliced
1 (8 ounce) jar plum jelly
½ cup sugar
⅓ cup lemon juice
¼ teaspoon ground nutmeg

- Place apples in 2-quart casserole dish.
- In saucepan, combine jelly, sugar and ⅔ cup water and heat until jelly melts.
- Remove from heat, stir in lemon juice and nutmeg and pour over apples.
- Bake covered at 350° for 1 hour 15 minutes or until apples are soft. Delicious served with pork.

Tequila Baby-Back Ribs

4 pounds baby-back pork ribs
1 (12 ounce) bottle tequila-lime marinade, divided
Black pepper

- Cut ribs in lengths to fit in large, resealable plastic bag.
- Place ribs in bag, add ¾ cup marinade, seal bag and shake to coat. Marinate in refrigerator overnight.
- Place ribs in sprayed shallow baking dish and discard used marinade.
- Cover ribs with foil and bake at 375° for 30 minutes.
- Remove from oven and spread remaining marinade over ribs.
- Lower heat to 300° and cook for 1 hour.
- Uncover to let ribs brown and bake 30 minutes longer.

Spunky Spareribs

5 to 6 pounds spareribs
1 (6 ounce) can frozen orange juice concentrate, thawed
2 teaspoons Worcestershire sauce
½ teaspoon garlic powder

- Place spareribs in shallow baking pan, meat side down and sprinkle with a little salt and pepper.
- Roast at 375° for 30 minutes. Turn ribs, roast another 15 minutes and drain off fat.
- Combine orange juice, Worcestershire and garlic powder and brush mixture on ribs.
- Reduce heat to 300°.
- Cover ribs, roast 2 hours or until tender and baste occasionally.

Orange Spareribs

4 to 5 pounds pork spareribs
1 (6 ounce) can orange juice concentrate, thawed
½ teaspoon garlic salt
⅔ cup honey

- Place ribs, meaty side down in shallow roasting pan and bake at 350° for 30 minutes.
- Drain off fat, turn ribs and bake for another 30 minutes.
- Combine orange juice concentrate, garlic salt and honey and brush on ribs.
- Reduce temperature to 325°.
- Cover pan, bake for 1 hour 30 minutes or until ribs are tender and brush with sauce several times.

Tangy Apricot Ribs

3 to 4 pounds baby-back pork loin ribs
1 (16 ounce) jar apricot preserves
⅓ cup soy sauce
¼ cup packed light brown sugar
2 teaspoons garlic powder

- Place ribs in large roasting pan.
- Whisk preserves, soy sauce, brown sugar and garlic powder until blended and pour over ribs. Cover and refrigerate overnight.
- Remove ribs from marinade and reserve marinade in small saucepan.
- Line baking pan with foil, add ribs and sprinkle with a little salt and pepper.
- Bring marinade to a boil, cover, reduce heat and simmer 5 minutes.
- Bake ribs at 325° for 1 hour 30 minutes or until tender and baste frequently with marinade.

Lemonade Spareribs

4 pounds pork spareribs
1 (6 ounce) can lemonade concentrate
½ teaspoon garlic salt
⅓ cup soy sauce

- Place ribs, meaty side down, in shallow roasting pan and cook covered at 350° for 40 minutes.
- Remove cover, drain fat and return ribs to oven.
- Bake 30 minutes and drain fat again.
- Combine lemonade concentrate, garlic salt and soy sauce and brush on ribs.
- Reduce temperature to 325°, cover and bake for 1 more hour or until ribs are tender. Brush occasionally with sauce.

Sweet and Sour Spareribs

3 to 4 pounds spareribs
3 tablespoons soy sauce
⅓ cup prepared mustard
1 cup packed brown sugar
½ teaspoon garlic salt

- Place spareribs in roasting pan, bake at 325° for 45 minutes and drain.
- Make sauce with soy sauce, mustard, brown sugar and garlic salt and brush on ribs.
- Return to oven, reduce heat to 300° and bake for 2 hours or until ribs are tender. Baste several times while cooking.

Dijon Baby-Back Ribs

4 pounds baby-back pork ribs
1 (12 ounce) bottle dijon-honey marinade with lemon juice, divided

- If needed, cut ribs in lengths to fit in large, resealable plastic bag.
- Place ribs in bag with ¾ cup marinade, seal bag and shake to coat.
- Marinate in refrigerator overnight. (Refrigerate remaining marinade.)
- Discard used marinade and place ribs on sprayed broiler pan.
- Bake uncovered at 300° for about 2 hours.
- Finish browning and cooking on grill and baste often with remaining marinade.

Italian Sausage and Ravioli

1 pound sweet Italian pork sausage
1 (26 ounce) jar extra chunky mushroom and green pepper
    spaghetti sauce
1 (24 ounce) package frozen cheese-filled ravioli, cooked, drained
Grated parmesan cheese

- Remove casing from sausage and cook in large skillet over medium heat until brown and no longer pink inside. Stir to separate sausage or slice sausage and drain.
- Stir in spaghetti sauce and heat to boiling.
- Add cooked ravioli to spaghetti sauce and sausage.
- Sprinkle with parmesan cheese and pour into serving dish.

Sausage Casserole

1 pound pork sausage
2 (15 ounce) cans pork and beans
1 (15 ounce) can Mexican-style stewed tomatoes
1 (8 ounce) package cornbread muffin mix

- Brown sausage and drain fat.
- Add beans and tomatoes, blend and bring to a boil.
- Pour mixture into 3-quart greased casserole dish.
- Prepare muffin mix according to package directions and drop by teaspoonfuls over meat-bean mixture.
- Bake at 400° for 30 minutes or until top browns.

Baked Fish

1 pound fish fillets
3 tablespoons butter
1 teaspoon tarragon
2 teaspoons capers
2 tablespoons lemon juice

- Place fish fillets with a little butter in greased shallow pan and sprinkle with salt and pepper.
- Bake at 375° for about 8 to 10 minutes, turn and bake another 6 minutes or until fish flakes.
- For sauce, melt butter with tarragon, capers and lemon juice and serve over warm fish.

Crispy Fish and Cheese Fillets

2 pounds fish fillets
½ cup prepared creamy ranch-style salad dressing
1½ cups crushed cheese crackers
2 tablespoons (¼ stick) butter, melted

- Cut fish into serving portions, dip into dressing and roll in cracker crumbs.
- Place in greased shallow pan and drizzle butter over fish.
- Bake uncovered at 425° for 15 minutes or until fish flakes easily.

Chips and Fish

3 to 4 fish fillets, rinsed, dried
1 cup mayonnaise
2 tablespoons fresh lime juice and lime wedges
1½ cups crushed corn chips

- Preheat oven to 425°.
- Mix mayonnaise and lime juice and spread on both sides of fish fillets.
- Place crushed corn chips on wax paper, dredge both sides of fish in chips and shake off excess chips.
- Place fillets on foil-covered baking sheet and bake for 15 minutes or until fish flakes.
- ·Serve with lime wedges.

Spicy Catfish Amandine

¼ cup (½ stick) butter, melted
3 tablespoons lemon juice
6 to 8 catfish fillets
1½ teaspoons Creole seasoning
½ cup sliced almonds

- Combine butter and lemon juice.
- Dip each fillet in butter mixture, arrange in 9 x 13-inch baking dish and sprinkle fish with Creole seasoning.
- Bake at 375° for 25 to 30 minutes or until fish flakes easily when tested with fork.
- Sprinkle almonds over fish for last 5 minutes of baking.

Golden Catfish Fillets

3 eggs
¾ cup flour
¾ cup cornmeal
1 teaspoon garlic powder
6 to 8 (4 to 8 ounce) catfish fillets

- In shallow bowl, beat eggs until foamy.
- In another shallow bowl, combine flour, cornmeal, garlic powder and a little salt.
- Dip fillets in eggs and coat with cornmeal mixture.
- Heat ¼ inch oil in large skillet and fry fish over medium-high heat for about 4 minutes on each side or until fish flakes easily with fork.

Home-Fried Fish

1½ pounds haddock, sole or cod
1 egg beaten
2 tablespoons milk
2 cups corn flake crumbs

- Cut fish into serving-size pieces.
- Combine egg and milk, dip fish in egg mixture and coat with crushed corn flakes on both sides.
- Fry in thin layer of oil in skillet until brown on both sides.

Chipper Fish

2 pounds sole or orange roughy
½ cup caesar salad dressing
1 cup crushed potato chips
½ cup shredded cheddar cheese

- Dip fish in dressing and place in greased baking dish.
- Combine potato chips and cheese and sprinkle over fish.
- Bake at 375° for about 20 to 25 minutes.

Orange Roughy with Peppers

1 pound orange roughy fillets
1 onion, sliced
2 red bell peppers, cut into julienne strips
1 teaspoon dried thyme leaves
¼ teaspoon black pepper

- Cut fish into 4 serving-size pieces.
- Heat a little oil in skillet, layer onion and bell peppers in oil and sprinkle with half thyme and pepper.
- Place fish over peppers and sprinkle with remaining thyme and pepper.
- Turn burner on high just until fish begins to cook.
- Lower heat, cover and cook fish for 15 to 20 minutes or until fish flakes easily.

Lemon-Dill Fillets

½ cup mayonnaise
2 tablespoons lemon juice
½ teaspoon grated lemon peel
1 teaspoon dillweed
1 pound cod or flounder fillets

- Combine mayonnaise, lemon juice, lemon peel and dillweed until they blend well.
- Place fish on greased grill or broiler rack and brush with half mayonnaise mixture.
- Grill or broil 5 to 8 minutes, turn and brush with remaining mayonnaise mixture.
- Continue grilling or broiling 5 to 8 minutes or until fish flakes easily with fork.

Crispy Flounder

⅓ cup mayonnaise
1 pound flounder fillets
1 cup dry, seasoned breadcrumbs
¼ cup grated parmesan cheese

- Place mayonnaise in small dish.
- Coat fish with mayonnaise and dip in crumbs to coat well.
- Arrange in shallow baking dish and bake uncovered at 375° for 25 minutes.

Flounder au Gratin

½ cup fine dry breadcrumbs
¼ cup grated parmesan cheese
1 pound flounder
⅓ cup mayonnaise

- In shallow dish, combine crumbs and cheese.
- Brush both sides of fish with mayonnaise and coat with crumb mixture.
- Arrange fillets in single layer in shallow pan and bake at 375° for 20 to 25 minutes or until fish flakes easily.

Lemon Baked Fish

1 pound sole or halibut fillets
2 tablespoons (¼ stick) butter
1 teaspoon dried tarragon
2 tablespoons lemon juice

- Place fish fillets in greased shallow pan with a little butter and sprinkle with salt and pepper.
- Bake at 375° for 8 to 10 minutes, turn and bake another 6 minutes or until fish flakes.
- Melt butter with tarragon and lemon juice and serve over warm fish fillets.

Baked Halibut

2 (1-inch thick) halibut steaks
1 (8 ounce) carton sour cream
½ cup grated parmesan cheese
¾ teaspoon dillweed

- Place halibut in greased 9 x 13-inch baking dish.
- Combine sour cream, parmesan cheese and dillweed (and salt and pepper if desired) and spoon over halibut.
- Cover and bake at 325° for 20 minutes.
- Uncover and sprinkle with paprika.
- Bake another 10 minutes or until fish flakes easily with fork.

Broiled Salmon Steaks

4 (1-inch thick) salmon steaks
Garlic salt
Worcestershire sauce
¼ to ½ cup (½ to 1 stick) butter, melted

- Place salmon steaks on baking sheet and sprinkle both sides with garlic salt.
- Splash Worcestershire and butter on top of each steak and broil for 2 to 3 minutes.
- Remove from oven and turn each steak.
- Splash Worcestershire and butter over top and broil for 2 to 3 more minutes. (Do not overcook. Fish will flake but should not be dry inside.)
- Top with a little melted butter just before serving.

Salmon Patties

1 (15 ounce) can pink salmon with juice
1 egg
½ cup cracker crumbs
1 teaspoon baking powder

- Drain juice from salmon and set juice aside.
- Remove bones and skin from salmon.
- Combine egg and cracker crumbs with salmon.
- In small bowl, add baking powder to ¼ cup salmon juice. (Mixture will foam.)
- After foaming, add to salmon mixture and drop by large tablespoonfuls into hot oil in skillet. Flatten into patties.
- Brown lightly on both sides and serve hot.

Salmon Croquettes

1 (15 ounce) can pink salmon, drained, flaked
1 egg
½ cup biscuit mix
¼ cup ketchup

- Combine salmon (discard skin and bones) and egg in bowl.
- Add biscuit mix and ketchup and mix well. Shape croquet into triangle-shaped logs about 3 inches long.
- Heat a little oil in skillet and place each croquet into skillet.
- Cook each side until brown.

Tuna-Asparagus Pot Pie

1 (8 ounce) package crescent rolls, divided
1 (6 ounce) can solid white tuna in water, drained, flaked
1 (15 ounce) can cut asparagus, drained
1 cup shredded cheddar cheese

- Form 7-inch square using 4 crescent rolls, pinch edges together to seal and place in sprayed 8 x 8 x 2-inch baking pan.
- Spread dough with tuna, then asparagus, followed by shredded cheese.
- Form remaining 4 crescent rolls into 7-inch square and place on top of cheese.
- Bake at 375° for 20 minutes or until top is brown and cheese bubbles.

Tuna Noodles

1 (8 ounce) package wide noodles, cooked, drained
2 (6 ounce) cans white tuna, drained
1 (10 ounce) can cream of chicken soup
¾ cup milk
¾ cup chopped black olives

- Place half noodles in buttered 2-quart casserole dish.
- In saucepan, combine tuna, soup, milk and olives and heat just enough to mix well.
- Pour half soup mixture over noodles and repeat layers.
- Cover and bake at 300° for 20 minutes.

Tuna and Chips

1 (6 ounce) can tuna, drained
1 (10 ounce) can cream of chicken soup
¾ cup milk
1½ cups crushed potato chips, divided

- Break chunks of tuna into bowl and stir in soup and milk.
- Add ¾ cups crushed potato chips and mix well.
- Pour mixture into greased baking dish and sprinkle remaining chips over top.
- Bake uncovered at 350° for 30 minutes or until chips are light brown.

Beer Batter Shrimp

1 (12 ounce) can beer
1 cup flour
2 teaspoons garlic powder
1 pound shrimp, peeled, veined

- Combine beer, flour and garlic powder and stir to creamy consistency to make batter.
- Dip shrimp into batter to cover and deep fry in hot oil.

Boiled Shrimp

3 pounds fresh shrimp
1 teaspoon salt
2 teaspoons seafood seasoning
½ cup vinegar

- Remove heads from shrimp.
- Place all ingredients in large saucepan, cover shrimp with water and bring to a boil.
- Reduce heat and boil for 10 minutes.
- Remove from heat, drain and refrigerate.

Shrimp Scampi

½ cup (1 stick) butter
3 cloves garlic, pressed
¼ cup lemon juice
Hot sauce
2 pounds raw shrimp, peeled

- Melt butter, sauté garlic and add lemon juice and a few dashes of hot sauce.
- Arrange shrimp in single layer in shallow pan, pour butter mixture over shrimp and salt lightly.
- Broil 2 minutes, turn shrimp and broil 2 more minutes.
- Reserve garlic butter and serve separately.

TIP: This recipe requires real butter – no substitutions.

Skillet Shrimp Scampi

2 teaspoons olive oil
2 pounds uncooked shrimp, peeled, veined
⅔ cup herb-garlic marinade with lemon juice
¼ cup finely chopped green onion with tops

- In large non-stick skillet, heat oil.
- Add shrimp and marinade and cook, stirring often, until shrimp turn pink.
- Stir in green onions.
- Serve over hot, cooked rice or your favorite pasta.

Broiled Lemon-Garlic Shrimp

1 pound shrimp, peeled, veined
1 teaspoon garlic salt
2 tablespoons lemon juice
2 tablespoons (¼ stick) butter

- Place shrimp in shallow baking pan.
- Sprinkle with garlic salt and lemon juice and dot with butter.
- Broil on 1 side for 3 minutes, turn and broil 3 minutes more.

TIP: If shrimp are large, split them down the middle and butterfly them before seasoning.

Creamed Shrimp Over Rice

3 (10 ounce) cans frozen cream of shrimp soup
1 pint sour cream
1½ teaspoons curry powder
2 (5 ounce) cans veined shrimp

- Combine all ingredients in double boiler.
- Heat and stir constantly but do not boil.
- Serve over hot, cooked rice.

Seafood Delight

1 (6 ounce) can shrimp, drained
1 (6 ounce) can crabmeat, drained, flaked
1 (10 ounce) can corn or potato chowder
2 to 3 cups dry, seasoned breadcrumbs, divided

- Mix shrimp, crabmeat, chowder and ⅓ cup breadcrumbs.
- Place mixture in prepared 1½-quart casserole dish and sprinkle with remaining breadcrumbs.
- Bake at 350° for 30 minutes or until casserole bubbles and breadcrumbs are light brown.

Crab Mornay

2 (6 ounce) cans crabmeat, drained
1 cup cream of mushroom soup
½ cup shredded Swiss cheese
½ cup seasoned breadcrumbs

- Combine crabmeat, soup and cheese and mix well.
- Pour into greased 1½-quart casserole dish and sprinkle with breadcrumbs.
- Bake uncovered at 350° for 30 minutes or until soup bubbles and breadcrumbs are brown.

Crabmeat Casserole

2 (6 ounce) cans crabmeat, drained, picked
1 (2.8 ounce) can french-fried onions, divided
1 (10 ounce) can cream of chicken soup
¾ cup cracker crumbs

- In bowl, combine crabmeat, half onions, soup and cracker crumbs and mix well.
- Place in buttered casserole dish and top with remaining onions.
- Bake covered at 350° for 30 minutes.

Baked Oysters

1 cup oysters, drained, rinsed
2 cups cracker crumbs
¼ cup (½ stick) butter, melted
½ cup milk

- Make alternating layers of oysters, cracker crumbs and butter in 7 x 11-inch baking dish.
- Pour warmed milk over layers and add lots of salt and pepper.
- Bake at 350° for 35 minutes.

Your Guide to Leftover Turkey, Chicken and Ham

Add 3 cups cooked, cubed chicken or turkey to Salads I–VIII.

Chicken or Turkey Salad I

⅔ cup chopped celery
¾ cup sweet pickle relish
1 bunch fresh green onions with tops, chopped
3 hard-boiled eggs, chopped
¾ cup mayonnaise

- Combine 3 cups chicken, celery, relish, onions and eggs.
- Toss with mayonnaise and refrigerate.
- Serve on lettuce leaves.

Chicken or Turkey Salad II

⅔ cup chopped celery
⅔ cup slivered almonds, toasted
2 small, firm bananas, sliced
1 (8 ounce) can pineapple tidbits, drained
¾ cup mayonnaise

- Combine 3 cups chicken, celery, almonds, bananas and pineapple and toss with mayonnaise.
- Refrigerate and serve on lettuce leaves.

Add 3 cups cooked, cubed chicken or turkey to Salads I–VIII.

Chicken or Turkey Salad III

1 cup chopped celery
1 cup tart green apple, peeled, cubed
1 (11 ounce) can mandarin oranges, drained
¾ cup chopped macadamia nuts
1 teaspoon curry powder
¾ cup mayonnaise

- Combine 3 cups chicken, celery, apple, oranges and nuts.
- Toss with curry powder and mayonnaise and refrigerate.
- Serve on lettuce leaves.

Chicken or Turkey Salad IV

1 cup chopped celery
1½ cups halved green grapes
¾ cup cashews
¾ cup mayonnaise
1 cup chow mein noodles

- Combine 3 cups chicken, celery, grapes and cashews and toss with mayonnaise.
- Just before serving, mix in noodles and serve on cabbage leaves.

Chicken or Turkey Salad V

⅔ cup chopped celery
½ cup chopped pecans
⅔ cup chopped sweet yellow bell pepper
1 bunch fresh green onions with tops, chopped
⅔ cup pickle relish
⅔ cup mayonnaise

- Combine 3 cups chicken, celery, pecans, bell pepper, onions and relish and toss with mayonnaise.
- Refrigerate and serve on shredded lettuce.

Add 3 cups cooked, cubed chicken or turkey to Salads I–VIII.

Chicken or Turkey Salad VI

⅔ cup chopped celery
1 (8 ounce) can sliced water chestnuts
1½ cups halved seedless red grapes
⅔ cup chopped pecans
¾ cup mayonnaise
½ teaspoon curry powder

- Combine 3 cups chicken, celery, water chestnuts, grapes and pecans.
- Toss with mayonnaise and curry powder and serve on cabbage leaves.

Chicken or Turkey Salad VII

1 (6 ounce) box long-grain, wild rice, cooked, drained
1 bunch fresh green onions with tops, chopped
1 cup chopped walnuts
1 (8 ounce) can sliced water chestnuts
1 cup mayonnaise
¾ teaspoon curry powder

- Combine 3 cups chicken, rice, onions, walnuts and water chestnuts.
- Toss with mayonnaise and curry powder and refrigerate.
- Serve on bed of lettuce.

Chicken or Turkey Salad VIII

⅔ cup chopped celery
1 (15 ounce) can pineapple tidbits, drained
¾ cup slivered almonds, toasted
¾ cup chopped red bell pepper
⅔ cup mayonnaise

- Combine 3 cups chicken, celery, pineapple, almonds and bell pepper, toss with mayonnaise and refrigerate.
- Serve on lettuce leaves.

Add 3 cups cooked, chopped chicken or turkey to Casseroles I–VI.

Chicken Casserole I

1 (16 ounce) package frozen broccoli florets, thawed
1 (10 ounce) can cream of chicken soup, diluted with ¼ cup water
⅔ cup mayonnaise
1 cup shredded cheddar cheese
1½ cups crushed cheese crackers

- Combine 3 cups chicken, broccoli, soup, mayonnaise and cheese and mix well.
- Pour into buttered 3-quart casserole dish and spread cheese crackers over top.
- Bake uncovered at 350° for 40 minutes.

Chicken Casserole II

1 (4 ounce) can sliced mushrooms, drained
1 (10 ounce) can cream of chicken soup, diluted with ¼ cup water
1 (8 ounce) carton sour cream
⅓ cup cooking sherry
1 (1 ounce) envelope dry onion soup mix

- Combine 3 cups chicken, mushrooms, soup, sour cream, sherry and onion soup mix and pour into buttered 3-quart casserole dish.
- Bake covered at 350° for 40 minutes and serve over hot rice.

Chicken Casserole III

1 (6.9 ounce) box chicken-flavored rice and macaroni
1 (10 ounce) can cream of mushroom soup
1 (10 ounce) can cream of celery soup
1 (10 ounce) package frozen peas, thawed
1 cup shredded cheddar cheese

- Cook rice and macaroni according to package directions.
- Combine 3 cups chicken, cooked rice and macaroni, soups, peas, cheese and ½ cup water and mix well.
- Pour into buttered 3-quart casserole dish and bake covered at 350° for 40 minutes.

Add 3 cups cooked, chopped chicken or turkey to Casseroles I–VI.

Chicken Casserole IV

1 (10 ounce) bag tortilla chips
1 onion, chopped
1 (10 ounce) can cream of chicken soup
1 (10 ounce) can tomatoes and green chiles
1 (16 ounce) package cubed processed cheese

- Place half tortilla chips in sprayed 9 x 13-inch baking dish and crush with palm.
- In large saucepan, combine onion, soup, tomatoes and chiles and cheese, heat on medium and stir until cheese melts.
- Add 3 cups chicken and pour over tortilla chips.
- Crush remaining tortilla chips in resealable plastic bag with rolling pin and sprinkle over chicken-cheese mixture.
- Bake uncovered at 350° about 40 minutes or until bubbly around edges.

Chicken Casserole V

2 (10 ounce) cans cream of mushroom soup
1 soup can milk
2 teaspoons curry powder
1 (4 ounce) can sliced mushrooms, drained
2½ cups cooked instant rice
3 bacon slices, fried, chopped

- In large saucepan, combine 3 cups chicken, soup, milk, curry powder, mushrooms, rice and bacon.
- Pour into sprayed 9 x 13-inch baking dish.
- Bake covered at 350° for 40 minutes.

Add 3 cups cooked, chopped chicken or turkey to Casseroles I–VI.

Chicken Casserole VI

1 (10 ounce) can cream of celery soup
1 (8 ounce) carton sour cream
1 (1 ounce) package dry onion soup mix
1 (8 ounce) can green peas, drained
2 cups cracker crumbs

- In large saucepan, combine 3 cups chicken, soup, sour cream and onion soup mix and heat just enough to mix well.
- Add green peas, spoon into buttered 3-quart baking dish and sprinkle crumbs over top of casserole.
- Bake uncovered at 350° for 35 minutes or until bubbly.

Use leftover turkey, chicken or ham.

Turkey (or Chicken) and Dressing Pie

1 (6 ounce) box stuffing mix
3 tablespoons butter, melted
2½ cups finely chopped, cooked turkey or chicken
1 cup shredded cheddar cheese
4 eggs, beaten
2 cups half-and-half cream

- Combine stuffing mix and butter and mix well.
- Press into bottom and sides of buttered 2-quart baking dish.
- Bake at 400° for 5 minutes and cool.
- Combine turkey and cheese and spread over dressing mixture in pan.
- Beat eggs and cream until well blended and pour over turkey mixture.
- Reduce heat to 325° and bake uncovered for 35 to 40 minutes or until set.

Use leftover turkey, chicken or ham.

Ranch Pasta and Turkey

1 (8 ounce) package pasta
½ cup (1 stick) butter
1 (1 ounce) packet dry ranch-style salad dressing mix
1 (15 ounce) can peas and carrots with liquid
3 cups cubed turkey or chicken

- Cook pasta according to directions on package.
- In saucepan, combine butter, dressing mix and peas and carrots and heat until butter melts.
- Toss with pasta and turkey and place in 2-quart casserole dish.
- Heat at 350° for about 20 minutes. (If you like, sprinkle some grated cheese over top after casserole bakes.)

Chicken (or Turkey) Jambalaya

1 (15 ounce) can stewed tomatoes with liquid
1 (1 ounce) package dry vegetable soup/dip mix
¾ teaspoon crushed red pepper
2 cups chopped chicken or turkey
1 cup ham, cut into julienne strips

- In large skillet, combine tomatoes, 2 cups water, soup mix and red pepper.
- Bring to a boil and stir well.
- Reduce heat, cover and simmer 15 minutes.
- Stir in chicken or turkey and ham, cook 5 minutes longer and serve over hot white rice.

Chicken-Broccoli Casserole

1 (10 ounce) can cream of chicken soup
¾ cup milk
3 cups diced, cooked chicken or turkey
1 (10 ounce) box frozen broccoli spears, thawed
1 (6 ounce) box chicken stuffing mix

- Heat soup and milk just enough to mix well and pour into greased 9 x 13-inch baking dish.
- Layer chicken over soup and place broccoli on top.
- Prepare stuffing mix according to package directions and spread over broccoli.
- Bake covered at 350° for 50 minutes.

Use leftover turkey, chicken or ham.

Golden Chicken (or Turkey) Casserole

2½ cups cooked, cubed chicken or turkey
1 (8 ounce) can pineapple chunks or tidbits, drained
½ cup apricot preserves
1 (10 ounce) can cream of chicken soup
1 (8 ounce) can sliced water chestnuts

- In bowl, combine all ingredients plus ⅓ cup water and mix well.
- Transfer to buttered 2-quart baking dish and bake uncovered at 350° for 35 minutes or until thoroughly heated.
- Serve over hot cooked rice.

Ham Salads

Add 3 cups cooked, chopped ham to Salads I–V.

Ham Salad I

½ cup chopped celery
1 bunch fresh green onions with tops, chopped
⅓ cup sweet pickle relish
1 teaspoon mustard
⅔ cup mayonnaise
1 (1.5 ounce) can shoe-string potato sticks

- Combine 3 cups ham, celery, onions and relish, toss with mustard and mayonnaise and refrigerate.
- When ready to serve, fold in potato sticks and serve on cabbage leaves.

Ham Salad II

1 bunch fresh green onions with tops, chopped
½ cup slivered almonds, toasted
½ cup sunflower seeds
2 cups chopped fresh broccoli florets
¾ cup mayonnaise

- Combine 3 cups ham, green onions, almonds, sunflower seeds and broccoli florets, toss with mayonnaise and refrigerate.
- Serve on lettuce leaves.

Add 3 cups cooked, chopped ham to Salads I–V.

Ham Salad III

1 (15 ounce) can pinto beans, drained
½ large purple onion, chopped
1 (11 ounce) can mexicorn, drained
1 cup chopped celery
About ½ to ¾ (8 ounce) bottle Italian salad dressing

- Combine 3 cups ham, beans, onion, corn and celery, toss with salad dressing and refrigerate.
- Serve on bed of shredded lettuce.

Ham Salad IV

¾ cup chopped celery
1 cup small-curd cottage cheese, drained
1 cup chopped cauliflower florets
1 cup chopped broccoli florets
Prepared honey mustard dressing

- Combine 3 cups ham, celery, cottage cheese, cauliflower and broccoli, toss with dressing and refrigerate.
- Serve on lettuce leaves.

Ham Salad V

⅔ cup chopped celery
1 (15 ounce) can English peas, drained
1 red bell pepper, chopped
8 ounces mozzarella cheese, cubed
¾ cup Garlic Mayonnaise (see page 148)

- Combine 3 cups ham, celery, peas, bell pepper and cheese, toss with Garlic Mayonnaise and refrigerate.
- Serve on cabbage leaves.

Ham-Potato Casserole

1 (24 ounce) package frozen hash browns with onions and peppers
3 cups cooked, cubed ham
1 (10 ounce) can cream of chicken soup
1 (10 ounce) can cream of celery soup
1 (8 ounce) package shredded cheddar cheese

- In large bowl, combine hash browns, ham, soups, ⅓ cup water and some salt and pepper.
- Spoon into sprayed 9 x 13-inch baking dish and bake covered at 350° for 40 minutes.
- Remove from oven, uncover, sprinkle cheese over casserole and bake another 5 minutes.

Ham-Broccoli Stromboli

1 (10 ounce) package refrigerated pizza dough
1 (10 ounce) package frozen chopped broccoli
1 (10 ounce) can cream of celery soup
3 cups diced, cooked ham
1 cup shredded cheddar cheese

- Unroll dough onto greased baking sheet and set aside.
- Cook broccoli according to package directions and drain.
- Mix broccoli, soup and ham. Spread ham mixture down center of dough and top with cheese.
- Fold long sides of dough over filling, pinch to seal and pinch short side to seal.
- Bake uncovered at 400° for 20 minutes or until golden brown.
- Slice and serve.

Ham 'n Cheese Mashed Potatoes

2 cups instant mashed potatoes
¾ teaspoon garlic powder
2 cups diced, cooked ham
1 (8 ounce) package shredded cheddar cheese
½ cup whipping cream

- In bowl, combine potatoes and garlic powder.
- Spread in buttered 2-quart baking dish and sprinkle with ham.
- Fold cheese into whipping cream and spoon over ham.
- Bake uncovered at 400° for 15 minutes or until golden brown.

Ham or Beef Spread

2 cups cooked ham or roast beef
¾ cup sweet pickle relish
2 celery ribs, finely chopped
2 hard-boiled eggs, chopped
½ onion, finely chopped
Mayonnaise

- Chop meat in food processor, add relish, celery, eggs and onion and add a little salt and pepper.
- Fold in enough mayonnaise to make mixture spreadable and refrigerate.
- Spread on crackers or bread for sandwiches.

Desserts

Special Desserts

Cakes

Pies & Cobblers

Cookies, Bars
& Brownies

Candies

Amaretto Ice Cream

1 (8 ounce) carton whipping cream, whipped
1 pint vanilla ice cream, softened
⅓ cup amaretto liqueur
⅓ cup chopped almonds, toasted

- Combine whipped cream, ice cream and amaretto and freeze in sherbet glasses.
- When ready to serve, drizzle a little additional amaretto over top of each individual serving and sprinkle with toasted almonds.

Amaretto Peaches

4½ cups peeled, sliced fresh peaches
½ cup amaretto liqueur
½ cup sour cream
½ cup packed brown sugar

- Lay peaches in 2-quart baking dish.
- Pour amaretto over peaches and spread with sour cream.
- Sprinkle brown sugar evenly over all.
- Broil mixture until it heats thoroughly and sugar melts.
- Serve over ice cream or pound cake.

Amaretto Sauce for Pound Cake

1 (3.4 ounce) package French vanilla pudding (not instant)
1 cup milk
1 (8 ounce) carton whipping cream, whipped
¼ cup amaretto liqueur

- Cook pudding with milk according to package directions.
- Cover and cool to room temperature.
- With wire whisk, stir in whipped cream and amaretto.
- Pour over pound cake (or vanilla ice cream).

Baked Custard

3 cups milk
3 eggs
¾ cup sugar
¼ teaspoon salt
1 teaspoon vanilla extract

- Preheat oven to 350°.
- Scald milk.
- Beat eggs and add sugar, salt and vanilla.
- Slowly add scalded milk to egg mixture.
- Pour into 2-quart baking dish and sprinkle a little cinnamon on top. Bake at 350° in hot water bath for 45 minutes.

Fun Fruit Fajitas

1 (20 ounce) can cherry pie filling
8 large flour tortillas
1½ cups sugar
¾ cup (1½ sticks) butter
1 teaspoon almond flavoring

- Divide fruit equally on tortillas, roll up and place in 9 x 13-inch baking dish.
- Mix sugar and butter in saucepan with 2 cups water and bring to boil.
- Add almond flavoring and pour sugar mixture over flour tortillas.
- Place in refrigerator and soak 1 to 24 hours.
- Bake at 350° for 20 minutes or until brown and bubbly. Serve hot or room temperature.

TIP: Use any flavor of pie filling you like.

Divine Strawberries

1 quart fresh strawberries
1 (20 ounce) can pineapple chunks, well drained
2 bananas, sliced
1 (18 ounce) carton strawberry glaze

- Cut strawberries in half (or in quarters if strawberries are very large).
- Add pineapple chunks and bananas.
- Fold in strawberry glaze and refrigerate.

TIP: This is wonderful over pound cake or just served in sherbet glasses.

Brandied Apples

1 (12 ounce) loaf pound cake
1 (20 ounce) can apple pie filling
½ teaspoon allspice
2 tablespoons brandy
Vanilla ice cream

- Slice pound cake and place on dessert plates.
- In saucepan, combine pie filling, allspice and brandy. Heat and stir just until heated thoroughly.
- Place several spoonfuls pie filling mixture over cake and top with scoop of vanilla ice cream.

Brandied Apple Topping

1 (20 ounce) can apple pie filling
¼ teaspoon allspice
¼ teaspoon cinnamon
4½ tablespoons brandy

- Pour apple pie filling onto dinner plate or into shallow bowl and cut apple slices into smaller chunks.
- Place pie filling, allspice, cinnamon and brandy in saucepan and cook over medium heat for 5 minutes.
- Pour topping over pound cake or vanilla ice cream.

Brandied Fruit

2 (20 ounce) cans crushed pineapple
1 (16 ounce) can sliced peaches
2 (11 ounce) cans mandarin oranges
1 (10 ounce) jar maraschino cherries
Sugar
1 cup brandy

- Let all fruit drain for 12 hours.
- For every cup of drained fruit, add ½ cup sugar. Let stand for 12 hours.
- Add brandy, spoon into large jar and store in refrigerator for 3 weeks.
- Serve over ice cream.

Blueberry Fluff

1 (20 ounce) can blueberry pie filling
1 (20 ounce) can crushed pineapple, drained
1 (14 ounce) can sweetened condensed milk
1 (8 ounce) carton whipped topping, thawed

- Mix pie filling, pineapple and condensed milk.
- Fold in whipped topping. (This dessert is even better if you add ¾ cup chopped pecans.)
- Pour into parfait glasses and refrigerate.

White Velvet

1 (8 ounce) carton whipping cream
1½ teaspoons unflavored gelatin
⅓ cup sugar
1 (8 ounce) carton sour cream
¾ teaspoon rum flavoring

- Heat cream over moderate heat.
- Soak gelatin in ¼ cup cold water.
- When cream is hot, stir in sugar and gelatin until they dissolve and remove from heat.
- Fold in sour cream and rum flavoring.
- Pour into individual molds, cover with plastic wrap and refrigerate.
- Unmold to serve. Serve with fresh fruit.

Blueberry-Angel Dessert

1 (8 ounce) package cream cheese, softened
1 cup powdered sugar
1 (8 ounce) carton whipped topping, thawed
1 (14 ounce) prepared angel food cake
2 (20 ounce) cans blueberry pie filling

- In large mixing bowl, beat cream cheese and sugar and fold in whipped topping.
- Tear cake into small 1 or 2-inch cubes and fold into cream cheese mixture.
- Spread mixture evenly in 9 x 13-inch dish and top with pie filling.
- Cover and refrigerate for at least 3 hours before cutting into squares to serve.

Caramel-Amaretto Dessert

1 (9 ounce) bag small chocolate-covered toffee candy bars, crumbled
30 caramels
⅓ cup amaretto liqueur
½ cup sour cream
1 cup whipping cream

- Reserve about ⅓ cup crumbled toffee bars.
- In buttered 7 x 11-inch dish, spread remaining candy crumbs.
- In saucepan, melt caramels with amaretto and cool to room temperature.
- Stir in creams, whip until thick and pour into individual dessert dishes.
- Top with reserved candy crumbs, cover and freeze.

Grasshopper Dessert

26 chocolate sandwich cookies, crushed
¼ cup (½ stick) butter, melted
¼ cup creme de menthe liqueur
2 (7 ounce) jars marshmallow cream
2 (8 ounce) cartons whipping cream

- Reserve about ⅓ cup crumbs for topping.
- Combine remaining cookie crumbs and butter and press into bottom of greased 9-inch springform pan.
- Gradually add creme de menthe to marshmallow cream.
- Whip cream until very thick and fold into marshmallow cream mixture. Pour over crumbs in pan.
- Sprinkle reserved cookie crumbs on top and freeze.

Ice Cream Dessert

19 ice cream sandwiches
1 (12 ounce) carton whipped topping, thawed, divided
1 (12 ounce) jar hot fudge ice cream topping
1 cup salted peanuts, divided

- Cut 1 ice cream sandwich in half. Place 1 whole and 1 half sandwich along short side of ungreased 9 x 13-inch pan.
- Arrange 8 sandwiches in opposite direction in pan.
- Spread with half whipped topping.
- Spoon fudge topping by teaspoonfuls onto whipped topping and sprinkle with ½ cup peanuts.
- Layer with remaining ice cream sandwiches, whipped topping and peanuts. (Pan will be full.)
- Cover and freeze. Take out of freezer 20 minutes before serving.

Lime-Angel Dessert

1 (6 ounce) package lime gelatin
1 (20 ounce) can crushed pineapple with juice
1 tablespoon lime juice
1 tablespoon sugar
1 (8 ounce) cartons whipping cream, whipped
1 (14 ounce) angel food cake

- Dissolve gelatin in 1 cup boiling water and mix well.
- Stir in pineapple, lime juice and sugar.
- Cool in refrigerator until mixture thickens.
- Fold in whipped cream.
- Break cake into pieces and place in 9 x 13-inch dish.
- Pour gelatin mixture over cake and refrigerate overnight.
- Cut into squares to serve.

Orange-Cream Dessert

2 cups (about 20) crushed chocolate sandwich cookies
⅓ cup (⅔ stick) butter, melted
1 (6 ounce) package orange gelatin
1½ cups boiling water
½ gallon vanilla ice cream, softened

- In bowl, combine cookie crumbs and butter and set aside ¼ cup crumb mixture for topping.
- Press remaining crumb mixture into greased 9 x 13-inch dish.
- In large bowl, dissolve gelatin in boiling water, cover and refrigerate for 30 minutes.
- Blend ice cream and gelatin until smooth. Work fast.
- Pour ice cream mixture over crust and sprinkle with reserved crumb mixture.
- Freeze and remove from freezer 10 or 15 minutes before serving.

Strawberry-Angel Dessert

1 (6 ounce) package strawberry gelatin
2 (10 ounce) cartons frozen strawberries with juice
2 (8 ounce) carton whipping cream, whipped
1 (14 ounce) large angel food cake

- Dissolve gelatin in 1 cup boiling water and mix well.
- Stir in strawberries and cool in refrigerator until mixture begins to thicken.
- Fold in whipped cream.
- Break cake into pieces and place in 9 x 13-inch dish.
- Pour gelatin mixture over cake and refrigerate overnight.
- Cut into squares to serve.

Butterscotch Finale

1 (16 ounce) carton whipping cream
¾ cup butterscotch ice cream topping
1 (14 ounce) angel food cake
¾ pound toffee bars, crushed, divided

- In mixing bowl, whip cream until thick.
- Slowly add butterscotch topping and continue to beat until mixture is thick.
- Slice cake into 3 equal horizontal layers.
- Place bottom layer on cake plate, spread with 1½ cups whipped cream mixture and sprinkle with one-fourth crushed toffee.
- Repeat layers and frost top and sides of cake with remaining whipped cream mixture.
- Sprinkle toffee over top of cake. Refrigerate for at least 8 hours before serving.

Caramel-Apple Delight

3 (2.07 ounce) Snickers candy bars, frozen
2 Granny Smith apples, chopped
1 (12 ounce) carton whipped topping, thawed
1 (3.4 ounce) package dry instant vanilla pudding mix

- Smash frozen candy bars in wrappers with hammer.
- Combine all ingredients and mix well. Refrigerate.

TIP: Place in a pretty crystal bowl or serve in individual sherbet glasses.

Cherry Trifle

1 (12 ounce) pound cake
⅓ cup amaretto
2 (20 ounce) cans cherry pie filling
4 cups vanilla pudding
1 (8 ounce) carton whipped topping, thawed

- Cut cake into 1-inch slices.
- Line bottom of 3-quart trifle bowl with cake and brush with amaretto.
- Top with 1 cup pie filling followed by 1 cup pudding. Repeat layers 3 times.
- Top with whipped topping and refrigerate several hours.

Cinnamon Cream

1 (14.4 ounce) box cinnamon graham crackers
2 (5 ounce) packages instant French vanilla pudding mix
3 cups milk
1 (8 ounce) carton whipped topping, thawed
1 (18 ounce) can prepared caramel frosting

- Line bottom of 9 x 13-inch casserole dish with graham crackers. (You will use ⅓ graham crackers.)
- With mixer, combine vanilla pudding and milk and whip until thick and creamy. Fold in whipped topping.
- Pour half pudding mixture over graham crackers.
- Top with another layer of graham crackers and add remaining pudding mixture.
- Top with final layer of graham crackers. (You will have a few crackers left.) Spread frosting over last layer of graham crackers and refrigerate overnight.

TIP: *This dessert must be made the day before serving.*

Coffee Mallow

3 cups miniature marshmallows
½ cup hot, strong coffee
1 cup whipping cream, whipped
½ teaspoon vanilla

- In large saucepan, combine marshmallows and coffee.
- On low heat, stir constantly and cook until marshmallows melt. Cool mixture.
- Fold in whipped cream and vanilla and stir.
- Pour into individual dessert glasses.

Coffee Surprise

This is a super dessert – no slicing, no "dishing up" – just bring it right from the fridge to the table.

1 cup strong coffee
1 (10 ounce) package large marshmallows
1 (8 ounce) package chopped dates
1¼ cups chopped pecans
1 (8 ounce) carton whipping cream, whipped

- Melt marshmallows in hot coffee.
- Add dates and pecans and refrigerate.
- When mixture thickens, fold in whipped cream.
- Pour into sherbet glasses. Place plastic wrap over top and refrigerate.

Candy Store Pudding

A special family dessert!

1 cup cold milk
1 (3.9 ounce) package instant chocolate pudding mix
1 (8 ounce) carton whipped topping, thawed
1 cup miniature marshmallows
½ cup chopped salted peanuts

- In bowl, whisk milk and pudding mix for 2 minutes.
- Fold in whipped topping, marshmallows and peanuts.
- Spoon into individual dessert dishes, place plastic wrap over top and refrigerate.

Creamy Banana Pudding

This is a quick and easy way to make the old favorite banana pudding.

1 (14 ounce) can sweetened condensed milk
1 (3.4 ounce) package instant vanilla pudding mix
1 (8 ounce) carton whipped topping, thawed
36 vanilla wafers
3 bananas

- In large bowl, combine condensed milk and 1½ cups cold water.
- Add pudding mix and beat well.
- Refrigerate 5 minutes then fold in whipped topping.
- Spoon 1 cup pudding mixture into 3-quart glass serving bowl. Top with wafers, bananas and pudding. Repeat layers twice and end with pudding.
- Cover and refrigerate.

Grape Fluff

1 cup grape juice
2 cups miniature marshmallows
2 tablespoons lemon juice
1 (8 ounce) carton whipping cream. whipped

- In saucepan, heat grape juice to boiling.
- Add marshmallows and stir constantly until they melt.
- Add lemon juice and cool.
- Fold in whipped cream and spoon into individual serving dishes. Refrigerate.

Kahlua Mousse

Light but rich and absolutely delicious!

1 (12 ounce) carton whipped topping, thawed
2 teaspoons dry instant coffee granules
5 teaspoons cocoa
5 tablespoons sugar
½ cup Kahlua® liqueur

- In large bowl, combine whipped topping, coffee, cocoa and sugar and blend well.
- Fold in Kahlua® and spoon into sherbet dessert glasses.
- Place plastic wrap over dessert glasses until ready to serve.

Mango Cream

2 soft mangoes
½ gallon vanilla ice cream, softened
1 (6 ounce) can frozen lemonade concentrate, thawed
1 (8 ounce) carton whipped topping, thawed

- Peel mangoes, cut slices around seeds and cut into small chunks.
- In large bowl, mix ice cream, lemonade and whipped topping and fold in mango chunks.
- Quickly spoon mixture into parfait or sherbet glasses and cover with plastic wrap.
- Freeze.

Oreo Sundae

A kids' favorite!

½ cup (1 stick) butter
1 (19 ounce) package chocolate sandwich cookies, crushed, divided
½ gallon vanilla ice cream, softened
2 (12 ounce) jars hot fudge topping
1 (12 ounce) carton whipped topping, thawed

- Melt butter in 9 x 13-inch pan.
- Reserve about ½ cup crushed cookies for top and mix remaining cookie crumbs with butter to form crust. Press crumbs into pan.
- Spread softened ice cream over crust (work fast) and add fudge sauce on top.
- Top with whipped topping and sprinkle with remaining cookie crumbs. Freeze.

Peachy Sundaes

1 pint vanilla ice cream
¾ cup peach preserves, warmed
¼ cup chopped almonds, toasted
¼ cup flaked coconut

- Divide ice cream into 4 sherbet dishes.
- Top with preserves.
- Sprinkle with almonds and coconut.

Peanut Butter Sundae

1 cup light corn syrup
1 cup chunky peanut butter
¼ cup milk
Ice cream or pound cake

- In mixing bowl, stir corn syrup, peanut butter and milk until they blend well.
- Serve over ice cream or pound cake.
- Store in refrigerator.

Strawberry Trifle

1 (5 ounce) package instant French vanilla pudding mix
1 (12 ounce) loaf pound cake
2 cups fresh strawberries, sliced
½ cup sherry
Whipped topping, thawed

- Prepare pudding according to package directions.
- Place layer of pound cake slices in 8-inch crystal bowl and sprinkle with ¼ cup sherry.
- Layer half of strawberries and half pudding on top.
- Repeat layers and refrigerate overnight or several hours.
- Before serving, top with whipped topping.

Twinkies Dessert

1 (10 count) box Twinkies®
4 bananas, sliced
1 (5 ounce) package vanilla instant pudding mix
1 (20 ounce) can crushed pineapple, drained
1 (8 ounce) carton whipped topping, thawed

- Slice Twinkies in half lengthwise and place in buttered 9 x 13-inch pan cream side up.
- Make layer of sliced bananas.
- Prepare pudding according to package directions (use 2 cups milk).
- Pour over bananas and add pineapple.
- Top with whipped topping and refrigerate.
- Cut into squares to serve.

Individual Meringues

1 (1 pound) box powdered sugar
6 egg whites, room temperature
1 teaspoon cream of tartar
½ teaspoon vanilla extract
1 teaspoon vinegar

- Preheat oven to 250°.
- With mixer, beat sugar and egg whites at high speed for 10 minutes.
- Add cream of tartar, vanilla and vinegar and beat another 10 minutes.
- Spoon individual meringues on greased baking sheet and bake at 250° for 15 minutes.
- Raise temperature to 300° and bake another 12 minutes.
- Remove immediately from baking sheet and store between sheets of wax paper in tightly closed containers.

Pavlova

3 large egg whites
1 cup sugar
1 teaspoon vanilla extract
2 teaspoons white vinegar
3 tablespoons cornstarch

- Preheat oven to 300°.
- Beat egg whites until stiff and add 3 tablespoons COLD water.
- Beat again and add sugar very gradually while beating.
- Continue beating slowly and add vanilla, vinegar and cornstarch.
- On parchment-covered baking sheet, draw 9-inch circle and mound mixture within circle.
- Bake at 300° for 45 minutes. LEAVE in oven to cool.
- To serve, peel paper from bottom while sliding Pavlova onto serving plate. Cover with whipped cream and top with assortment of fresh fruit such as kiwi, strawberries, blueberries, etc.

Chocolate Pudding Cake

1 (18 ounce) box milk chocolate cake mix
1¼ cups milk
⅓ cup oil
3 eggs

- Preheat oven to 350°.
- In mixing bowl, combine all ingredients and beat well.
- Pour into greased 9 x 13-inch baking pan.
- Bake at 350° for 35 minutes or until cake tester comes out clean.

Frosting for Chocolate Pudding Cake:

1 (14 ounce) can sweetened condensed milk
¾ (16 ounce) can chocolate syrup
1 (8 ounce) carton whipped topping, thawed
⅓ cup chopped pecans

- In small bowl, combine condensed milk and chocolate syrup and mix well.
- Pour frosting over cake and let soak.
- Refrigerate for several hours.
- Spread whipped topping over cake and sprinkle pecans over top. Refrigerate.

Chocolate-Cherry Cake

This is a chocolate lover's dream.

1 (18 ounce) milk chocolate cake mix
1 (20 ounce) can cherry pie filling
3 eggs

- Preheat oven to 350°.
- In mixing bowl, combine cake mix, pie filling and eggs.
- Mix by hand and pour into greased, floured 9 x 13-inch baking dish.
- Bake at 350° for 35 to 40 minutes. Test with toothpick for doneness.
- Spread Chocolate-Cherry Cake Frosting over hot cake.

Chocolate-Cherry Cake Frosting:

5 tablespoons (⅔ stick) butter
1¼ cups sugar
½ cup milk
1 (6 ounce) package chocolate chips

- When cake is done, combine butter, sugar and milk in medium saucepan.
- Boil 1 minute and stir constantly.
- Add chocolate chips and stir until chips melt.
- Pour over hot cake.

Golden Rum Cake

1 (18 ounce) box yellow cake mix with pudding
3 eggs
⅓ cup oil
½ cup rum
1 cup chopped pecans

- Preheat oven to 325°.
- Blend cake mix, eggs, 1⅓ cups water, oil and rum with mixer.
- Stir in pecans and pour into greased, floured 10-inch tube or bundt pan.
- Bake for 1 hour.
- If you like, sprinkle powdered sugar over cooled cake.

Chocolate-Orange Cake

1 (16 ounce) loaf frozen pound cake, thawed
1 (12 ounce) jar orange marmalade
1 (16 ounce) can ready-to-spread chocolate-fudge frosting

- Cut cake horizontally into 3 equal layers.
- Place 1 layer on cake platter and spread with half marmalade.
- Place second layer over first and spread with remaining marmalade.
- Top with third cake layer and spread frosting liberally on top and sides of cake.
- Refrigerate.

Oreo Cake

1 (18 ounce) box white cake mix
⅓ cup oil
4 egg whites
1¼ cup coarsely chopped Oreo cookies

- Preheat oven to 350°.
- In mixing bowl, combine cake mix, oil, egg whites and 1¼ cups water.
- Blend on low speed until moist and then beat for 2 minutes at high speed.
- Gently fold in coarsely chopped cookies and pour batter into 2 greased, floured 8-inch round cake pans.
- Bake for 25 to 30 minutes or until toothpick inserted in center comes out clean.
- Cool for 15 minutes and remove from pan. Cool completely and frost.

Frosting for Oreo Cake:

4¼ cups powdered sugar
1 cup (2 sticks) butter, softened
1 cup shortening
1 teaspoon almond flavoring

- With mixer, combine all frosting ingredients and beat until creamy.
- Frost first layer of cake, place second layer on top and frost top and sides.
- Sprinkle with extra crushed Oreo cookies on top.

TIP: Do not use butter-flavored shortening.

Coconut Cake Deluxe

This is a fabulous cake!

1 (18 ounce) box yellow cake mix
1 (14 ounce) can sweetened condensed milk
1 (15 ounce) can coconut cream
1 (3 ounce) can flaked coconut
1 (8 ounce) carton whipped topping, thawed

- Preheat oven to 350°.
- Mix cake mix according to package directions.
- Pour batter into greased, floured 9 x 13-inch baking pan and bake for 30 to 35 minutes or until toothpick inserted in center comes out clean.
- While cake is warm, punch holes in cake about 2 inches apart.
- Pour sweetened condensed milk over cake and spread until all milk soaks into cake.
- Pour coconut cream over cake and sprinkle with coconut.
- Cool, frost with whipped topping and refrigerate.

Gooey Butter Cake

4 eggs, divided
1 (18 ounce) box butter cake mix
½ cup (1 stick) butter, melted
1 (16 ounce) box powdered sugar
1 (8 ounce) package cream cheese, softened

- Preheat oven to 350°.
- With mixer, beat 2 eggs with cake mix and butter and spread mixture into greased, floured 9 x-13 inch baking pan.
- Reserve ¾ cup powdered sugar for topping. Mix remaining powdered sugar, 2 remaining eggs and cream cheese and beat until smooth.
- Spread mixture on top of batter and sprinkle remaining powdered sugar on top.
- Bake for 40 minutes. Cake will puff up and then go down when it cools.

Poppy Seed Bundt Cake

1 (18 ounce) box yellow cake mix
1 (3.4 ounce) package instant coconut cream pudding mix
½ cup oil
3 eggs
2 tablespoons poppy seeds

- Preheat oven to 350°.
- In mixing bowl, combine cake and pudding mixes, oil, eggs and 1 cup water and beat on low speed until moist.
- Beat on medium speed for 2 minutes.
- Stir in poppy seeds and pour into greased, floured bundt pan.
- Bake for 50 minutes or until toothpick inserted near the center comes out clean.
- Cool for 10 minutes, remove from pan and dust with powdered sugar.

Pecan Cake

1 (18 ounce) box butter pecan cake mix
½ cup (1 stick) butter, melted
1 egg
1 cup chopped pecans

- Combine cake mix, butter, egg and ¾ cup water.
- Mix well and stir in pecans.
- Pour into 9 x 13-inch baking dish.

Topping for Pecan Cake:

1 (8 ounce) package cream cheese, softened
2 eggs
1 (16 ounce) box powdered sugar

- Use mixer to combine all topping ingredients.
- Pour over cake mixture and bake at 350° for 40 minutes or until toothpick inserted in center of cake comes out clean.

Pound Cake

1 cup (2 sticks) butter, softened
2 cups sugar
5 eggs
2 cups flour
1 tablespoon almond flavoring

- Preheat oven to 325°.
- Combine all ingredients in mixing bowl and beat for 10 minutes at medium speed.
- Pour into greased, floured tube pan. (Batter will be very thick.)
- Bake for 1 hour. Test with toothpick for doneness.

TIP: If you would like a sauce for this cake, there's a wonderful recipe for Amaretto Sauce for Pound Cake on page 272.

Pound Cake Deluxe

1 (14 ounce) bakery pound cake
1 (20 ounce) can crushed pineapple with juice
1 (3.4 ounce) package instant coconut cream pudding mix
1 (8 ounce) carton whipped topping, thawed
½ cup flaked coconut

- Slice cake horizontally into 3 equal layers.
- Mix pineapple, pudding mix and whipped topping and blend well.
- Spread on each cake layer and over top.
- Sprinkle top of cake with coconut and refrigerate.

Strawberry Pound Cake

1 (18 ounce) box strawberry cake mix
1 (3.4 ounce) package instant pineapple pudding mix
⅓ cup oil
4 eggs
1 (3 ounce) package strawberry gelatin

- Preheat oven to 325°.
- Mix all ingredients plus 1 cup water and beat for 2 minutes at medium speed.
- Pour into greased, floured bundt pan.
- Bake for 55 to 60 minutes. Cake is done when toothpick comes out clean.
- Cool for 20 minutes before removing cake from pan. If you would like an icing, use commercial vanilla icing.

TIP: If you like coconut better than pineapple, use coconut cream pudding mix.

O'Shaughnessy's Special

1 (14 ounce) pound cake loaf
1 (15 ounce) can crushed pineapple with juice
1 (3.4 ounce) package pistachio pudding mix
1 (8 ounce) carton whipped topping, thawed

- Slice cake horizontally into 3 equal layers.
- Combine pineapple and pudding mix and beat until mixture begins to thicken.
- Fold in whipped topping and blend well. (You may add a few drops of green food coloring if you would like the cake to be a brighter green.)
- Spread pineapple mixture on each cake layer and on top. Refrigerate.

Blueberry Pound Cake

1 (18 ounce) box yellow cake mix
1 (8 ounce) package cream cheese, softened
½ cup oil
4 eggs
1 (15 ounce) can whole blueberries, drained
Powdered sugar

- Preheat oven to 350°.
- With mixer, combine all ingredients and beat for 3 minutes.
- Pour batter into greased, floured bundt or tube pan.
- Bake for 50 minutes. Test with toothpick to be sure cake is done.
- Sprinkle powdered sugar over top of cake.

Chess Cake

    1 (18 ounce) box yellow cake mix
    2 eggs
    ½ cup (1 stick) butter, softened
- Preheat oven to 350°.
- Beat cake mix, 2 eggs and butter and press into greased 9 x 13-inch baking pan.

Topping for Chess Cake:

    2 eggs
    1 (8 ounce) package cream cheese, softened
    1 (1 pound) box powdered sugar
- Beat 2 eggs, cream cheese and powdered sugar and pour over cake.
- Bake for 35 minutes.

Two-Surprise Cake

The first surprise is how easy it is and the second surprise is how good it is! You'll make this more than once.

    1 bakery orange-chiffon cake
    1 (15 ounce) can crushed pineapple with juice
    1 (3.4 ounce) package vanilla instant pudding mix
    1 (8 ounce) carton whipped topping, thawed
    ½ cup slivered almonds, toasted
- Slice cake horizontally into 3 equal layers.
- Mix pineapple, pudding mix and whipped topping and blend well.
- Spread pineapple mixture on each cake layer and cover top of cake. Sprinkle almonds on top and refrigerate.

Fruit Cocktail Cake

2 cups sugar
2 cups flour
1 teaspoon baking soda
2 (15 ounce) cans fruit cocktail, divided

- Preheat oven to 350°.
- Use mixer to combine sugar, flour, baking soda and 1 can fruit cocktail with juice. Drain other can fruit cocktail and add half fruit to sugar mixture. (Reserve half can fruit cocktail.)
- Beat several minutes with mixer (fruit will be chopped up).
- Pour into greased, floured 9 x 13-inch baking pan and bake for 30 to 33 minutes. Test with toothpick to make sure cake is done.
- While cake is cooking, prepare icing.

Fruit Cocktail Cake Icing:

1 (8 ounce) package cream cheese, softened
½ cup (1 stick) butter, softened
Coconut
Powdered sugar
Reserved fruit cocktail

- Combine cream cheese and butter and beat until creamy.
- Add coconut, powdered sugar and reserved fruit.
- Beat several minutes until fruit chops well and pour mixture over hot cake.
- When cool, store in refrigerator.

TIP: *Pecans can be substituted for coconut.*

Cherry-Pineapple Cake

1 (20 ounce) can crushed pineapple, drained
1 (20 ounce) can cherry pie filling
1 (18 ounce) box yellow cake mix
1 cup (2 sticks) butter, softened
1¼ cups chopped pecans

- Preheat oven to 350°.
- Place all ingredients in mixing bowl and mix by hand.
- Pour into greased, floured 9 x 13-inch baking dish.
- Bake for 1 hour 10 minutes.

Hawaiian Dream Cake

This looks like a lot of trouble to make, but it really isn't. And it is a wonderful cake!

1 (18 ounce) box yellow cake mix
4 eggs
¾ cup oil
½ (20 ounce) can crushed pineapple with half juice

- Preheat oven to 350°.
- With mixer, beat all ingredients for 4 minutes.
- Pour into greased, floured 9 x 13-inch baking pan.
- Bake for 30 to 35 minutes or until cake tests done with toothpick. Cool and spread Coconut-Pineapple Icing over cake.

Coconut-Pineapple Icing:

½ (20 ounce) can crushed pineapple with juice
½ cup (1 stick) butter
1 (16 ounce) box powdered sugar
1 (6 ounce) can flaked coconut

- Heat pineapple and butter and boil for 2 minutes.
- Add powdered sugar and coconut.
- Punch holes in cake with knife and pour hot icing over cake.

Easy Pineapple Cake

2 cups sugar
2 cups flour
1 (20 ounce) can crushed pineapple with juice
1 teaspoon baking soda

- Preheat oven to 350°.
- Combine all cake ingredients and mix by hand.
- Pour into greased, floured 9 x 13-inch baking pan.
- Bake for 30 to 35 minutes.

Easy Pineapple Cake Icing:

1 (8 ounce) package cream cheese, softened
½ cup (1 stick) butter, melted
1 cup powdered sugar
1 cup chopped pecans

- Combine cream cheese, butter and powdered sugar and beat with mixer.
- Add chopped pecans and pour over hot cake.

Cherry Cake

1 (18 ounce) box French vanilla cake mix
½ cup (1 stick) butter, melted
2 eggs
1 (20 ounce) can cherry pie filling
1 cup chopped pecans

- Preheat oven to 350°.
- In large bowl, mix all ingredients by hand.
- Pour into greased, floured bundt or tube pan.
- Bake for 1 hour.
- Sprinkle powdered sugar on top of cake if you like.

Miracle Cake

1 (18 ounce) box lemon cake mix
3 eggs
⅓ cup oil
1 (20 ounce) can crushed pineapple with juice

- Preheat oven to 350°.
- In mixing bowl, combine all cake ingredients, blend on low speed and beat on medium for 2 minutes.
- Pour batter into greased, floured 9 x 13-inch baking dish.
- Bake for 30 to 35 minutes until cake tests done with toothpick.

Miracle Cake Topping:

1 (14 ounce) can sweetened condensed milk
¼ cup lemon juice
1 (8 ounce) carton whipped topping, thawed

- Blend all topping ingredients and mix well.
- Spread topping over cake and refrigerate.

Apple Cake

1 (18 ounce) box spiced cake mix
1 (20 ounce) can apple pie filling
2 eggs
½ cup chopped walnuts

- Preheat oven to 350°.
- Combine all ingredients and mix very thoroughly with spoon until all lumps from cake mix are gone.
- Pour into greased, floured bundt pan.
- Bake for 50 minutes. Check with toothpick for doneness.

TIP: You may substitute any other pie filling for this cake.

Lemon-Pineapple Cake

1 (18 ounce) box lemon cake mix
1 (20 ounce) can crushed pineapple with juice
3 eggs
⅓ cup oil

- Preheat oven to 350°.
- In mixing bowl, combine all cake ingredients. Blend on low speed to moisten and beat on medium for 2 minutes.
- Pour batter into greased, floured 9 x 13-inch baking pan.
- Bake for 30 minutes. Test with toothpick to be sure cake is done. (While cake is baking, prepare topping for cake.) Cool for 15 minutes.

Lemon-Pineapple Cake Topping:

1 (14 ounce) can sweetened condensed milk
1 cup sour cream
¼ cup lemon juice

- In medium bowl, combine all topping ingredients. Stir well to blend.
- Pour over warm cake. Refrigerate.

Fluffy Orange Cake

1 (18 ounce) box orange cake mix
4 eggs
⅔ cup oil
½ cup water

- Preheat oven to 350°.
- In mixing bowl, combine all cake ingredients.
- Beat on low speed to blend and beat on medium speed for 2 minutes.
- Pour into greased, floured 9 x 13-inch baking pan.
- Bake for 30 minutes or until cake tests done. Cool.

Fluffy Orange Cake Topping:

1 (14 ounce) can sweetened condensed milk
⅓ cup lemon juice
1 (8 ounce) carton whipped topping, thawed
2 (11 ounce) cans mandarin oranges, drained, halved, chilled

- In large bowl, blend condensed milk and lemon juice and mix well.
- Fold in whipped topping and orange slices and blend well.
- Pour mixture over cool cake, cover and refrigerate.

Delightful Pear Cake

1 (15 ounce) can pears in light syrup with juice
1 (18 ounce) box white cake mix
2 egg whites
1 egg

- Preheat oven to 350°.
- Drain pears, save liquid and chop pears.
- Place pears and liquid in mixing bowl and add cake mix, egg whites and egg.
- Beat on low speed for 30 seconds. Beat on high for 4 minutes.
- Pour batter into greased, floured 10-inch bundt pan.
- Bake for 50 to 55 minutes or until toothpick inserted in center comes out clean.
- Cool in pan for 10 minutes, remove cake and dust with sifted powdered sugar.

Quick Fruitcake

1 (15 ounce) package cranberry or blueberry quick-bread mix
½ cup chopped pecans
½ cup chopped dates
¼ cup chopped maraschino cherries
¼ cup crushed pineapple, drained

- Preheat oven to 350°.
- Prepare quick-bread batter according to package directions.
- Stir in pecans, dates, cherries and pineapple and pour into greased 9 x 5-inch loaf pan.
- Bake for 60 minutes or until toothpick inserted in cake comes out clean.
- Cool 10 minutes before removing from pan.

Old-Fashioned Applesauce Spice Cake

1 (18 ounce) box spice cake mix
3 eggs
1¼ cups applesauce
⅓ cup oil
1 cup chopped pecans

- Preheat oven to 350°.
- With mixer, combine cake mix, eggs, applesauce and oil and beat at medium speed for 2 minutes.
- Stir in pecans and pour into greased, floured 9 x 13-inch baking pan.
- Bake for 40 minutes. Test until toothpick comes out clean. Cool.
- For frosting, use prepared vanilla frosting and add ½ teaspoon cinnamon.

Coconut-Angel Cake

1 (14 ounce) round angel food cake
1 (20 ounce) can coconut pie filling
1 (12 ounce) carton whipped topping, thawed
3 tablespoons flaked coconut

- Cut angel food cake horizontally into 3 equal layers.
- Combine coconut pie filling and whipped topping.
- Spread one-third of mixture on first layer and top with second layer.
- Spread one-third mixture on second layer and top with third layer.
- Spread remaining whipped topping mixture on top of cake and sprinkle with coconut.
- Refrigerate.

Strawberry-Angel Delight Cake

1 cup sweetened condensed milk
¼ cup lemon juice
1 pint fresh strawberries, halved
1 (14 ounce) angel food cake
1 pint whipping cream, whipped

- Combine condensed milk and lemon juice and fold in strawberries.
- Slice cake in half.
- Spread strawberry filling on bottom layer and place top layer over filling.
- Cover with whipped cream and top with extra strawberries.

Angel Cream Cake

1 (14 ounce) angel food cake
1 (18 ounce) jar chocolate ice cream topping
½ gallon vanilla ice cream, softened
1 (12 ounce) carton whipped topping, thawed
½ cup slivered almonds, toasted

- Tear cake into large pieces and stir pieces in chocolate topping to coat.
- Mix in softened ice cream. (Work fast!)
- Spoon into tube pan and freeze overnight.
- Turn out onto large cake plate and frost with whipped topping. Decorate with almonds and freeze.

TIP: Cookies and cream ice cream is also great with this recipe.

Chiffon Torte

1 round bakery orange chiffon cake
1 (20 ounce) can crushed pineapple with juice
1 (5.1 ounce) package vanilla instant pudding mix
1 (8 ounce) carton whipped topping, thawed

- Slice cake horizontally into 3 equal layers.
- In mixing bowl, combine pineapple and pudding mix and beat by hand until mixture is thick.
- Fold in whipped topping, spread mixture on each layer and cover top of cake.
- Refrigerate overnight.

TIP: Toasted almonds may be sprinkled on top of cake.

Easy Cheesecake

2 (8 ounce) packages cream cheese, softened
½ cup sugar
½ teaspoon vanilla extract
2 eggs
1 (9 inch) graham cracker piecrust

- Preheat oven to 350°.
- In mixing bowl, beat cream cheese, sugar, vanilla and eggs and pour into piecrust.
- Bake for 40 minutes.
- Cool and serve with any pie filling.

Key Lime Pie

6 egg yolks
2 (14 ounce) cans sweetened condensed milk
1 (8 ounce) bottle lime juice from concentrate
1 (9 inch) graham cracker piecrust

- Preheat oven to 350°.
- In large mixing bowl, beat egg yolks with condensed milk.
- Stir in lime juice and green food coloring if you like.
- Pour mixture into piecrust and bake for 20 minutes.
- Refrigerate. Top with whipped cream.

Sunny Lime Pie

2 (6 ounce) cartons key lime pie yogurt
1 (3 ounce) package dry lime gelatin mix
1 (8 ounce) carton whipped topping, thawed
1 (9 inch) graham cracker piecrust

- In bowl, combine yogurt and lime gelatin mix and mix well.
- Fold in whipped topping, spread in piecrust and freeze.
- Remove from freezer 20 minutes before slicing.

Limeade Pie

1 (6 ounce) can frozen limeade concentrate, thawed
2 cups low-fat frozen yogurt, softened
1 (8 ounce) carton whipped topping, thawed
1 (7 inch) graham cracker piecrust

- In large mixing bowl, combine limeade concentrate and yogurt and mix well.
- Fold in whipped topping and pour into piecrust.
- Freeze for at least 4 hours or overnight.

Pink Lemonade Pie

1 (6 ounce) can pink lemonade frozen concentrate
1 (14 ounce) can sweetened condensed milk
1 (8 ounce) package whipped topping, thawed
1 (9 inch) graham cracker piecrust

- In bowl, combine lemonade concentrate and condensed milk and blend well.
- Fold in whipped topping and pour into piecrust.
- Refrigerate overnight.

Frozen Lemonade Pie

½ gallon vanilla ice cream, softened
1 (6 ounce) can frozen pink lemonade concentrate
1 (9 inch) graham cracker piecrust

- With mixer, combine ice cream and lemonade concentrate. (Work quickly.)
- Pile ice cream mixture in piecrust and freeze.

Creamy Lemon Pie

1 (8 ounce) package cream cheese, softened
1 (14 ounce) can sweetened condensed milk
¼ cup lemon juice
1 (20 ounce) can lemon pie filling
1 (9 inch) graham cracker piecrust

- In mixing bowl, beat cream cheese until creamy.
- Add sweetened condensed milk and lemon juice and beat until mixture is very creamy.
- Fold in lemon pie filling, stir until creamy and pour into piecrust.
- Refrigerate several hours before slicing and serving.

Pineapple-Lemon Pie

Eat one and freeze the other!

1 (14 ounce) can sweetened condensed milk
1 (20 ounce) can lemon pie filling
1 (20 ounce) can crushed pineapple, well drained
1 (8 ounce) carton whipped topping, thawed
2 (9 inch) cookie-flavored piecrusts

- With mixer, combine condensed milk and lemon pie filling and beat until smooth.
- Gently fold pineapple and whipped topping into pie filling mixture.
- Pour into 2 piecrusts and refrigerate.

Pineapple Fluff Pie

1 (20 ounce) can crushed pineapple with juice
1 (3.4 ounce) package instant lemon pudding mix
1 (8 ounce) carton whipped topping, thawed
1 (9 inch) graham cracker piecrust

- In mixing bowl, combine pineapple and pudding mix and beat until thick.
- Fold in whipped topping and spoon into piecrust.
- Refrigerate for several hours before serving.

Pineapple-Cheese Pie

1 (14 ounce) can sweetened condensed milk
¼ cup lemon juice
1 (8 ounce) package cream cheese, softened
1 (15 ounce) can crushed pineapple, well drained
1 (9 inch) graham cracker piecrust

- In mixing bowl, combine condensed milk, lemon juice and cream cheese.
- Beat slowly at first, then beat and increasae speed until smooth. Fold in well drained pineapple and mix well.
- Pour into prepared piecrust and refrigerate 8 hours before slicing.

Yum-Yum Strawberry Pie

2 pints fresh strawberries, divided
1¼ cups sugar
3 tablespoons cornstarch
1 (9 inch) graham cracker piecrust
1 (8 ounce) carton whipping cream, whipped

- Crush 1 pint strawberries, add sugar, cornstarch and a dash of salt and cook on low heat until thick and clear. Cool.
- Place other pint of strawberries in piecrust and cover with cooked mixture.
- Top with whipping cream and refrigerate.

Strawberry-Almond Pie

2 (10 ounce) packages frozen sweetened strawberries, thawed
24 large marshmallows
1 (8 ounce) carton whipped topping, thawed
¼ cup slivered almonds, chopped, toasted
1 (9 inch) prepared shortbread piecrust

- Drain strawberries but reserve juice.
- In saucepan, heat strawberry juice and slowly add marshmallows.
- Heat on low and stir until marshmallows melt.
- Refrigerate and fold in whipped topping and strawberries.
- Pour into piecrust, sprinkle chopped almonds over top and refrigerate for several hours.

Strawberry-Cream Cheese Pie

2 (10 ounce) packages frozen sweetened strawberries, thawed
2 (8 ounce) packages cream cheese, softened
⅔ cup powdered sugar
1 (8 ounce) carton whipped topping, thawed
1 (9 inch) prepared chocolate crumb piecrust

- Drain strawberries and reserve ¼ cup juice.
- In mixing bowl, combine cream cheese, reserved juice, strawberries and sugar and beat well.
- Fold in whipped topping and spoon into piecrust.
- Refrigerate overnight and garnish with fresh strawberries.

Peach-Mousse Pie

Incredibly good!

1 (16 ounce) package frozen peach slices, thawed
1 cup sugar
1 (1 ounce) packet unflavored gelatin
⅛ teaspoon ground nutmeg
¾ (8 ounce) carton whipped topping, thawed
1 (9 inch) prepared graham cracker piecrust

- Place peaches in blender and process until smooth.
- Transfer peaches to saucepan, bring to a boil and stir constantly.
- Combine sugar, gelatin and nutmeg and stir into hot purée until sugar and gelatin dissolve.
- Pour gelatin-peach mixture into large mixing bowl.
- Place in freezer until mixture mounds (about 20 minutes) and stir occasionally
- Beat mixture at high speed about 5 minutes until mixture becomes light and frothy.
- Fold in whipped topping and spoon into piecrust.

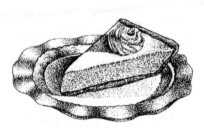

Merry Berry Pie

1 (6 ounce) package strawberry gelatin mix
1 cup whole cranberry sauce
½ cup cranberry juice cocktail
1 (8 ounce) carton whipped topping, thawed
1 (9 inch) baked piecrust

- Dissolve gelatin in 1 cup boiling water. Add cranberry sauce and juice and refrigerate until it begins to thicken.
- Fold in whipped topping, refrigerate again until mixture mounds and pour into piecrust.
- Refrigerate several hours before serving.

Cherry-Pecan Pie

1 (14 ounce) can sweetened condensed milk
¼ cup lemon juice
1 (8 ounce) carton whipped topping, thawed
1 cup chopped pecans
1 (20 ounce) can cherry pie filling
2 (9 inch) prepared graham cracker piecrusts

- Combine condensed milk and lemon juice, stir well and fold in whipped topping.
- Fold pecans and pie filling into mixture.
- Spoon into piecrusts. Refrigerate overnight.

Creamy Pecan Pie

1½ cups light corn syrup
1 (3 ounce) package vanilla instant pudding mix
3 eggs
2½ tablespoons (⅓ stick) butter, melted
2 cups pecan halves
1 (9 inch) deep-dish piecrust, unbaked

- Preheat oven to 325°.
- Combine corn syrup, pudding, eggs and butter, mix well and stir in pecans.
- Pour into piecrust. (Cover piecrust edges with strips of foil to prevent excessive browning.)
- Bake for 35 to 40 minutes or until center of pie sets.

Million Dollar Pie

24 round, buttery crackers, crumbled
1 cup chopped pecans
4 egg whites (absolutely no yolks at all)
1 cup sugar

- Preheat oven to 350°.
- In bowl, combine cracker crumbs with pecans.
- In separate mixing bowl, beat egg whites until stiff and slowly add sugar while still mixing.
- Gently fold crumb mixture into egg whites.
- Pour into 9 inch pie pan, bake for 20 minutes and cool before serving.

Cheesecake Pie

2 (8 ounce) packages cream cheese
3 eggs
1 cup sugar, divided
1½ teaspoons vanilla extract, divided
1 (8 ounce) carton sour cream

- Preheat oven to 350°.
- In mixing bowl, combine cream cheese, eggs, ¾ cup sugar and ½ teaspoon vanilla and beat for 5 minutes.
- Pour into sprayed 9-inch pie pan and bake for 25 minutes. Cool for 20 minutes.
- Combine sour cream, ¼ cup sugar and 1 teaspoon vanilla, pour over cooled cake and bake 10 minutes longer.
- Refrigerate for at least 4 hours and serve with your favorite fruit topping.

Cheesecake-Pudding Pie

1 (20 ounce) can strawberry pie filling, divided
1 (9 inch) prepared graham cracker piecrust
2 cups milk
2 (3.4 ounce) packages instant cheesecake pudding mix
½ (8 ounce) carton whipped topping, thawed

- Spoon ¾ cup pie filling into piecrust.
- In mixing bowl, combine milk and pudding mixes and beat for 2 minutes or until smooth. (Mixture will be thick.)
- Fold in whipped topping and spoon over pie filling in crust. Refrigerate for at least 3 hours.
- When ready to serve, top with remaining pie filling.

Holiday Pie

1 (8 ounce) package cream cheese, softened
1 (14 ounce) can sweetened condensed milk
1 (3.4 ounce) package instant vanilla pudding mix
1½ cups whipped topping, thawed
1 (9 inch) prepared graham cracker piecrust
Holiday candies

- Use mixer to beat cream cheese until smooth. Gradually add condensed milk and beat until smooth.
- Add ¾ cup water and pudding mix and beat until smooth.
- Fold in whipped topping and pour into piecrust.
- Top with crumbled holiday candies and refrigerate.

Peanut Butter Pie

⅔ cup crunchy peanut butter
1 (8 ounce) package cream cheese, softened
½ cup milk
1 cup powdered sugar
1 (8 ounce) carton whipped topping, thawed
1 (9 inch) prepared graham cracker piecrust

- With mixer, blend peanut butter, cream cheese, milk and powdered sugar and fold in whipped topping.
- Pour into piecrust and refrigerate several hours before serving.

Chess Pie

½ cup (1 stick) butter, softened
2 cups sugar
1 tablespoon cornstarch
4 eggs
1 (9 inch) piecrust, unbaked

- Preheat oven to 325°.
- Cream butter, sugar and cornstarch. Add eggs one at a time and beat well after each addition.
- Pour mixture into piecrust. (Cover piecrust edges with strips of foil to prevent excessive browning.)
- Bake for 45 minutes or until center sets.

Coffee-Mallow Pie

1 tablespoon instant coffee granules
4 cups miniature marshmallows
1 tablespoon butter
1 (8 ounce) carton whipping cream, whipped
½ cup chopped walnuts, toasted
1 (9 inch) prepared graham cracker piecrust

- In heavy saucepan, bring 1 cup water to a boil and stir in coffee until it dissolves.
- Reduce heat and add marshmallows and butter.
- Cook and stir over low heat until marshmallows melt and mixture is smooth.
- Set saucepan in ice and whisk mixture constantly until it cools.
- Fold in whipped cream, spoon into piecrust and sprinkle with walnuts.
- Refrigerate for at least 4 hours before serving.

Dixie Pie

24 large marshmallows
1 cup evaporated milk
1 (8 ounce) carton whipping cream, whipped
3 tablespoons bourbon
1 (9 inch) prepared chocolate piecrust

- In saucepan on low heat, melt marshmallows in milk and stir constantly. (Do not boil.) Cool in refrigerator.
- Fold into whipped cream while adding bourbon and pour into chocolate crust.
- Refrigerate at least 5 hours before serving.

Grasshopper Pie

22 large marshmallows
⅓ cup creme de menthe liqueur
1 (12 ounce) carton whipping cream, whipped
1 (9 inch) prepared chocolate piecrust

- In large saucepan, melt marshmallows with creme de menthe over low heat and cool.
- Fold whipped cream into marshmallow mixture.
- Pour filling into piecrust and freeze until ready to serve.

Tumbleweed Pie

½ gallon vanilla ice cream, softened
⅓ cup plus 1 tablespoon Kahlua® liqueur
⅓ cup plus 1 tablespoon amaretto
1 (9 inch) prepared chocolate cookie crust
¼ cup slivered almonds, toasted

- Place ice cream, Kahlua® and amaretto in mixing bowl and blend as quickly as possible.
- Pour into piecrust, sprinkle almonds over top and freeze.

Easy Chocolate Pie

1 (8 ounce) milk chocolate candy bar
1 (16 ounce) carton frozen whipped topping, thawed, divided
¾ cup chopped pecans
1 (9 inch) prepared piecrust

- In saucepan, break candy into small pieces and melt over low heat. Remove and cool several minutes.
- Fold in two-thirds whipped topping, mix well and stir in chopped pecans.
- Pour into piecrust, spread remaining whipped topping over top and refrigerate for at least 8 hours.

Caramel Ice Cream Pie

1 (14 ounce) roll butterscotch cookie dough
½ gallon vanilla ice cream
1 (12 ounce) jar caramel sauce

- Bake cookies according to package directions.
- When cookies cool, crumble and place in 10-inch pie pan. Set aside ½ cup to use for topping.
- Place ice cream in bowl to soften.
- Stir caramel sauce into ice cream (do not mix completely) and spoon mixture into pie pan.
- Sprinkle remaining crumbs over top of pie and freeze.

Chocolate-Cream Cheese Pie

1 (8 ounce) package cream cheese, softened
¾ cup powdered sugar
¼ cup cocoa
1 (8 ounce) container whipped topping, thawed
½ cup chopped pecans
1 (9 inch) prepared crumb piecrust

- Combine cream cheese, sugar and cocoa in mixing bowl and beat at medium speed until creamy.
- Add whipped topping and fold until smooth.
- Spread into piecrust, sprinkle pecans over top and refrigerate.

311

Cool Chocolate Pie

22 large marshmallows
2 (8 ounce) milk chocolate-almond candy bars
1 (8 ounce) carton whipped topping, thawed
½ cup chopped pecans
1 (9 inch) prepared graham cracker piecrust

- In double boiler, melt marshmallows and chocolate bars.
- Cool partially and fold in whipped topping and pecans.
- Pour into piecrust. Refrigerate for several hours before serving.

Black Forest Pie

This is definitely a party dessert, but the family will insist it should be served on a regular basis.

4 (1 ounce) squares unsweetened baking chocolate
1 (14 ounce) can sweetened condensed milk
1 teaspoon almond extract
1½ cups whipping cream, whipped
1 (9 inch) prepared piecrust
1 (20 ounce) can cherry pie filling, chilled

- In saucepan over medium low heat, melt chocolate with sweetened condensed milk and stir well to mix.
- Remove from heat and stir in extract. (This mixture needs to cool.)
- When mixture is about room temperature, pour chocolate into whipped cream and fold gently until combined.
- Pour into piecrust.
- To serve, spoon heaping spoonful of cherry filling over each piece of pie.

Sweet Potato Pie

1 (14 ounce) can sweet potatoes
¾ cup milk
1 cup firmly packed brown sugar
2 eggs
½ teaspoon ground cinnamon
½ teaspoon salt
1 (9 inch) piecrust, unbaked

- Preheat oven to 350°.
- Combine sweet potatoes, milk, brown sugar, eggs, cinnamon and salt in mixing bowl and blend until smooth.
- Pour into piecrust. (Cover piecrust edges with strips of foil to prevent excessive browning.)
- Bake for 40 minutes or until knife inserted in center comes out clean.

Easy Pumpkin Pie

2 eggs
1 (30 ounce) can pumpkin pie mix
1 (5 ounce) can evaporated milk
1 (9 inch) deep-dish piecrust, unbaked

- Preheat oven to 400°.
- Beat eggs lightly in large bowl and stir in pumpkin pie mix and evaporated milk.
- Pour into piecrust. (Cover piecrust edges with strips of foil to prevent excessive browning.)
- Bake for 15 minutes. Reduce temperature to 325° and bake for 40 more minutes or until knife inserted in center comes out clean and cool.

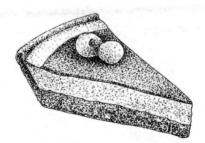

Cherry Cobbler

2 (20 ounce) cans cherry pie filling
1 (18 ounce) box white cake mix
¾ cup (1½ sticks) butter, melted
1 (4 ounce) package almonds, slivered

- Preheat oven to 350°.
- Spread pie filling in greased 9 x 13-inch baking pan.
- Sprinkle cake mix over cherries, drizzle with melted butter and sprinkle almonds over top.
- Bake for 45 minutes. Top with whipped topping.

Cherry-Strawberry Cobbler

1 (20 ounce) can strawberry pie filling
1 (20 ounce) can cherry pie filling
1 (18 ounce) box white cake mix
1 cup (2 sticks) butter, melted
¾ cup slivered almonds

- Preheat oven to 350°.
- Spread pie fillings into greased 9 x 13-inch baking pan and sprinkle cake mix over pie fillings.
- Drizzle melted butter over top and sprinkle with almonds.
- Bake for 55 minutes. Top with whipped topping.

Cherry-Cinnamon Cobbler

1 (20 ounce) can cherry pie filling
1 (12 ounce) tube refrigerated cinnamon rolls

- Preheat oven to 400°.
- Spread pie filling into greased 8-inch baking dish.
- Set aside icing from cinnamon rolls and arrange rolls around edge of baking dish.
- Bake for 15 minutes. Cover and bake 10 minutes longer.
- Spread icing over rolls and serve warm.

Apple-Crumb Cobbler

2 (20 ounce) cans apple slices
1¼ cups sugar
2 teaspoons lemon juice
¾ teaspoon cinnamon
1 (18 ounce) box white cake mix
½ cup (1 stick) butter, sliced

- Preheat oven to 350°.
- Place apples in greased 9 x 13-inch baking pan and sprinkle with sugar, lemon juice and cinnamon.
- Sprinkle cake mix over top and dot with butter.
- Bake for 40 minutes or until light brown.

Apricot Cobbler

So easy and so good!

1 (20 ounce) can apricot pie filling
1 (20 ounce) can crushed pineapple with juice
1 cup chopped pecans
1 (18 ounce) box yellow cake mix
1 cup (2 sticks) butter, melted

- Preheat oven to 375°.
- Spray 9 x 13-inch baking dish with non-stick spray, pour pie filling in pan and spread.
- Spoon pineapple and juice over pie filling and sprinkle pecans over pineapple.
- Sprinkle cake mix over pecans.
- Drizzle melted butter over cake mix and bake for 40 minutes or until light brown and crunchy.
- Serve hot or room temperature. (It's great topped with whipped topping.)

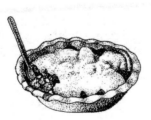

Blueberry Cobbler

½ cup (1 stick) butter, melted
1 cup self-rising flour
1¼ cups sugar
1 cup milk
1 (20 ounce) can blueberry pie filling

- Preheat oven to 300°.
- Pour butter in 9-inch baking pan.
- Mix flour and sugar in bowl, add milk and stir.
- Pour mixture over melted butter but do not stir.
- Spoon pie filling over batter and bake for 1 hour.
- To serve, top with whipped topping.

Easier Blueberry Cobbler

2 (20 ounce) cans blueberry pie filling
1 (18 ounce) box white cake mix
1 egg
½ cup (1 stick) butter, softened

- Preheat oven to 350°
- Spread pie filling in greased 9 x 13-inch baking dish.
- With mixer, combine cake mix, egg and butter and blend well. (Mixture will be stiff.)
- Spoon over filling and bake for 45 minutes or until golden brown.

Blueberry Crunch

1 (20 ounce) can crushed pineapple with juice
1 (18 ounce) box yellow cake mix
3 cups fresh or frozen blueberries
⅔ cup sugar
½ cup (1 stick) butter, melted

- Preheat oven to 350°.
- Spread pineapple in buttered 9 x 13-inch baking dish and sprinkle with cake mix, blueberries and sugar. (It is even better if you add 1 cup chopped pecans.)
- Drizzle with butter and bake for 45 minutes or until bubbly.

Peach Crisp

4¾ cups peeled, sliced peaches
3 tablespoons lemon juice
1 cup flour
1¾ cups sugar
1 egg, beaten

- Preheat oven to 375°.
- Place peaches in 9-inch baking dish and sprinkle lemon juice over top.
- Mix flour, sugar, egg and dash of salt.
- Spread mixture over top of peaches and dot with a little butter.
- Bake until golden brown.

Cherry Crisp

2 (20 ounce) cans cherry pie filling
1 (18 ounce) box white cake mix
½ cup (1 stick) butter
2 cups chopped pecans

- Preheat oven to 350°.
- Pour pie filling into greased 9 x 13-inch baking dish. Sprinkle cake mix over top of filling.
- Dot with butter and cover with pecans. Bake uncovered for 45 minutes.

Peach Crunch

2 (20 ounce) cans peach pie filling
1 (18 ounce) box white cake mix
1 cup slivered almonds
½ cup (1 stick) butter

- Preheat oven to 350°.
- Spread pie filling evenly in greased, floured 9 x 13-inch baking pan.
- Sprinkle cake mix evenly and smooth over top.
- Sprinkle almonds evenly over cake mix and cover with ⅛-inch slices butter.
- Bake for 40 to 45 minutes or until top is brown.

Vanishing Butter Cookies

1 (18 ounce) box butter cake mix
1 (3.4 ounce) package instant butterscotch pudding mix
1 cup oil
1 egg, beaten
1¼ cups chopped pecans

- Preheat oven to 350°.
- Mix cake and pudding mixes by hand and stir in oil. Add egg, mix thoroughly and stir in pecans.
- Place dough on baking sheet by teaspoonfuls about 2 inches apart.
- Bake for 8 or 9 minutes. (Do not overcook.)

Lemon Cookies

½ cup (1 stick) butter, softened
1 cup sugar
2 tablespoons lemon juice
2 cups flour

- Cream butter, sugar and lemon juice and slowly stir in flour.
- Drop by teaspoonfuls onto ungreased baking sheet.
- Bake at 350° for 14 to 15 minutes.

Brown Sugar Cookies

¾ cup packed brown sugar
1 cup (2 sticks) butter, softened
1 egg yolk
2 cups flour

- Cream sugar and butter until light and fluffy. Mix in egg yolk. Blend in flour. Refrigerate dough for 1 hour.
- Form dough into 1-inch balls, flatten and criss-cross with fork on lightly greased baking sheet.
- Bake at 325° for 10 to 12 minutes or until golden brown.

Yummy Cookies

3 egg whites
1¼ cups sugar
2 teaspoons vanilla extract
3½ cups frosted corn flakes
1 cup chopped pecans

- Preheat oven to 250°.
- Beat egg whites until stiff and gradually add sugar and vanilla.
- Fold in frosted corn flakes and pecans and drop by teaspoonfuls on baking sheet lined with wax paper.
- Bake for 40 minutes.

Peanut Butter-Date Cookies

1 egg, beaten
⅔ cup granulated sugar
⅓ cup packed brown sugar
1 cup chunky peanut butter
½ cup chopped dates

- Preheat oven to 350°.
- Blend egg, sugars and peanut butter and mix thoroughly. Stir in dates and roll dough into 1-inch balls.
- Place on ungreased baking sheet and use fork to press each ball down to about ½ inch.
- Bake for about 12 minutes and cool before storing.

Easy Peanut Butter Cookies

1 (18 ounce) package sugar cookie dough
½ cup creamy peanut butter
½ cup miniature chocolate chips
½ cup peanut butter chips
½ cup chopped peanuts

- Preheat oven to 350°.
- Beat cookie dough and peanut butter in large bowl until blended and smooth.
- Stir in chocolate chips, peanut butter chips and peanuts and mix well.
- Drop dough by heaping tablespoonfuls onto ungreased baking sheet.
- Bake for 15 minutes and cool on wire rack.

Devil's Food Cookies

1 (18 ounce) package devil's food cake mix
½ cup oil
2 eggs
¾ cup chopped pecans, optional

- Preheat oven to 350°.
- Combine cake mix, oil and eggs in bowl and mix well.
- Drop by teaspoons onto non-stick baking sheet.
- Bake for 10 to 12 minutes.
- Cool and remove to wire rack.

Butter Cookies

1 pound butter
¾ cup packed brown sugar
¾ cup granulated sugar
4½ cups flour

- Preheat oven to 350°.
- Cream butter and sugars, slowly add flour and mix well. (Batter will be very thick.)
- Roll into small balls and place on ungreased baking sheet.
- Bake for about 15 minutes until only slightly brown. Do not overbake.

Cheesecake Cookies

1 cup (2 sticks) butter, softened
2 (3 ounce) packages cream cheese, softened
2 cups sugar
2 cups flour

- Preheat oven to 350°.
- Cream butter and cream cheese, add sugar and beat until light and fluffy. Add flour and beat well.
- Drop by teaspoonfuls onto baking sheet and bake for 12 to 15 minutes or until edges are golden.

TIP: These are even better if you add 1 cup chopped pecans.

Chocolate-Coconut Cookies

1 cup sweetened condensed milk
4 cups flaked coconut
⅔ cup miniature semi-sweet chocolate bits
1 teaspoon vanilla extract
½ teaspoon almond extract

- Preheat oven to 325°.
- Combine milk and coconut. (Mixture will be gooey.)
- Add chocolate bits and extracts and stir until well blended.
- Drop by teaspoonfuls onto sprayed baking sheet and bake for 12 minutes.
- Store in airtight container.

Brown Sugar Wafers

1 cup (2 sticks) butter, softened
¾ cup packed dark brown sugar
1 egg yolk
1 tablespoon vanilla extract
1¼ cups flour

- With mixer, beat butter and gradually add brown sugar.
- Add egg yolk and vanilla and beat well. Add flour and dash salt and mix well.
- Shape dough into 1-inch balls and refrigerate 2 hours.
- Preheat oven to 350°.
- Place on baking sheet, flatten each cookie and bake for 10 to 12 minutes.

Chocolate Kisses

2 egg whites, room temperature
⅔ cup sugar
1 teaspoon vanilla extract
1¼ cups chopped pecans
1 (6 ounce) package chocolate chips

- Preheat oven to 375º.
- Beat egg whites until very stiff and blend in sugar, vanilla and a dash of salt. Fold in pecans and chocolate chips.
- Cover baking sheet with foil (shiny side up) and drop dough onto foil by teaspoonfuls.
- Put cookies in oven, TURN OVEN OFF and leave overnight. If cookies are a little sticky, leave out in air to dry.

Coconut Macaroons

2 (7 ounce) packages flaked coconut
1 (14 ounce) can sweetened condensed milk
2 teaspoons vanilla extract
½ teaspoon almond extract

- Preheat oven to 350°.
- In mixing bowl, combine coconut, condensed milk and extracts and mix well.
- Drop by rounded teaspoons onto foil-lined baking sheet.
- Bake for 8 to 10 minutes or until light brown around edges.
- Immediately remove from foil. (Macaroons will stick if allowed to cool.) Store at room temperature.

Coconut Moments

1 cup (2 sticks) butter, softened
½ cup powdered sugar
½ cup cornstarch
1⅓ cups flour
Flaked coconut

- Beat butter and powdered sugar until light and fluffy.
- Add cornstarch and flour and beat until they blend well.
- Cover and refrigerate for 1 hour.
- Preheat oven to 325°.
- Shape into 1-inch balls, roll in flaked coconut and place on ungreased baking sheet.
- Bake for 12 to 15 minutes. Watch closely and don't let coconut burn.
- Cool 2 to 3 minutes before removing from pan.

Hello Dollies

1½ cups graham cracker crumbs
1 (6 ounce) package chocolate chips
1 cup flaked coconut
1¼ cups chopped pecans
1 (14 ounce) can sweetened condensed milk

- Preheat oven to 350°.
- Sprinkle cracker crumbs in 9 x 9-inch pan.
- Layer chocolate chips, coconut and pecans and pour condensed milk over top of layered ingredients.
- Bake for 25 to 30 minutes. Cool and cut into squares.

Lemon Drops

½ (8 ounce) carton whipped topping, thawed
1 (18 ounce) box lemon cake mix
1 egg
Powdered sugar

- Preheat oven to 350°.
- Stir whipped topping into lemon cake mix by hand, add egg and mix thoroughly.
- Shape dough into balls and roll in powdered sugar
- Bake for 8 to 10 minutes. Do not overcook.

Nutty Fudgies

1 (18 ounce) box fudge cake mix
1 (8 ounce) carton sour cream
⅔ cup peanut butter chips
½ cup chopped peanuts

- Preheat oven to 350°.
- Beat cake mix and sour cream until mixture blends well and is smooth.
- Stir in peanut butter chips and peanuts. Drop by teaspoonfuls onto greased baking sheet.
- Bake for 10 to 12 minutes, remove from oven and cool.

Pecan Puffs

2 egg whites
¾ cup packed light brown sugar
1 teaspoon vanilla extract
1 cup chopped pecans

- Preheat oven to 250°.
- Beat egg whites until foamy and add brown sugar, ¼ cup at a time.
- Add vanilla, continue beating until stiff peaks form (about 3 or 4 minutes) and fold in pecans.
- Line baking sheet with freezer paper and drop mixture by teaspoonfuls onto paper.
- Bake for 45 minutes.

Potato Chip Crispies

These are really good and crunchy!

1 cup (2 sticks) butter, softened
⅔ cup sugar
1 teaspoon vanilla extract
1½ cups flour
½ cup crushed potato chips

- Preheat oven to 350°.
- Cream butter, sugar and vanilla. Add flour and chips and mix well.
- Drop by teaspoonfuls on ungreased baking sheet.
- Bake for about 12 minutes or until light brown.

Praline Grahams

⅓ (16 ounce) box graham crackers (1 package)
¾ cup (1½ sticks)butter
½ cup sugar
1 cup chopped pecans

- Preheat oven to 300°.
- Separate each graham cracker into 4 sections and arrange in jellyroll pan with edges touching.
- Melt butter in saucepan and stir in sugar and pecans.
- Bring to a boil and cook 3 minutes. Stir frequently. Spread mixture evenly over graham crackers.
- Bake for 10 to 12 minutes.
- Remove from pan, cool on wax paper and break up to serve.

Sand Tarts

1 cup (2 sticks) butter, softened
¾ cup powdered sugar
2 cups sifted flour
1 cup chopped pecans
1 teaspoon vanilla

- Preheat oven to 325°.
- With mixer, cream butter and sugar and add flour, pecans and vanilla.
- Roll into crescents and place on ungreased baking sheet.
- Bake for 20 minutes and roll in extra powdered sugar after tarts cool.

Scotch Shortbread

½ cup (1 stick) unsalted butter, softened
⅓ cup sugar
1¼ cups flour
Powdered sugar

- Preheat oven to 325°.
- Cream butter and sugar until light and fluffy. Add flour and a dash of salt and mix well.
- Spread dough into 8-inch square pan and bake for 20 minutes or until light brown.
- Let shortbread cool in pan, dust with powdered sugar and cut into squares.

Pumpkin Cupcakes

1 (18 ounce) box spice cake mix
1 (15 ounce) can pumpkin
3 eggs
⅓ cup oil
⅓ cup water

- Preheat oven to 350°.
- With mixer, blend all ingredients and beat for 2 minutes.
- Pour batter into 24 paper-lined muffin cups and fill three-fourths full.
- Bake for 18 to 20 minutes or until toothpick inserted in center comes out clean. (You might want to spread with commercial frosting.)

Porcupine Clusters

¼ cup corn syrup
1 (12 ounce) package white chocolate morsels
2 cups chow mein noodles
¾ cup salted peanuts

- On low heat, melt corn syrup and white chocolate morsels.
- Pour over noodles and peanuts and mix well.
- Drop by teaspoonfuls onto wax paper.
- Refrigerate to harden and store in airtight container.

Peanutty Cocoa Puff

¾ cup light corn syrup
1¼ cups sugar
1¼ cups chunky peanut butter
4½ cups cocoa puff cereal

- In large saucepan, bring syrup and sugar to rolling boil.
- Stir in peanut butter and mix well. Stir in cocoa puffs and drop on wax paper by teaspoonfuls.

Peanut Butter Crunchies

1 cup sugar
½ cup white corn syrup
2 cups peanut butter
4 cups crispy rice cereal

- In saucepan, mix sugar and syrup and bring to rolling boil.
- Remove from stove and stir in peanut butter. Add crispy rice cereal and mix well.
- Drop by teaspoonfuls onto wax paper and place in refrigerator for a few minutes to set.

Peanut Clusters

1 (24 ounce) package almond bark
1 (12 ounce) package milk chocolate chips
5 cups salted peanuts

- In double boiler, melt almond bark and chocolate chips.
- Stir in peanuts and drop by teaspoonfuls onto wax paper.
- Place in refrigerator for 30 minutes to set and store in airtight container.

No-Cook Lemon Balls

2 cups almond or pecan shortbread cookie crumbs, divided
1 (6 ounce) can frozen lemonade concentrate, thawed
½ cup (1 stick) butter, softened
1 (16 ounce) box powdered sugar, sifted

- Combine 1½ cups cookie crumbs, lemonade concentrate, butter and powdered sugar and shape into small balls.
- Roll in reserved cookie crumbs and put on wax paper.
- Refrigerate 3 to 4 hours in sealed container or freeze to serve later.

Orange Balls

1 (12 ounce) box vanilla wafers, crushed
½ cup (1 stick) butter, melted
1 (16 ounce) box powdered sugar
1 (6 ounce) can frozen orange juice concentrate
1 cup finely chopped pecans

- Combine wafer crumbs, butter, sugar and orange juice concentrate and mix well.
- Form into balls, roll in chopped pecans and store in airtight container.

TIP: Make these in finger shapes for something different. They make neat cookies for a party or a tea.

Marshmallow Treats

¼ cup (½ stick) butter
4 cups miniature marshmallows
½ cup chunky peanut butter
5 cups crispy rice cereal

- In saucepan, melt butter. Add marshmallows, stir until they melt and add peanut butter.
- Remove from heat. Add cereal and stir well.
- Press mixture into 9 x 13-inch pan. Cut in squares when cool.

Haystacks

1 (12 ounce) package butterscotch chips
1 cup salted peanuts
1½ cups chow mein noodles

- Melt butterscotch chips in top of double boiler.
- Remove from heat and stir in peanuts and noodles.
- Drop by teaspoonfuls on wax paper.
- Cool and store in airtight container.

Crazy Cocoa Crisps

1 (24 ounce) package almond bark
2¼ cups cocoa-flavored crispy rice cereal
2 cups dry-roasted peanuts

- Place almond bark in double boiler, heat and stir while bark melts.
- Stir in cereal and peanuts. Drop by teaspoonfuls on baking sheet.
- Place in refrigerator for about 30 minutes to set. Store in airtight container.

Coconut Yummies

1 (12 ounce) package white chocolate baking chips
¼ cup (½ stick) butter
16 large marshmallows
2 cups quick-cooking oats
1 cup flaked coconut

- In saucepan over low heat, melt chocolate chips, butter and marshmallows and stir until smooth.
- Stir in oats and coconut and mix well.
- Drop by rounded teaspoonfuls onto wax paper-lined baking sheets.
- Refrigerate until set and store in airtight container.

Chocolate Crunchies

1 (20 ounce) package chocolate
¾ cup light corn syrup
2 tablespoons (¼ stick) butter
2 teaspoons vanilla extract
8 cups crispy rice cereal

- Combine chocolate, corn syrup and butter in top of double boiler.
- Heat on low and cook until chocolate melts. Remove from heat and stir in vanilla.
- Place cereal in large mixing bowl, pour chocolate mixture on top and stir until well coated.
- Quickly spoon mixture into buttered 9 x 13-inch dish and press firmly, using back of spoon.
- Cool completely and cut into bars.

Chinese Cookies

1 (6 ounce) package butterscotch chips
1 (6 ounce) package chocolate chips
2 cups chow mein noodles
1¼ cups salted peanuts

- On low heat, melt butterscotch and chocolate chips. Add noodles and peanuts and mix well.
- Drop by teaspoonfuls onto wax paper and refrigerate to harden.
- Store in airtight container.

Butterscotch Cookies

1 (12 ounce) and 1 (6 ounce) package butterscotch chips
2¼ cups chow mein noodles
½ cup chopped walnuts
¼ cup flaked coconut

- Melt butterscotch chips in double boiler. Add noodles, walnuts and coconut.
- Drop by tablespoonfuls onto wax paper.

Peanut Butter Cookies

1 cup sugar
¾ cup light corn syrup
1 (16 ounce) jar crunchy peanut butter
4½ cups chow mein noodles

- In saucepan over medium heat, bring sugar and corn syrup to boil and stir in peanut butter.
- Remove from heat and stir in noodles.
- Drop by spoonfuls onto wax paper and allow to cool.

Corn Flake Cookies

1 (12 ounce) package butterscotch morsels
¾ cup peanut butter
3½ to 4 cups corn flakes, crushed

- Melt butterscotch morsels on very low heat and add peanut butter.
- When mixed thoroughly, add corn flake crumbs.
- Drop by teaspoonfuls onto wax paper.

Walnut Bars

1⅔ cups graham cracker crumbs
1½ cups coarsely chopped walnuts
1 (14 ounce) can sweetened condensed milk
¼ cup flaked coconut, optional

- Preheat oven to 350°.
- Place graham cracker crumbs and walnuts in bowl.
- Slowly add condensed milk, coconut and pinch of salt. (Mixture will be very thick.)
- Pack into greased 9-inch square pan and press mixture down with back of spoon.
- Bake for 35 minutes and cut into squares when cool.

Rainbow Cookie Bars

½ cup (1 stick) butter
2 cups graham cracker crumbs
1 (14 ounce) can sweetened condensed milk
⅔ cup flaked coconut
1 cup chopped pecans
1 cup M&M's® plain chocolate candies

- Preheat oven to 350°.
- In 9 x 13-inch baking pan, melt butter in oven.
- Sprinkle crumbs over butter and pour condensed milk over crumbs.
- Top with coconut, pecans and M&M's® and press down firmly.
- Bake for 25 to 30 minutes or until light brown. Cool and cut into bars.

TIP: When making these one time, I realized I was missing the M&M's®, so I substituted white chocolate bits. They were great (just not "rainbow").

Rocky Road Bars

1 (12 ounce) package semi-sweet chocolate morsels
1 (14 ounce) can sweetened condensed milk
2 tablespoons (¼ stick) butter
2 cups dry-roasted peanuts
1 (10 ounce) package miniature marshmallows

- Place chocolate morsels, condensed milk and butter in top of double boiler and heat until chocolate and butter melt, stirring constantly.
- Remove from heat and stir in peanuts and marshmallows.
- Spread mixture quickly on wax paper-lined 9 x 13-inch pan.
- Refrigerate at least 2 hours, cut into bars and store in refrigerator.

Pecan Squares

1 (24 ounce) package almond bark
1 cup cinnamon chips
1 cup chopped pecans
8 cups frosted crispy rice cereal

- Melt almond bark and cinnamon chips in very large saucepan or roasting pan on low heat and stir constantly until they melt.
- Remove from heat and add pecans and cereal.
- Mix well and stir into 9 x 13-inch pan.
- Pat down with back of spoon, refrigerate just until set and cut into squares.

Honey-Nut Bars

⅓ cup (⅔ stick) butter
¼ cup cocoa
1 (10 ounce) package miniature marshmallows
6 cups honey-nut clusters cereal

- Melt butter in large saucepan and stir in cocoa and marshmallows.
- Cook over low heat, stirring constantly, until marshmallows melt and mixture is smooth.
- Remove from heat and stir in cereal.
- Pour into sprayed 7 x 11-inch pan and smooth mixture with spatula.
- Cool completely and cut into bars.

Kids' Bars

1 cup sugar
1 cup light corn syrup
1½ cups crunchy peanut butter
6 cups crispy rice cereal
1 (12 ounce) package chocolate chips

- In saucepan, combine sugar and corn syrup and bring to a boil, stirring constantly.
- Remove from heat and stir in peanut butter and crispy rice cereal. Spread into buttered 9 x 13-inch pan.
- In saucepan over low heat, melt chocolate chips and spread over cereal layer.
- Refrigerate until set and cut into bars. Store in refrigerator.

Gooey Turtle Bars

½ cup (1 stick) butter, melted
2 cups vanilla wafer crumbs
1 (12 ounce) semi-sweet chocolate morsels
1 cup pecan pieces
1 (12 ounce) jar caramel topping

- Preheat oven to 350°.
- Combine butter and wafer crumbs in 9 x 13-inch baking pan and press into bottom of pan. Sprinkle with chocolate morsels and pecans.
- Remove lid from caramel topping and microwave on HIGH for 30 seconds or until hot and drizzle over pecans.
- Bake for about 15 minutes or until morsels melt.
- Cool in pan and refrigerate at least 30 minutes before cutting into squares.

TIP: Watch bars closely – you want the chips to melt, but you don't want the crumbs to burn.

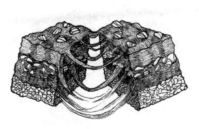

Chocolate Chip Cheese Bars

1 (18 ounce) tube refrigerated chocolate chip cookie dough
1 (8 ounce) package cream cheese, softened
½ cup sugar
1 egg

- Preheat oven to 350°.
- Cut cookie dough in half.
- For crust, press half dough into bottom of greased 9-inch square baking pan or 7 x 11-inch baking pan.
- In mixing bowl, beat cream cheese, sugar and egg until smooth.
- Spread cream cheese mixture over crust and crumble remaining dough over top.
- Bake for 35 to 40 minutes or until toothpick inserted near center comes out clean.
- Cool on wire rack, cut into bars and refrigerate leftovers.

Apricot Bars

1¼ cups flour
¾ cup packed brown sugar
6 tablespoons (¾ stick) butter
¾ cup apricot preserves

- Preheat oven to 350°.
- In mixing bowl, combine flour, brown sugar and butter and mix well.
- Place half mixture in 9-inch square baking pan, spread apricot preserves over top and sprinkle with remaining flour mixture.
- Bake for 30 minutes. Cut into squares.

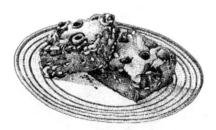

Chocolate-Cherry Bars

1 (18 ounce) devil's food cake mix
1 (20 ounce) can cherry pie filling
2 eggs
1 cup milk chocolate chips

- Preheat oven to 350°.
- In large bowl, mix all bar ingredients by hand and blend well.
- Pour batter into greased, floured 9 x 13-inch baking dish.
- Bake for 25 to 30 minutes or until toothpick inserted in center comes out clean. Cool and frost.

Chocolate-Cherry Bar Frosting:

1 (3 ounce) square semi-sweet chocolate, melted
1 (3 ounce) package cream cheese, softened
½ teaspoon vanilla extract
1½ cups powdered sugar

- In medium bowl beat chocolate, cream cheese and vanilla until smooth.
- Gradually beat in powdered sugar and spread over Chocolate-Cherry Bars.

Snickers Brownies

1 (18 ounce) box German chocolate cake mix
¾ cup (1½ sticks) butter, melted
½ cup evaporated milk
4 (2.7 ounce) Snickers® candy bars, cut in ⅛-inch slices

- Preheat oven to 350°.
- In large bowl, combine cake mix, butter and evaporated milk and beat on low speed until mixture blends well.
- Place half batter in greased, floured 9 x 13-inch baking pan and bake for 10 minutes.
- Remove from oven and place candy bar slices evenly over brownies.
- Drop remaining half of batter by spoonfuls over candy bars and spread as evenly as possible.
- Return to oven and bake for another 20 minutes. When cool, cut into bars.

Nutty Blonde Brownies

1 (1 pound) box light brown sugar
4 eggs
2 cups biscuit mix
2 cups chopped pecans

- Preheat oven to 350°.
- In mixing bowl, beat brown sugar, eggs and biscuit mix.
- Stir in pecans and pour into greased 9 x 13-inch baking pan.
- Bake for 35 minutes, cool and cut into squares.

Peanut Krispies

¾ cup (1½ sticks) butter
2 cups peanut butter
1 (16 ounce) box powdered sugar
3½ cups crispy rice cereal
¾ cup chopped peanuts

- Melt butter in large saucepan, add peanut butter and mix well.
- Add powdered sugar, cereal and peanuts and mix.
- Drop by teaspoonfuls on wax paper.

Microwave Fudge

3 cups semi-sweet chocolate morsels
1 (14 ounce) can sweetened condensed milk
¼ cup (½ stick) butter, sliced
1 cup chopped walnuts

- Combine chocolate morsels, condensed milk and butter in 2-quart glass bowl.
- Microwave on MEDIUM for 4 to 5 minutes and stir at 1½-minute intervals.
- Stir in walnuts and pour into buttered 8-inch square dish.
- Refrigerate 2 hours and cut into squares.

Diamond Fudge

1 (6 ounce) package semi-sweet chocolate morsels
1 cup creamy peanut butter
½ cup (1 stick) butter
1 cup powdered sugar

- Combine morsels, peanut butter and butter in saucepan over low heat. Stir constantly, just until mixture melts and is smooth.
- Remove from heat, add powdered sugar and stir until smooth.
- Spoon into buttered 8-inch square pan and refrigerate until firm.
- Let stand 10 minutes at room temperature before cutting into squares and store in refrigerator.

Raisin Fudge

1 (12 ounce) package semi-sweet chocolate chips
1 cup chunky peanut butter
3 cups miniature marshmallows
¾ cup raisins

- In saucepan melt chocolate chips and peanut butter over medium-low heat.
- Fold in marshmallows and raisins and stir until marshmallows melt.
- Pour into 7 x 11-inch pan.
- Refrigerate until firm. Cut into squares and store in cool spot.

Crispy Fudge Treats

6 cups crispy rice cereal
¾ cup powdered sugar
1¾ cups semi-sweet chocolate chips
½ cup light corn syrup
⅓ cup (⅔ stick) butter

- Combine cereal and sugar in large bowl and set aside.
- Place chocolate chips, corn syrup and butter in 1-quart microwave-safe dish.
- Microwave uncovered on HIGH for about 1 minute and stir until smooth. (If you have vanilla extract on hand, stir in 2 teaspoons vanilla.)
- Pour over cereal mixture and mix well.
- Spoon into greased 9 x 13-inch pan, refrigerate for 30 minutes and cut into squares.

Peanut Butter Fudge

1 (12 ounce) jar chunky peanut butter
1 (12 ounce) package milk chocolate chips
1 (14 ounce) can sweetened condensed milk
1 cup chopped pecans

- Melt peanut butter and chocolate chips.
- Add condensed milk and heat.
- Add pecans and mix well.
- Pour into buttered 9 x 9-inch dish, refrigerate until firm and cut into squares.

Creamy Peanut Butter Fudge

3 cups sugar
¾ cup (1½ sticks) butter
⅔ cup evaporated milk
1 (10 ounce) package peanut butter-flavored morsels
1 (7 ounce) jar marshmallow cream
1 teaspoon vanilla extract

- Combine sugar, butter and evaporated milk in large saucepan.
- Bring to boil over medium heat and stir constantly. Cover and cook 3 minutes without stirring.
- Uncover and boil 5 minutes (do not stir).
- Remove from heat, add morsels and stir until morsels melt.
- Stir in marshmallow cream and vanilla.
- Pour into buttered 9 x 13-inch pan and place in freezer for 10 minutes.

White Chocolate Fudge

1 (8 ounce) package cream cheese, softened
4 cups powdered sugar
1½ teaspoons vanilla extract
12 ounces almond bark, melted
¾ cup chopped pecans

- Beat cream cheese at medium speed with mixer until smooth, gradually add sugar and vanilla and beat well.
- Stir in melted almond bark and pecans and spread into buttered 8-inch square pan.
- Refrigerate until firm and cut into small squares.

TIP: This is a little different slant to fudge – really creamy and really good!

Peanut Brittle

2 cups sugar
½ cup light corn syrup
2 cups dry-roasted peanuts
1 tablespoon butter
1 teaspoon baking soda

- Combine sugar and corn syrup in saucepan.
- Cook over low heat and stir constantly until sugar dissolves.
- Cover and cook over medium heat another 2 minutes.
- Uncover, add peanuts and cook, stirring occasionally, to hard-crack stage (300°).
- Stir in butter and baking soda, pour into buttered jelly-roll pan and spread thinly.
- Cool and break into pieces.

Caramel Crunch

½ cup firmly packed brown sugar
½ cup light corn syrup
4 tablespoons (½ stick) butter
6 cups bite-size crispy corn cereal squares
2 cups peanuts

- In large saucepan, heat brown sugar, syrup and butter. Stir constantly until sugar and butter melt.
- Add cereal and peanuts and stir until all ingredients are well coated.
- Spread mixture on lightly greased baking sheet and bake at 250° for 30 minutes. Stir occasionally while baking.
- Cool and store in airtight container.

Karo Caramels

2 cups sugar
1¾ cups light corn syrup
½ cup (1 stick) butter
2 (8 ounce) cartons whipping cream, divided
1¼ cups chopped pecans, toasted

- In saucepan, combine sugar, syrup, butter and 1 carton cream and bring to a boil.
- While boiling, add second carton of cream and cook to soft-ball stage (234° on candy thermometer).
- Beat by hand for 3 to 4 minutes.
- Add pecans and pour on buttered platter. Cut when cool.

Chocolate-Peanut Butter Drops

1 cup sugar
½ cup light corn syrup
¼ cup honey
1 (12 ounce) jar chunky peanut butter
4 cups chocolate-flavored frosted corn puff cereal

- Combine sugar, corn syrup and honey in Dutch oven. Bring to a boil and stir constantly.
- Remove from heat, add peanut butter and stir until it blends.
- Stir in cereal and drop by tablespoonfuls onto wax paper. Cool.

Easy Holiday Mints

1 (16 ounce) box powdered sugar
3 tablespoons butter, softened
3½ tablespoons evaporated milk
¼ to ½ teaspoon peppermint or almond extract
Few drops desired food coloring

- Combine all ingredients in large mixing bowl and knead mixture in bowl until smooth.
- Shape mints in rubber candy molds and place on baking sheets.
- Cover with paper towel and dry.
- Store in airtight container.

Dream Candy

2 (8 ounce) cartons whipping cream
3 cups sugar
1 cup light corn syrup
1 cup chopped pecans

- In saucepan, combine whipping cream, sugar and corn syrup and cook to soft-ball stage (234° on candy thermometer).
- Stir and beat until candy is cool.
- Add pecans and pour into buttered 9-inch pan.

Yummy Pralines

½ cup (1 stick) butter
1 (16 ounce) box light brown sugar
1 (8 ounce) carton whipping cream
2½ cups whole pecans

- In heavy saucepan, combine butter, brown sugar and whipping cream.
- Cook for 20 minutes or until temperature comes to soft-ball stage (234° on candy thermometer) and stir constantly.
- Remove from heat and set aside for 5 minutes.
- Fold in pecans and stir until ingredients are glassy. (This will take several minutes of stirring.)
- With large spoon, drop onto wax paper. Remove from paper after pralines cool.

Microwave Pralines

1½ cups packed brown sugar
⅔ cup half-and-half cream
Dash of salt
2 tablespoons (¼ stick) butter, melted
1⅔ cups chopped pecans

- Combine brown sugar, cream and salt in deep glass dish and mix well. Blend in butter.
- Microwave on HIGH for 10 minutes, stir once and add pecans. Cool for 1 minute.
- Beat by hand until creamy and thick, about 4 to 5 minutes. (The mixture will lose some of its gloss.)
- Drop by tablespoonfuls onto wax paper.

Nutty Haystacks

1 pound candy orange slices, chopped
2 cups flaked coconut
2 cups chopped pecans
1 (14 ounce) can sweetened condensed milk
2 cups powdered sugar

- Place orange slices, coconut, pecans and condensed milk in baking dish and cook at 350° for 12 minutes or until bubbly.
- Add powdered sugar and mix well.
- Drop by teaspoonfuls on wax paper.

Macadamia Candy

2 (3 ounce) jars macadamia nuts
1 (20 ounce) package almond bark
¾ cup flaked coconut

- Heat dry skillet and toast nuts until slightly golden. (Some brands of macadamia nuts are already toasted.) Set aside.
- In double boiler, melt almond bark.
- As soon as almond bark melts, pour in macadamia nuts and coconut and stir well.
- Place wax paper on baking sheet, pour candy on wax paper and spread out.
- Refrigerate for 30 minutes to set and break into pieces.

Pecan-Topped Toffee

1 cup (2 sticks) butter
1¼ cups packed brown sugar
6 (1.5 ounce) milk chocolate bars
⅔ cup finely chopped pecans

- In saucepan, combine butter and brown sugar and cook on medium-high heat.
- Stir constantly until mixture reaches 300° on candy thermometer and pour immediately into greased 9-inch baking pan.
- Lay chocolate bars evenly over hot candy.
- When chocolate is soft, spread into smooth layer.
- Sprinkle pecans over chocolate and press lightly with back of spoon.
- Refrigerate for 1 hour.
- Invert candy onto wax paper and break into small, irregular pieces.

Quick Pralines

1 (3 ounce) box butterscotch cook-and-serve pudding mix
1¼ cups sugar
½ cup evaporated milk
2 cups pecan pieces

- In large saucepan, mix butterscotch pudding mix, sugar and milk.
- Bring to a boil and stir constantly for 2 minutes.
- Add pecans, boil another 1½ minutes and stir constantly.
- Remove from heat and beat until candy begins to cool.
- Drop by tablespoonfuls on wax paper.

Sugar Plum Candy

1¼ pounds vanilla-flavored almond bark, chopped
1½ cups tiny red and green marshmallows
1½ cups peanut butter cereal
1½ cups crispy rice cereal
1½ cups mixed nuts

- In double boiler on low heat, melt almond bark.
- Place marshmallows, cereals and nuts in large bowl, pour melted bark over mixture and stir to coat.
- Drop mixture by teaspoonfuls on wax paper-lined baking sheet.
- Let stand until set and store in airtight container.

Date Loaf Candy

3 cups sugar
1 cup milk
1 (16 ounce) box chopped dates
1 cup chopped pecans

- Combine sugar and milk in large saucepan.
- Cook mixture to soft-ball stage (234° on candy thermometer). Stir in dates.
- Cook mixture again to hard-ball stage (260°). Stir constantly.
- Remove from heat, add pecans and mix well. Stir and cool until stiff. Pour mixture onto damp tea towel.
- Roll into log and set aside until set.
- When candy is set, remove tea towel and slice.

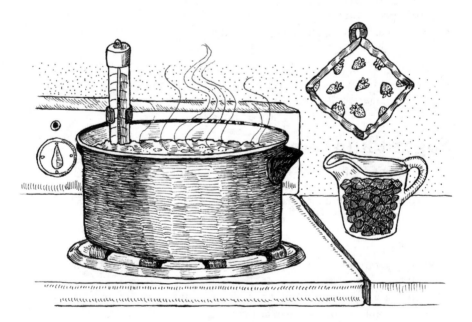

The Best 1001 Short, Easy Recipes

That Everyone Should Have

Index of Recipe Names and Categories

A

B

■ ▫ ▪ ▪ ▫ ▪ ■ ▫ ■ ▫ ▪ ▫ ▫ ▪ ▫ ■ ▪ ▫ ▪ ▫ ■ ▪ ▫

Breakfast & Brunch

Cheese

Chicken & Turkey

Chocolate

Cobblers

Cookies, Bars & Brownies

Cornbread

D

Desserts

Dips

G

H

I

Ice Cream

J

K

L

Leftovers

M

Main Dishes

N

Pork

Q

R

S

Sandwich Spreads

Sandwiches

Sandwiches Extraordinaire

Seafood

Special Desserts

Spreads

T

U

V

W

Y

Z

Cookbooks Published by Cookbook Resources
Bringing Family and Friends to the Table

The Best 1001 Short, Easy Recipes

1001 Slow Cooker Recipes

1001 Short, Easy, Inexpensive Recipes

1001 Fast Easy Recipes

1001 Community Recipes

Easy Slow Cooker Cookbook

Busy Woman's Slow Cooker Recipes

Busy Woman's Quick & Easy Recipes

Easy Diabetic Recipes

365 Easy Soups and Stews

365 Easy Chicken Recipes

365 Easy One-Dish Recipes

365 Easy Soup Recipes

365 Easy Vegetarian Recipes

365 Easy Casserole Recipes

365 Easy Pasta Recipes

365 Easy Slow Cooker Recipes

Super Simple Cupcake Recipes

*Leaving Home Cookbook
and Survival Guide*

Essential 3-4-5 Ingredient Recipes

Ultimate 4 Ingredient Cookbook

Easy Cooking with 5 Ingredients

The Best of Cooking with 3 Ingredients

Ultimate 4 Ingredient Diabetic Cookbook

4-Ingredient Recipes for 30-Minute Meals

Cooking with Beer

The Pennsylvania Cookbook

The California Cookbook

Best-Loved New England Recipes

Best-Loved Canadian Recipes

*Best-Loved Recipes
from the Pacific Northwest*

Easy Slow Cooker Recipes (with Photos)

Cool Smoothies (with Photos)

Easy Cupcake Recipes (with Photos)

Easy Soup Recipes (with Photos)

Classic Tex-Mex and Texas Cooking

Best-Loved Southern Recipes

Classic Southwest Cooking

Miss Sadie's Southern Cooking

Classic Pennsylvania Dutch Cooking

Healthy Cooking with 4 Ingredients

Trophy Hunters' Wild Game Cookbook

Recipe Keeper

Simple Old-Fashioned Baking

Quick Fixes with Cake Mixes

Kitchen Keepsakes

& More Kitchen Keepsakes

Cookbook 25 Years

Texas Longhorn Cookbook

Gifts for the Cookie Jar

All New Gifts for the Cookie Jar

The Big Bake Sale Cookbook

Easy One-Dish Meals

Easy Potluck Recipes

Easy Casseroles Cookbook

Easy Desserts

Sunday Night Suppers

Easy Church Suppers

365 Easy Meals

Gourmet Cooking with 5 Ingredients

Muffins In A Jar

A Little Taste of Texas

A Little Taste of Texas II

cookbook resources® LLC

www.cookbookresources.com
Toll-free: 1-866-229-2665
Your Ultimate Source for Easy Cookbooks

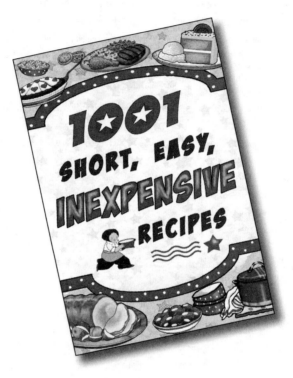

www.cookbookresources.com
Toll-free: 1-866-229-2665